The Campus History Series

UNIVERSITY OF IDAHO

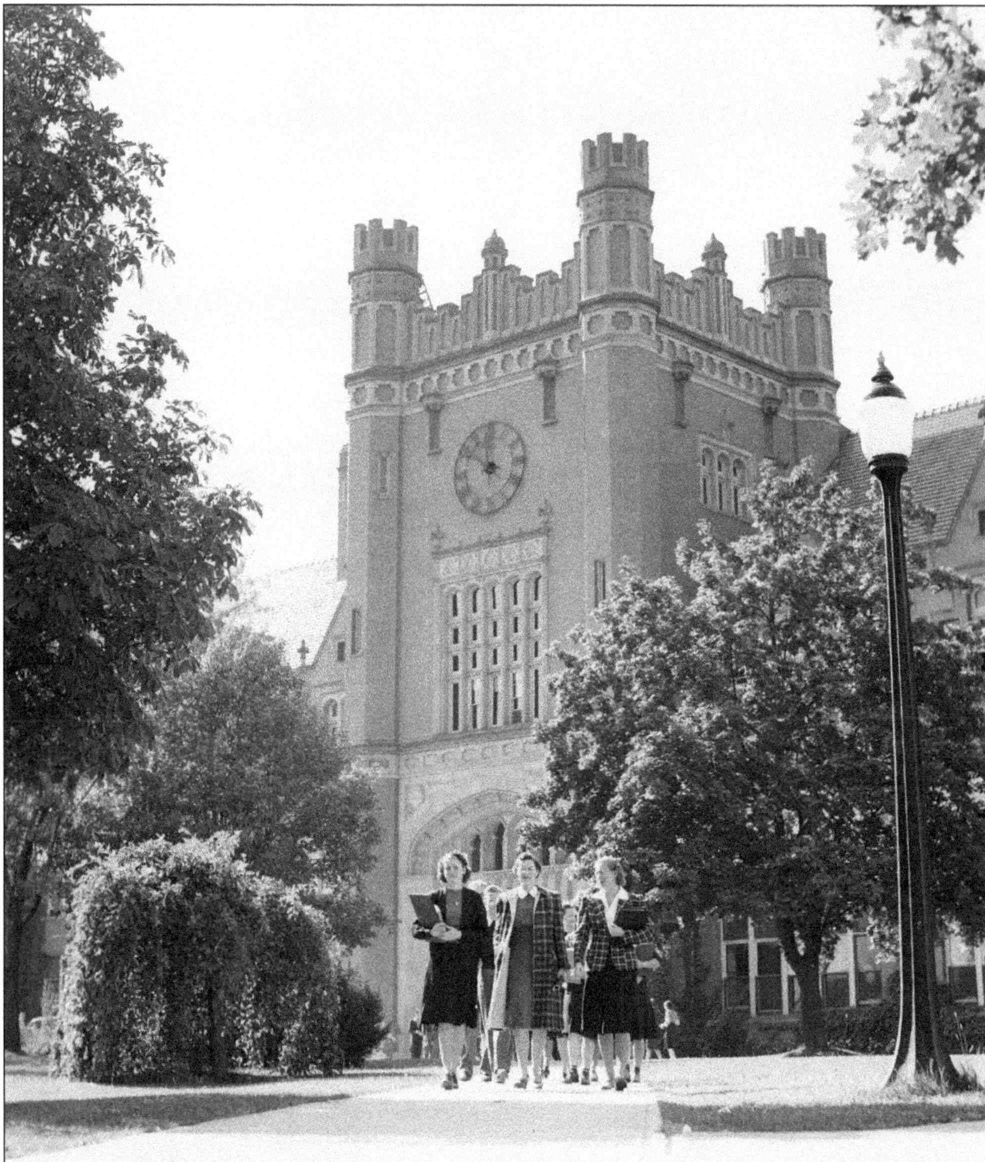

Rebuilt after the 1906 fire, the Administration Building remains the most identifiable building on campus. Students walk outside the picturesque building in 1945. (University of Idaho Special Collections and Archives, PG 1-52-114.)

On the Front Cover: Two students socialize near the university landmark concrete seat shaped like the letter *I* outside the Administration Building in 1961. The "I" bench served as a central gathering and meeting spot for students, although in years past it was reserved for senior students. (University of Idaho Special Collections and Archives, PG 1-101-03.)

On the Back Cover: This panoramic view of campus was taken in 1923. (University of Idaho Special Collections and Archives, PG 1-002-20.)

The Campus History Series

UNIVERSITY OF IDAHO

ERIN PASSEHL-STODDART AND KATHERINE G. AIKEN

FOREWORD BY CHUCK STABEN, PRESIDENT

ARCADIA PUBLISHING

ISBN 978-1-4671-1732-6

Published by Arcadia Publishing
Charleston, South Carolina

Library of Congress Control Number: 2016932227

For all general information, please contact Arcadia Publishing:
Telephone 843-853-2070
Fax 843-853-0044
E-mail sales@arcadiapublishing.com
For customer service and orders:
Toll-Free 1-888-313-2665

Visit us on the Internet at www.arcadiapublishing.com

To past, present, and future Vandals.

CONTENTS

Foreword

The University of Idaho is a special place, a fact that has been reinforced daily and amplified in my time as the 18th president of our state's land-grant research university. Our role in helping our society and individuals realize their human potential is the most uplifting part of what we do.

In Moscow, on the beautiful Palouse hills next to the mountains, our historic campus comes to life with the bustling energy and boundless optimism of students and faculty members. From its humble beginnings in the muddy fields outside of Moscow before Idaho's statehood, we have grown up alongside our state to be a leading, national research university, drawing students nationally and internationally and contributing unique research, scholarship, and creative work to Idaho, the region, and the world. In this remarkable book, you'll see how our Vandal family has made and remade our university with their talent, passion, and commitment.

As president, it's a great joy to meet students who have come to explore options for their lives and who, in the process, develop lifelong relationships. After their graduation, they'll join the many Vandal alumni who are doers and dreamers in all walks of life—as leaders in organizations and industries, as dedicated community members, and as volunteers and civic champions. This is the University of Idaho story, a tale of success as a special institution in Idaho and as a launching pad for the success of thousands of individuals, for discovery and innovation that changes lives, and for service and outreach of relevance to our state and its citizens.

I would be hard-pressed to find two better chroniclers of the UI story than Katherine Aiken, historian and former interim provost, and Erin Passehl-Stoddart, head of Special Collections and Archives. They bring our university's proud history to vivid life, and their care for the institution and its legacy, for its values and its heritage, for its excellence and its accomplishments, all speak to a confidence in our bright future and a passionate belief in the men and women who so proudly wear the nickname "Vandal."

—Chuck Staben
President

Acknowledgments

We thank everyone who assisted with this project. Members of the university community responded to our questions and requests for information quickly and with unfailing good humor—no matter how many times we asked. Staff in the Special Collections and Archives department took on the brunt of the requests, as the majority of material featured in this book came directly from the archives—a big thank-you to Amy Thompson, Darcie Riedner, Jordan Wrigley, and Rachel Kerr. Three other significant sources of material were UI Photo Services staff Joe Pallen and Melissa Hartley, UI Athletics staff Becky Paull and Athletic Director Rob Spear, and Bill Loftus in the College of Agricultural and Life Sciences. We also appreciate the willingness of Pres. Chuck Staben to contribute the book's foreword, and assistance from Brian Keenan, Kevin Ketchie, and Brenda Helbling from the President's Office; Provost John Wiencek and Lodi Price from the Provost's Office; and Dean of Libraries Lynn Baird, Samm Green, and the Library Advisory Board. Additional faculty and staff helped throughout the writing process, including the late Paul Joyce, Eric Bennett, Jennie Hall, Peter Mundt, Andy Kersten, Torrey Lawrence, Cori Mantle-Bromley, Kurt Pregitzer, Tom Gorman, Mark Hoversten, Martha McClintock, Allison Stormo, Mario Reyes, and Phil Scruggs. Thank you to Kristin Becker for taking photographs of the new building construction on campus. And last but certainly not least, we thank our partners, Rick Stoddart and Joe Schwartz.

This book builds upon two histories of the University of Idaho: *The Beacon for Mountain and Plain* by Rafe Gibbs (1962) and *This Crested Hill* by former Idaho state historian Keith Petersen (1988). The Vandal family can now trace its 125-plus-year history through these narratives and images.

The majority of the images compiled for this work are housed within the University of Idaho Library Special Collections and Archives (SPEC). The Library's identification numbers are listed with the corresponding caption for reference purposes.

Introduction

In a speech entitled "This is Your University of Idaho," delivered in 1961, Pres. Donald R. Theophilus proclaimed, "The university serves the people of Idaho on a state-wide basis, so all the people have a stake in ***their*** university." Theophilus's notion of the "people's university" resonates across the University of Idaho's 125-plus-year history and continues to define UI's mission as it looks forward into the 21st century.

In 1861, Congressman Justin Smith Morrill of Vermont sponsored "An Act Donating Public Lands to the Several States and Territories Which May Provide Colleges for the Benefit of Agriculture and Mechanic Arts." Pres. Abraham Lincoln signed the act into law on July 2, 1862. The Morrill Land Grant Act provided states a vast amount of land, and each recipient state was to create a permanent endowment for the support "of at least one college where the leading object shall be, without excluding other subjects, scientific and classical studies, and including military tactics . . . agriculture and mechanic arts, in such manner as the legislatures of the State may respectively prescribe, in order to promote the liberal and practical education of the industrial classes in the several pursuits and professions in life." Thus, the United States became the first nation in the world to provide federal governmental funds to support higher education. The legislation stipulated that states would have complete control of the institutions of higher learning that resulted. On the 100th anniversary of the Morrill Act, Pres. John F. Kennedy praised it for creating "the most ambitious and fruitful system of higher education in the history of the world."

The state of Idaho's land-grant university dates from 1889, when a pair of Moscow community boosters, Willis Sweet and William McConnell, instigated a bold campaign to locate the university in Latah County. At their urging, territorial legislator John Warren Bingham submitted a bill establishing a university at Moscow. The bill received only one negative vote, and territorial governor Edward A. Stevenson signed the legislation on January 30, 1889. Wanting the university to be safe from any future political vagaries, McConnell, Sweet, and Bingham made sure that voters who later that year ratified the Idaho Constitution included specific wording regarding the University of Idaho—making it the state's only constitutionally authorized institution of higher education and requiring a constitutional amendment to locate the university anywhere else.

As the first president of a newly formed University of Idaho Board of Regents, Willis Sweet facilitated the purchase of 20 acres from Moscow landowner James Deakin; the university began actual operations on October 3, 1892, when 40 students joined a single professor, John Edwin Ostrander. It is apropos that the following Christmas the secretary of the interior presented Sweet a check for $15,000—the first Morrill Act funding.

The Morrill Act recognized that American society was in transition and sought to ensure that young Americans received an education that would allow them to navigate this changing economic landscape. The law codified the American conviction that an educated populace was a necessary component of the United States' continued progress. The Morrill Act vision for land-grant institutions did not include any restrictions regarding the gender, race, or religion of students. In keeping with this "people's universities" spirit, the University of Idaho's first graduating class in 1896 included two men and two women—Stella Allen, Florence Corbett, Charles Kirtley, and Arthur Adair. In 1899, Jennie Eva Hughes became the first African American graduate.

The first Administration Building was not very welcoming when students arrived in 1892; it was almost devoid of furniture and located in a nearly treeless landscape. Former University of Idaho history professor Carlos Schwantes rediscovered a terrific story about how the Moscow campus became a veritable showplace. After 1906, the Administration Building fire left 202 students homeless, at least in an academic sense. Pres. James MacLean chose Boise architect John E. Tourtellotte, who also designed the Idaho state capitol, to create a suitable replacement. He also contacted the country's premier landscape architectural firm, the Olmsted Brothers of Brookline, Massachusetts, whose founder, Frederick Law Olmsted, is considered a cofounder of the profession of landscape architecture. In 1899, his nephew John Charles and son Frederick Law Jr. were charter members of the American Society of Landscape Architecture, and John served as its first president. The Olmsted brothers and their associates designed countless public and private spaces, including New York City's Central Park and the US Capitol grounds, as well as the campus plans for Stanford, Johns Hopkins, and Duke Universities.

President MacLean telegraphed the Olmsted brothers in 1906 and asked if they could visit Moscow when their other business brought them west. In 1907, John C. Olmsted traveled to Seattle to consult regarding the Alaska-Yukon Exposition, and visited the University of Idaho on his way home. At that time, the campus included only a few buildings and the new Administration Building's foundation. Eleven months later, President MacLean received a 25-page report. Generations of Vandals owe the expansive Administration Building lawn to Olmsted's vision. The landscape architect warned University of Idaho officials to decide upon a building material and style of architecture. Redbrick Gothic buildings are predominant at UI—the Administration Building, Memorial Gymnasium, and Willis Sweet and Chrisman Halls (now Brink and Phinney) are examples. The College of Business and Economics' Albertson Building continued this tradition in 2002.

Following the eruption of Mount Saint Helens in 1980, ash blanketed the region, forcing the closure of several campus roads for safety reasons. Students urged Pres. Richard Gibb to turn some of these streets into walkways and thus modify the campus core to create a "walking campus." The campus community and visitors alike enjoy the results. The University of Idaho campus is indeed an Idaho gem and adheres to John Olmsted's advice to President MacLean: "the University as a whole, both grounds and buildings, without any suggestion of lavishness or over decoration, ought to exhibit clearly, in all its outward appearance, the fact that it is the place of work and of residence of cultivated and careful people."

Added dimensions to the land-grant mission came when the US Congress passed the Hatch Act (1887), creating experiment stations at land-grant institutions, and the Smith-Lever Act (1914), which provided for cooperative extension services. The first University of Idaho extension office opened before any students had even arrived at the Moscow campus. Extension offices in 42 of Idaho's 44 counties continue to provide Idaho residents with up-to-date information on topics from crops and livestock to gardens to personal finance—and everything in between. The Idaho Agricultural Experiment Station oversees statewide agricultural research at the Palouse, Aberdeen, Tetonia, Kimberly, Twin Falls, Caldwell, and Parma stations. Associated research sites include the US Sheep Experiment Station in Dubois, the Nancy M. Cummings Research Extension and Education Center in Salmon, the

Hagerman Fish Culture Experiment Station, and Caldwell's Caine Veterinary Teaching and Food Technology Centers.

In 1947, *Newsweek* magazine published a study showing that the University of Idaho had produced more Rhodes Scholars up to that time than any other university—public or private—west of the Great Lakes. That tradition of academic excellence continues as UI is home to one of the highest proportions of National Merit Scholars in the Pacific Northwest. More than 100,000 graduates have benefitted from the UI, which now includes seven academic colleges and the largest library in the state of Idaho.

Students are indeed the focus of the University of Idaho community. Today, over 3,000 faculty and staff work to combine first-rate academics with a comprehensive cocurricular program for nearly 12,000 students. Students come from all 50 states and almost 90 countries; 36 percent are first generation—the first in their families to attend college. The following pages illustrate the vibrancy of student life and activities and of the always-exciting Vandal athletic teams.

Without faculty and their scholarship and creative activities, the University of Idaho could not exist. While it was not possible to include every one of them in this book, every graduate has a story about a faculty or staff member who made a real difference in his or her professional or personal life. University of Idaho research confronts difficult problems and seeks solutions that benefit the state, the nation, and the world.

As Idaho's national land-grant, founding, comprehensive, constitutional institution, the University of Idaho continues to embrace its roots as the people's university for Idahoans and others. The sentiments recorded at the Administration Building's entrance, "Erected by the Commonwealth of Idaho for the training of her future citizens to their highest usefulness in private life and public service," continue to inform all aspects of the University of Idaho. Economic development and personal growth go hand-in-hand as students, faculty, and staff embark on this beloved university's next 125 years.

One

Idaho Is Our Campus

The stately Tudor Gothic Administration Building anchors the University of Idaho's almost 1,600-acre Moscow campus. It is the centerpiece of sweeping grounds, part of a campus plan designed by the famous Olmsted Brothers landscape architectural firm in 1908. The university occupies traditional Nez Perce tribal lands, a connection both the university and the tribe recognize.

After the 1906 fire and demolition of the original Administration Building, the university rebuilt in stages. The auditorium was added to the new Administration Building in 1912. This 437-seat performance space is a notable campus attraction that is known for its outstanding acoustics and its stained-glass windows that recognize University of Idaho presidents.

The ASUI-Kibbie Center (often referred to as the Kibbie Dome; ASUI stands for the Associated Students of the University of Idaho) is among the more prominent campus buildings. Athletic and campus events are held there, including commencement and the Lionel Hampton Jazz Festival. The American Society of Civil Engineers conferred it with the Outstanding Structural Engineering Achievement Award in 1976. At the time it was built, the Kibbie Dome was the largest indoor college facility in the nation. Other highly visible buildings are Theophilus Tower student residence, Memorial Gymnasium, and the Library. Opened in 2000, the Idaho Commons' central location makes it a meeting place for students, staff, and faculty. The facility includes various student services, a food court, and the offices of student government.

Three regional centers contribute to the university's statewide mission of teaching, scholarship, and engagement. Located in Coeur d'Alene, Boise, and Idaho Falls, the university centers serve their communities and regions and embrace their local focus. At the same time, they are integral to the fulfillment of the University of Idaho's overarching goal: serving the state of Idaho and its people. Online programs and dual-credit courses for high school students expand the university's reach as well.

The state of Idaho is truly the Idaho campus through extension offices. Often the result of partnerships with county governments, the university boasts extension offices in 42 of the 44 Idaho counties and on the Shoshone Bannock, Nez Perce, and Coeur d'Alene Indian Reservations. The university operates research stations across the state.

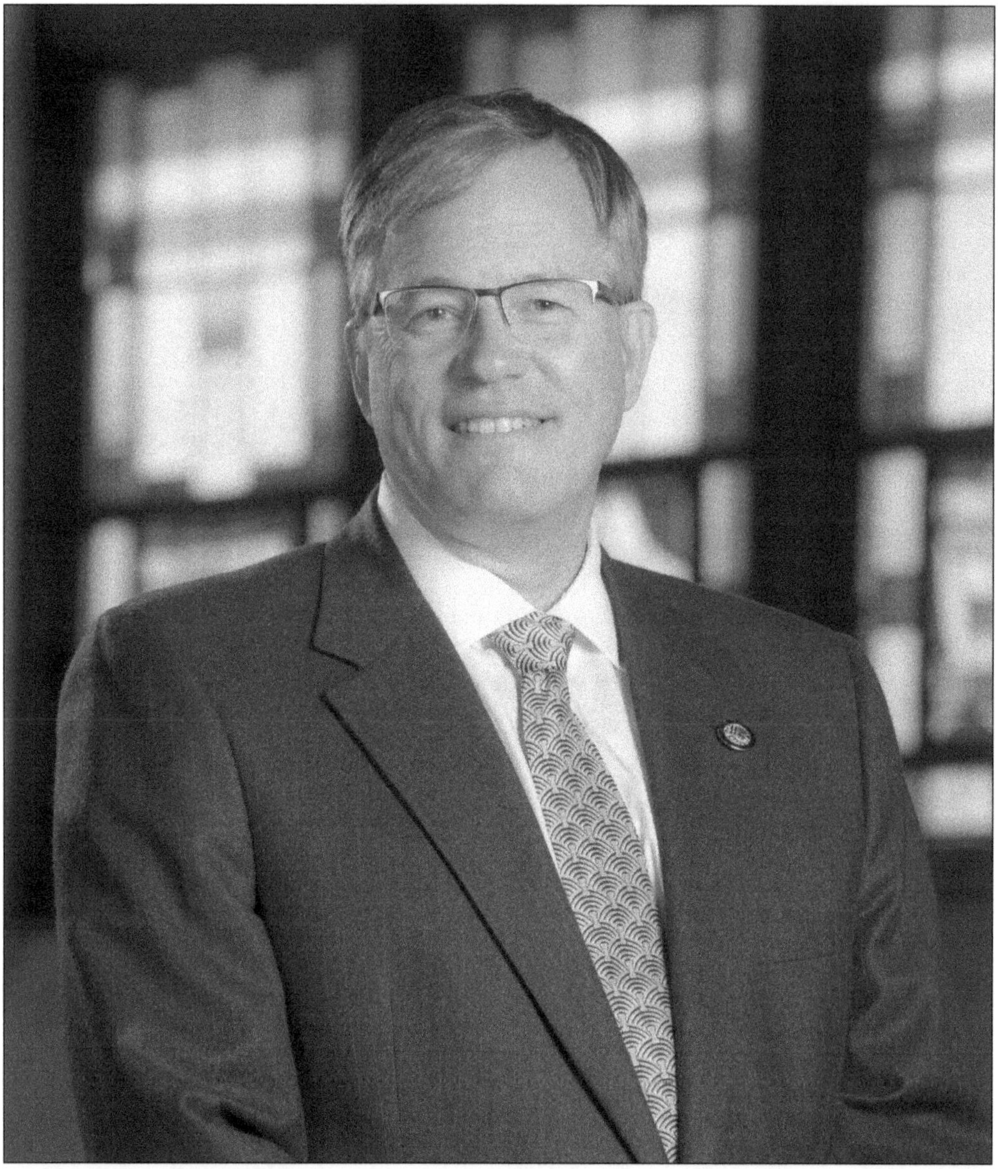

Chuck Staben is the University of Idaho's 18th president and has been in office since March 1, 2014. Franklin B. Gault served as the university's first president from 1892 to 1898. James A. MacLean was the longest serving president, from 1900 to 1913. He presided over the new Administration Building construction, hired the Olmsted Brothers to develop a campus plan, and created the university's first colleges. Melvin A. Brannon (1914–1917) and Ernest H. Lindley (1917–1920) both served as president during World War I. Alfred H. Upham (1920–1928) established the "Hello Walk" tradition. Joseph P. Blanton (1898–1900) and Frederick J. Kelley (1928–1930) each served for only two years. Other presidents include Mervin G. Neale (1930–1937), Harrison C. Dale (1937–1946), Jesse E. Buchanan (1946–1954, the first University of Idaho graduate to be president), Donald R. Theophilus (1954–1965), Ernest W. Hartung (1965–1977), Richard D. Gibb (1977–1989), Robert A. Hoover (1996–2003), Timothy P. White (2004–2008), and M. Duane Nellis (2009–2013). Elisabeth A. Zinser (1989–1995) is the only woman to have held the office of president at the University of Idaho. (UI Photo Services.)

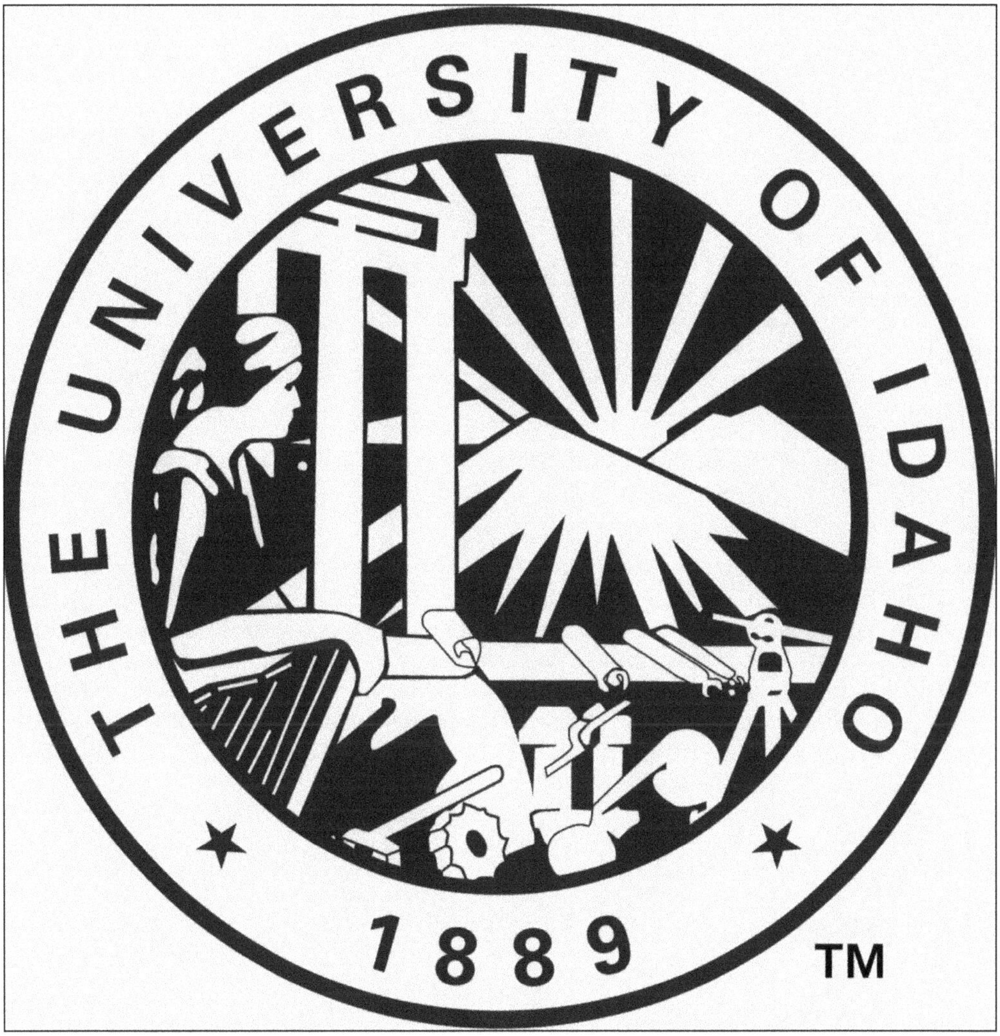

The University of Idaho Board of Regents approved a first seal design in 1908. The current seal, used for official documents including diplomas, features a seated woman perusing scrolls with a mountain sunrise in the background and a sledge, gear, chemical apparatus, and surveyor's transit in the foreground. (UI President's Office.)

Alma Mater (chorus):

And here we have Idaho,
Winning her way to fame;
Silver and Gold in the sunlight blaze,
And Romance lies in her name;
Singing, we're singing of you, ah, proudly, too;
All our lives through we'll go singing,
Singing of you, Alma Mater, our Idaho.

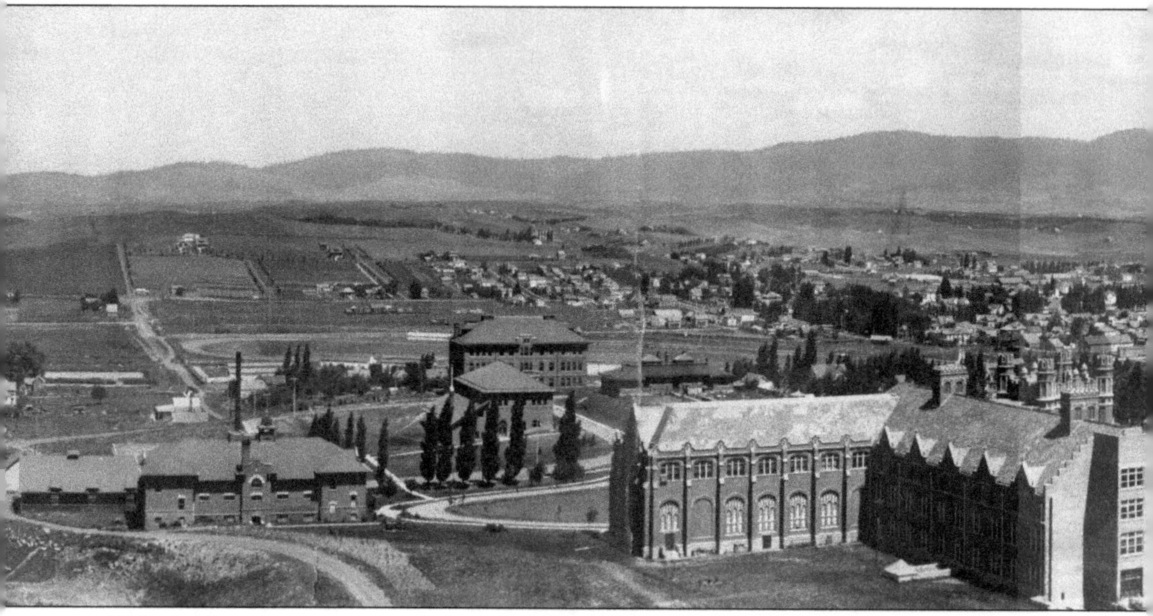

This 1916 panoramic view of the University of Idaho campus features the Administration Building. The proximity of downtown Moscow continues; it is difficult to know where the university ends and the city begins. The rolling Palouse hills in the background define the location. In 1916, there were 715 UI students; the population of Moscow was approximately 3,800. (SPEC, PG 1-2-22.)

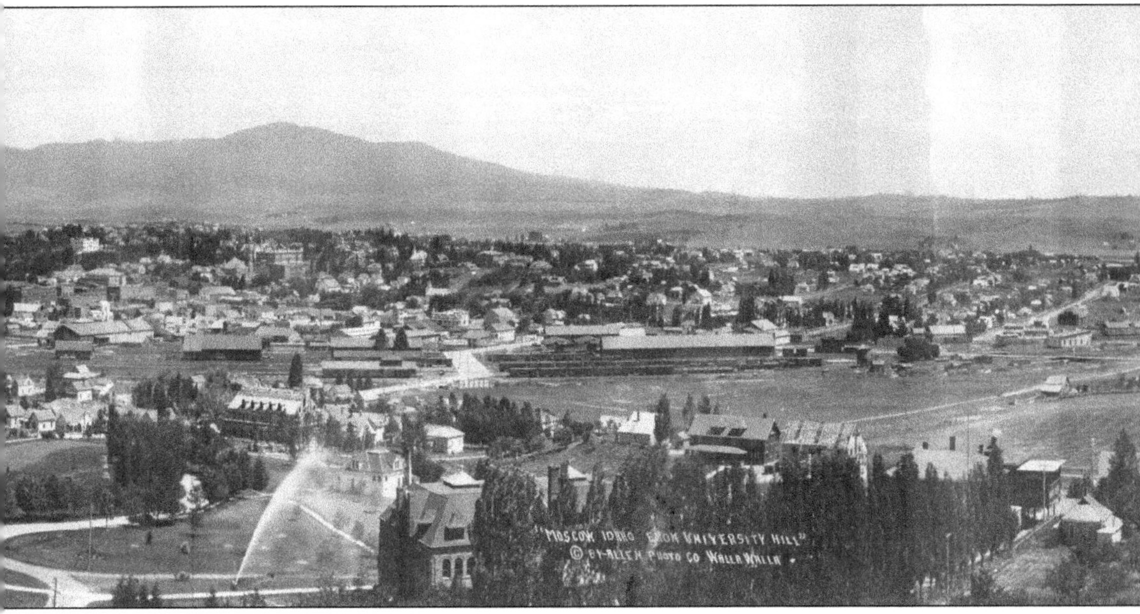

UNIVERSITY OF IDAHO FIGHT SONG:

Came a tribe from the North, brave and bold,
Bearing banners of Silver and Gold;
Tried and true to subdue all their foes
Go Vandals, go mighty Vandals!

C'mon go Vandals, go
Fight on with hearts true and bold,
Foes will fall before your Silver and your Gold,
The victory cannot be withheld from thee,
So all bear down for Idaho,
Come on old Vandals, go!

I-D-A-H-O
Idaho, Idaho, Go! Go! Go!

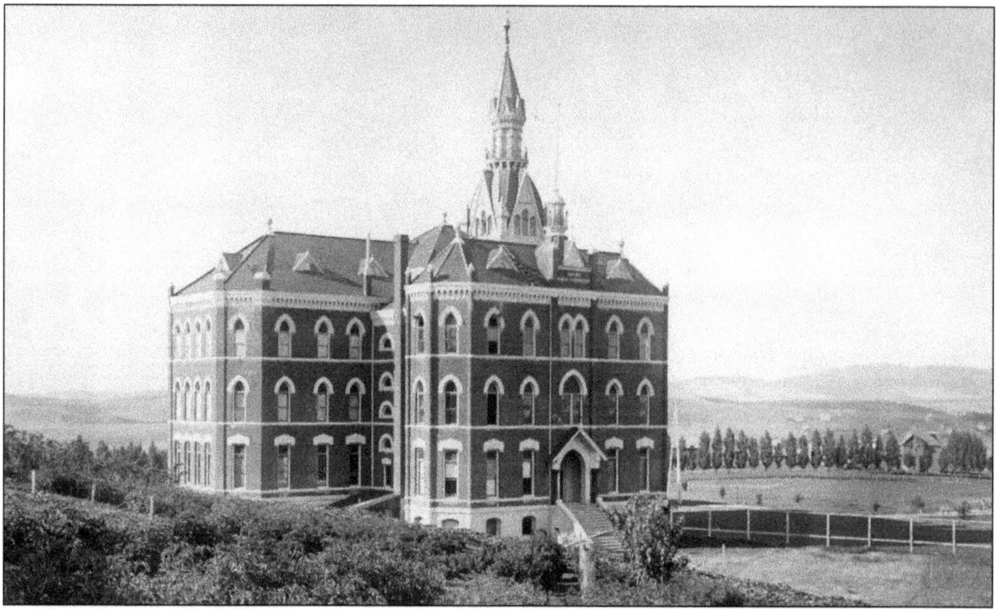

The original Administration Building (Old Admin) was constructed in 1892 at a cost of $131,068. With three stories and a 168-foot steeple, it featured a redbrick exterior and California redwood and native tamarack on the inside. The building was designed in a U-shape with east and west wings. The 1893–1894 catalog described it as "the most attractive building in Idaho." The building dominated the campus landscape. (SPEC, PG 1-51-17.)

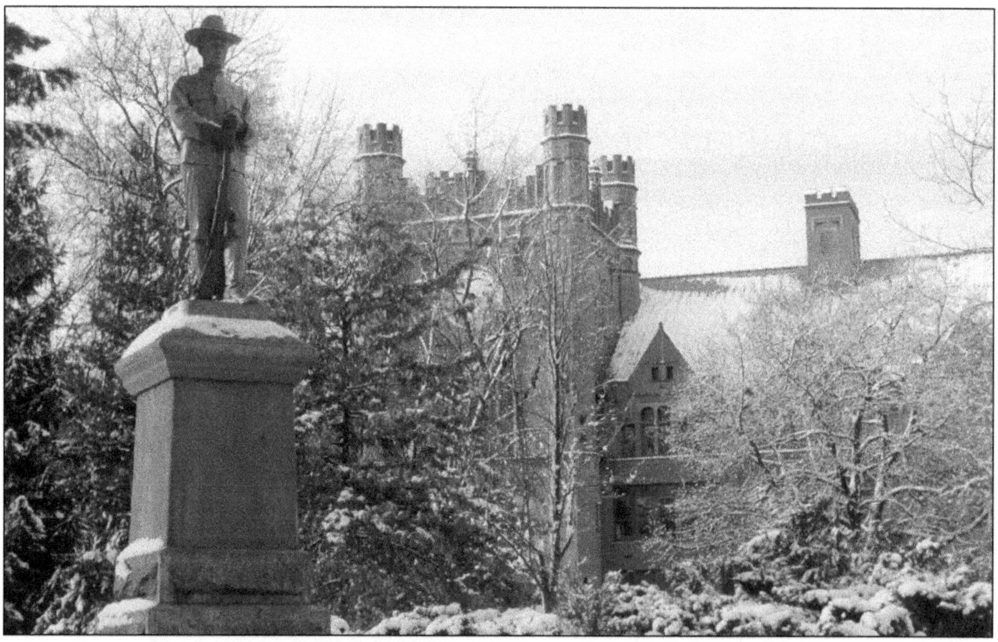

Erected in 1901, the Spanish American War Memorial honors Paul Draper and Ole Hagberg (the university's first international student), the only two UI students who died while serving during the conflict. UI president Joseph Blanton led fundraising efforts for the statue, one of the university's most frequently photographed icons. Each year, the campus community and ROTC students honor POWs and MIAs on the lawn near the statue. (UI Photo Services.)

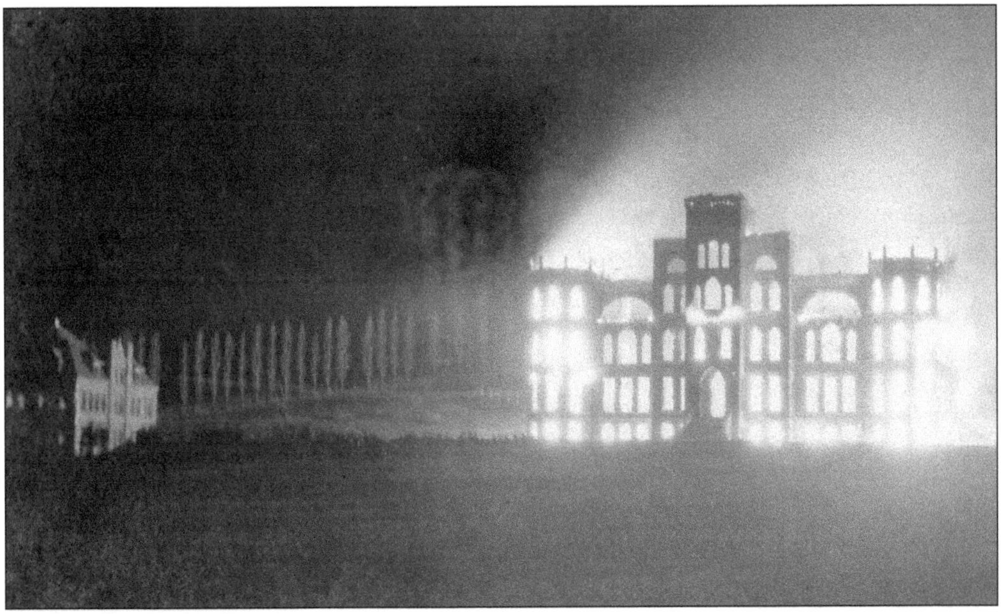

At 2:30 a.m. on March 30, 1906, Moscow was awakened to cries of "The university's burning!" Dean Eldridge threw student records from a second-story window to local druggist Roland Hodgins, waiting below. Students rushed in and saved two items—a stuffed mountain goat and the *Silver and Gold Book*. What was left of Old Admin was demolished to make way for a new building. The *Silver and Gold Book* was part of a Chicago World's Fair exhibit in 1893. Corner designs depict Idaho's major industries: mining, hunting, timber, and agriculture. Tradition says the gold and silver came from Coeur d'Alene mines, rubies from Ruby Creek, and an opal from Latah County. It was purportedly designed by art instructor Annette Brown and UI president Franklin Gault. (Above, SPEC, PG 1-51-24c; below, UI Photo Services.)

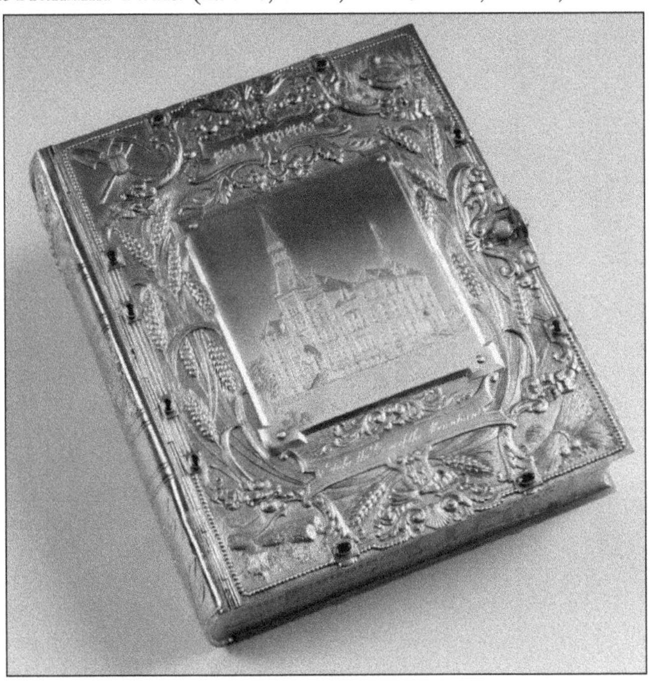

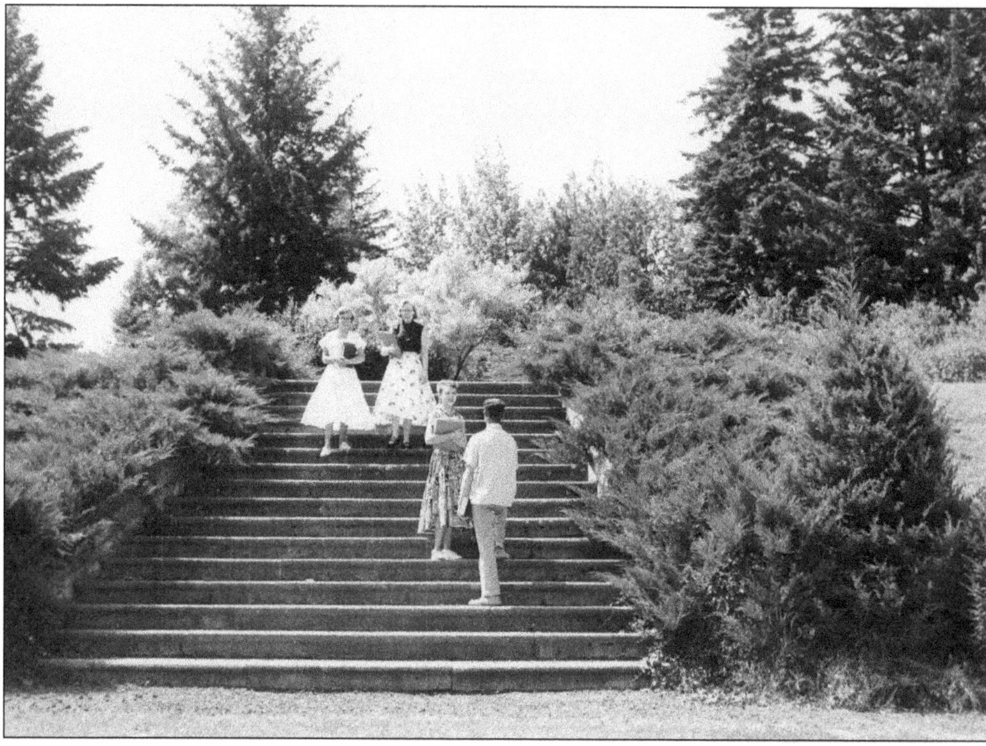

All that remains of the original Administration Building are stones that were scattered around the Moscow community and reassembled by class of 1901 alumni. Alum and congressman Burton French and Pres. Mervin Neale placed the stones in a commemorative 16-step stairway. Architecture professor Theodore Prichard designed two benches at the top of the stairs with the remaining stones. A plaque describes the origin of the stairs. (SPEC, PG 1-97-04.)

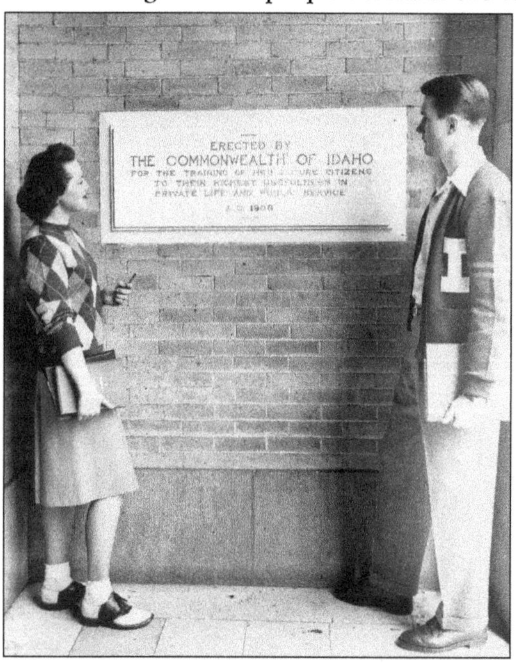

The Administration Building cornerstone is pictured in 1935. Idaho citizens have been generous in their support of the University of Idaho for its entire history. The sentiments expressed on the 1908 cornerstone remain an eloquent testament to the relationship between the University of Idaho and the people of Idaho: "For the training of her future citizens, to their highest usefulness in private life and public service." (SPEC, PG 1-52-151.)

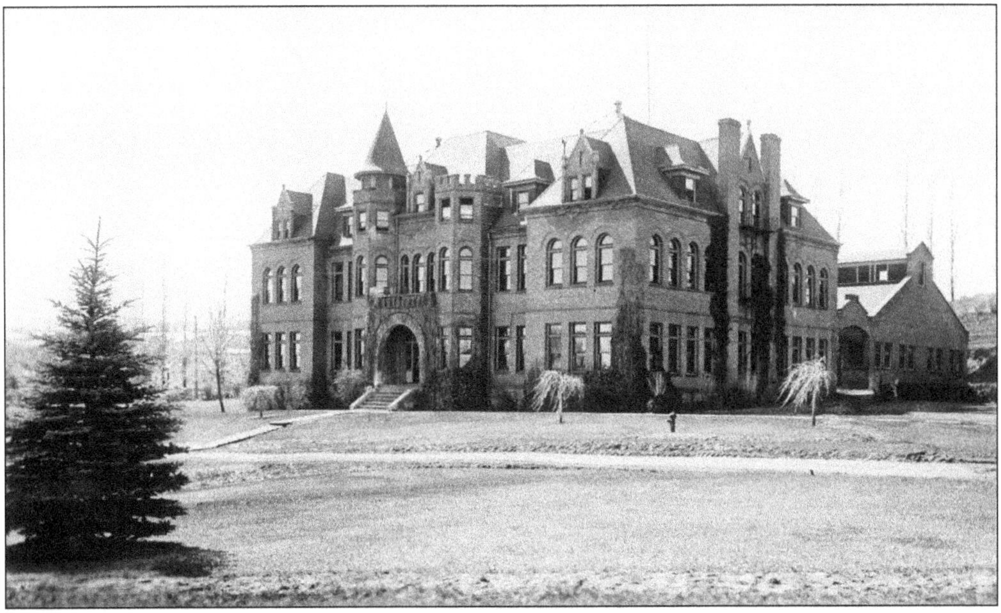

Shown here in 1925, the Old Engineering Building is an example of an early campus building that was torn down to make room for new construction. The College of Engineering Building was home to one of UI's original academic units. Replacement buildings include the Gauss-Johnson Engineering Building (1949), Janssen Engineering, and Buchanan Engineering, named for the first UI alum to become president, Jesse E. Buchanan. (SPEC, PG 1-56-5.)

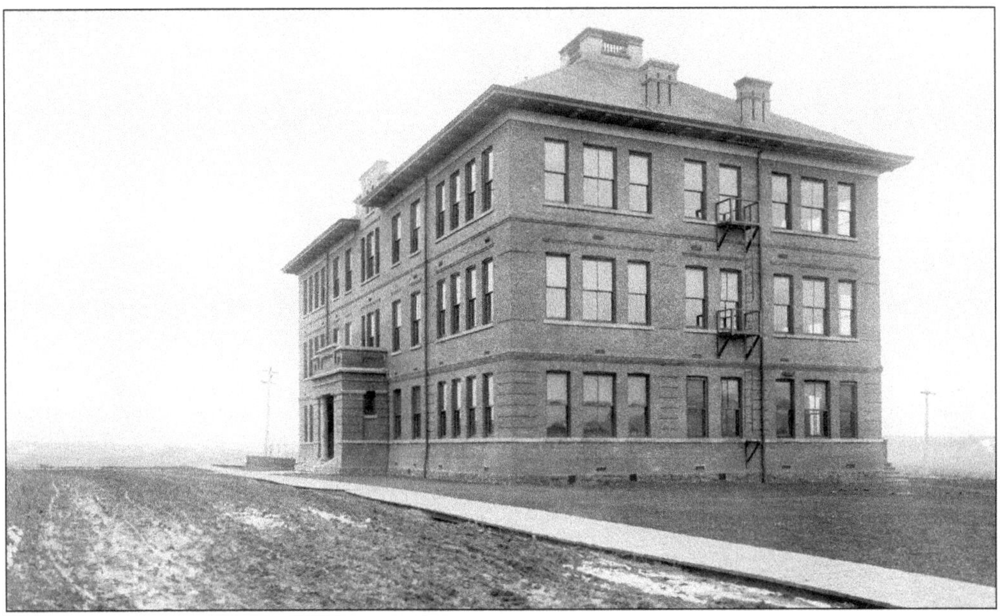

Pres. James MacLean used insurance proceeds from the Administration Building fire to finance construction of the university's first agricultural building, named for the sponsor of the 1862 Morrill Act. The classical Etruscan columns in the entry were covered with plywood; campus architects rediscovered the entry, which was brought back to its original state in 1987. The building currently houses the College of Graduate Studies and Sponsored Research. (SPEC, PG 67.)

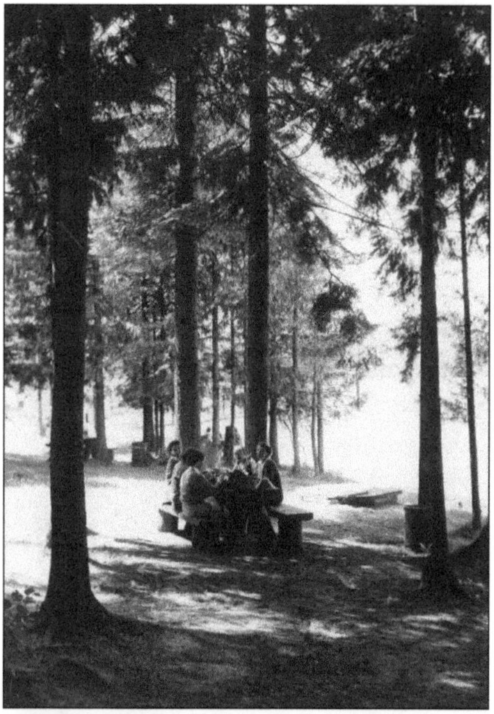

Charles Houston Shattuck came to the university in 1909 to develop one of the earliest forestry schools in the United States. The campus was nearly treeless when Shattuck planted a 14-acre spot west of the Administration Building. The first university arboretum in the West (pictured in 1951) was named for him in 1933. The Arboretum and Botanical Gardens includes 63 acres and panoramic views to the Blue Mountains. (SPEC, PG 1-6-8.)

First Lady Eleanor Roosevelt planted a Douglas fir tree in the Presidential Grove on the Administration Lawn during her visit in 1938, shown here with College of Forestry dean Dwight Smithson Jeffers. The tree still stands today just east of the Administration Building and is part of the Borah International Peace Grove. Other famous planters include Bethine Church and US presidents Theodore Roosevelt and William Taft. (SPEC, PG 3-36c.)

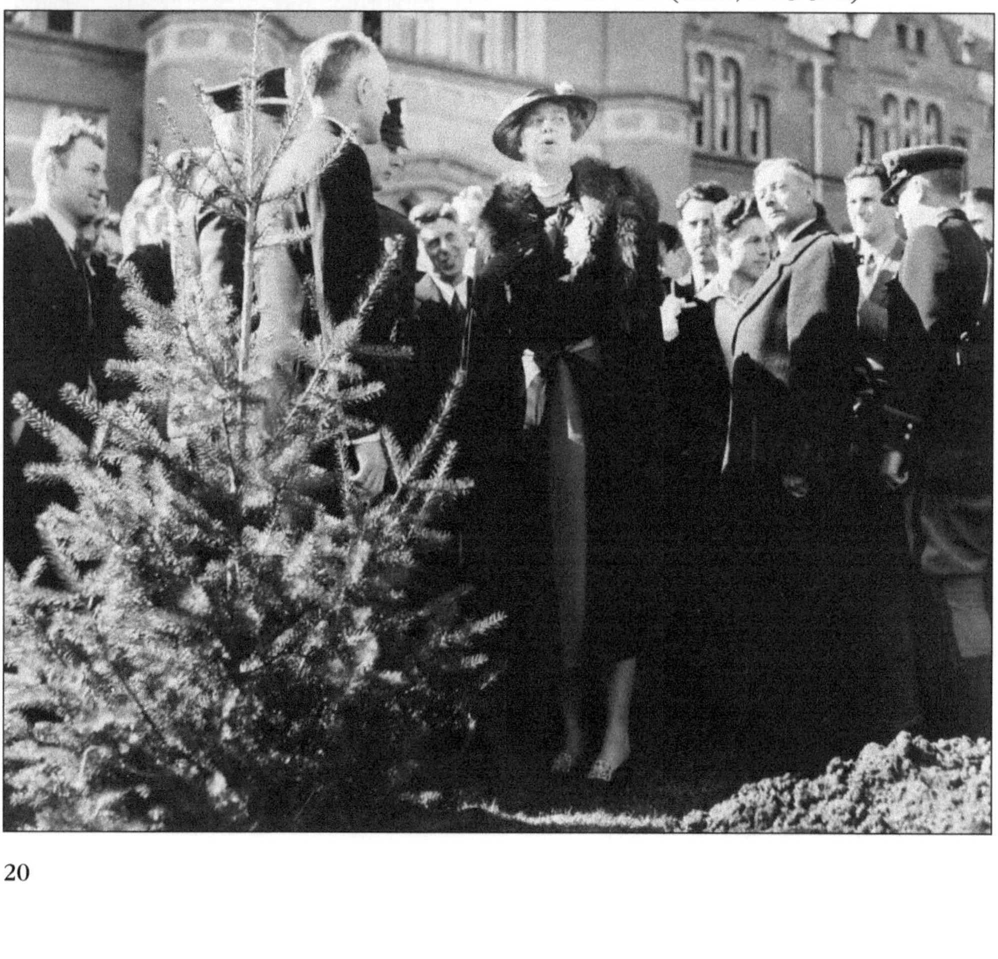

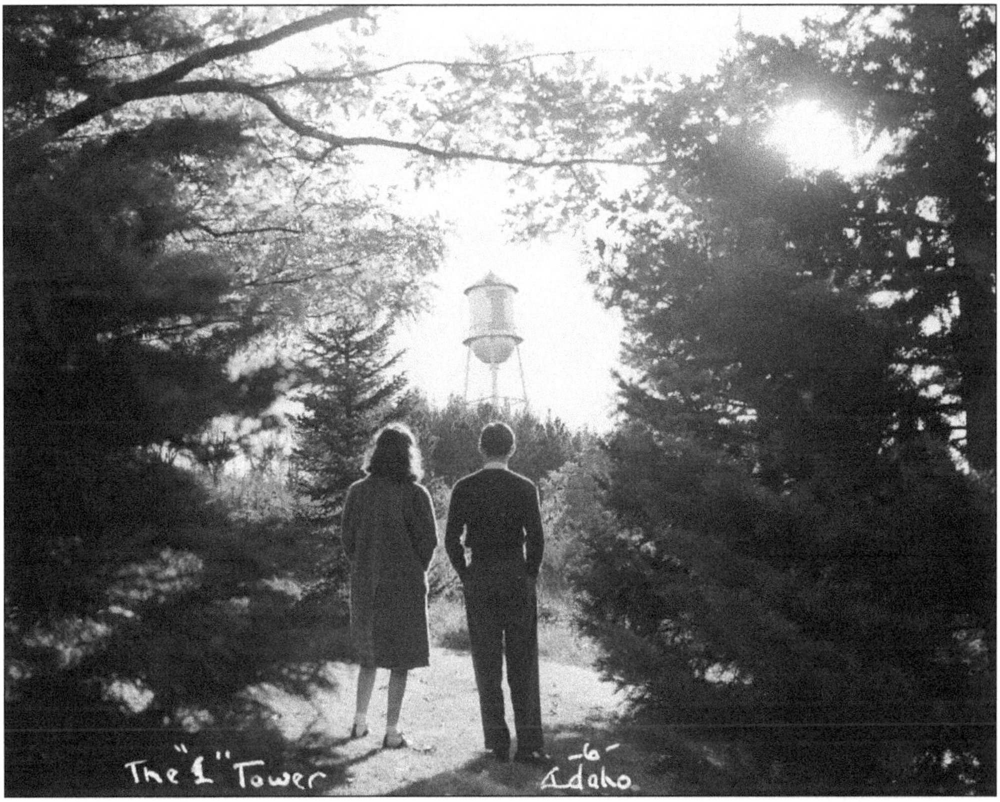

The old "I" Tower was constructed in 1916. In the early years, student groups repainted the tower as a service project, since it was frequently a target for Washington State College students prior to the Idaho-WSC football game. The tower was 79 feet high with a 60,000-gallon capacity. Dating couples often visited the tower, and many marriage proposals were made and accepted there. (SPEC, PG 1-88-10.)

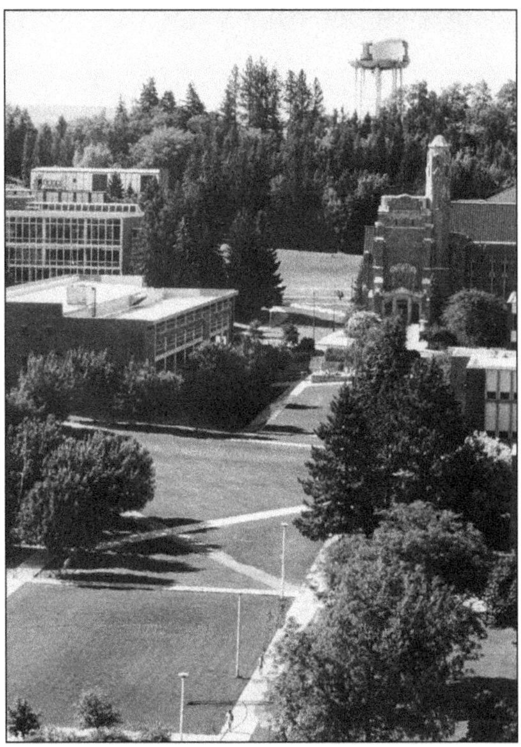

This view of the University of Idaho Academic Mall from the residence halls shows the new "I" Tower, built in 1952. Along the sidewalk are the College of Natural Resources, College of Agriculture, Renfrew Hall, the Library, Art & Architecture, College of Education, University Classroom Center, Swimming Center, and Physical Education. According to tradition, with the "I" of Idaho always upon them, students should act accordingly. (SPEC, UA 1987-17.)

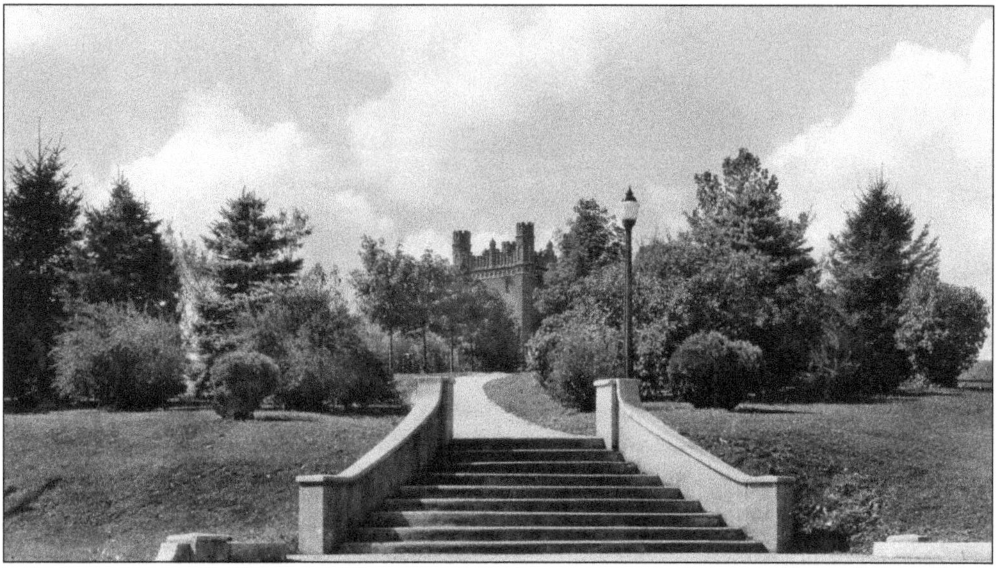

In the 1920s, Pres. Alfred Upham, ever friendly, greeted each passerby on his daily walks to and from his office, giving rise to "Hello Walk." Shown above are the original "Hello Walk" steps, which were refurbished in 2012. The newly remodeled steps feature a seal designed to commemorate the long-standing relationship between the University of Idaho and the Moscow community. (Above, SPEC, PG 1-102-01b; below, UI Photo Services.)

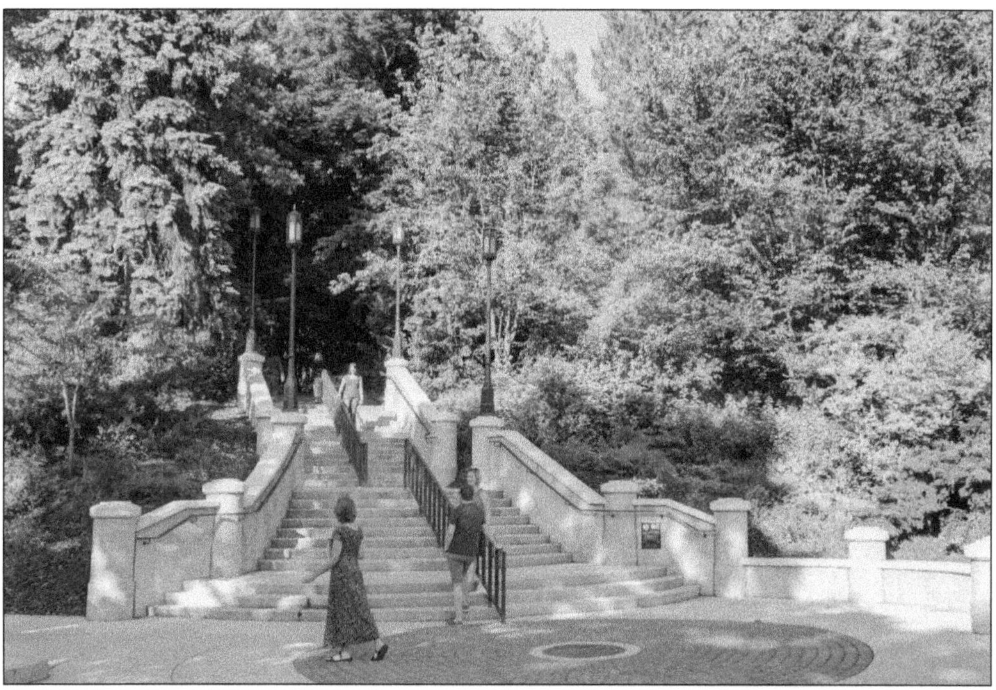

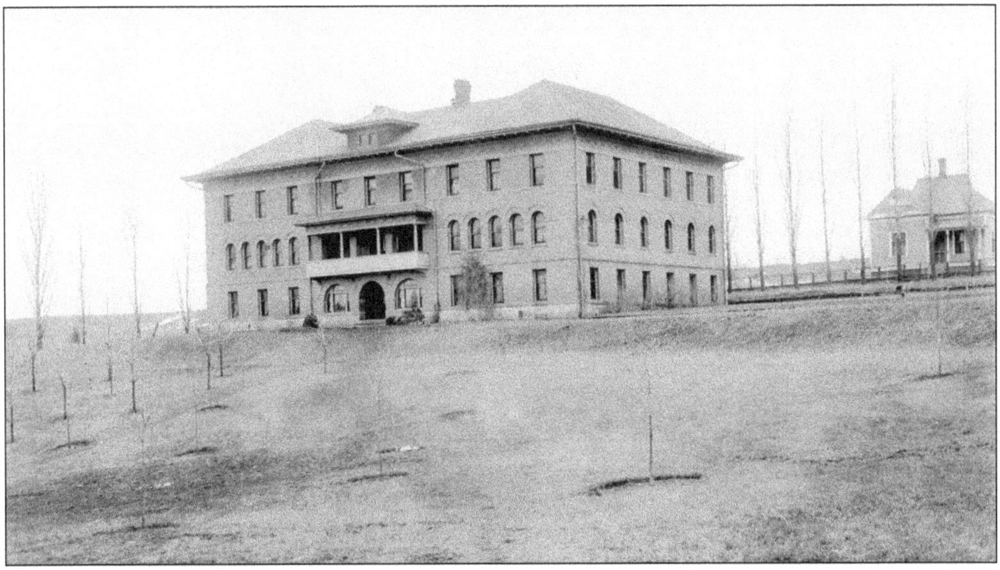

Convinced that University of Idaho women needed suitable housing where the institution could provide 24-hour oversight, the board of regents authorized the construction of Ridenbaugh Hall. Completed in 1901 at a cost of $17,000, it is the oldest extant building on campus. Recognizing Regent Mary E. Ridenbaugh, it is the first campus structure named for a person. The building is listed in the National Register of Historic Places. (SPEC, PG 67.)

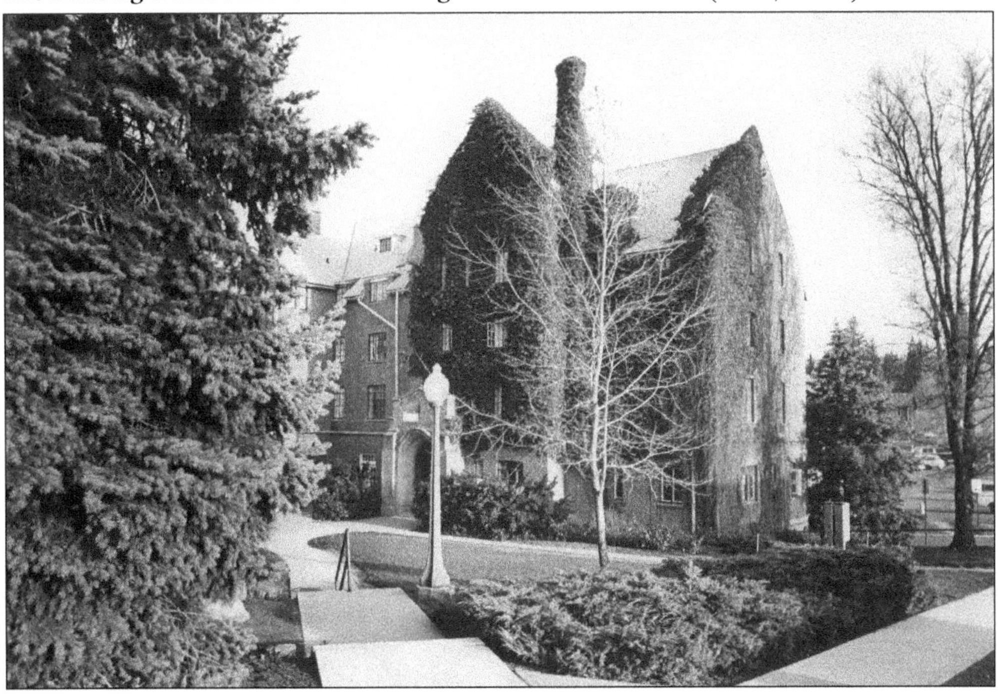

Gertrude Hays Hall opened in 1927 and was financed by the sale of bonds to Moscow businessmen. Hays was a member of the UI board of regents from 1906 to 1913. Originally a women's dormitory, Hays Hall now houses the Alumni Association offices. Founded in 1899, the association represents over 100,000 living alumni. It established Silver & Gold Day in 1981, which recognizes outstanding alumni at ceremonies around the state. (SPEC, UA 2001-001.)

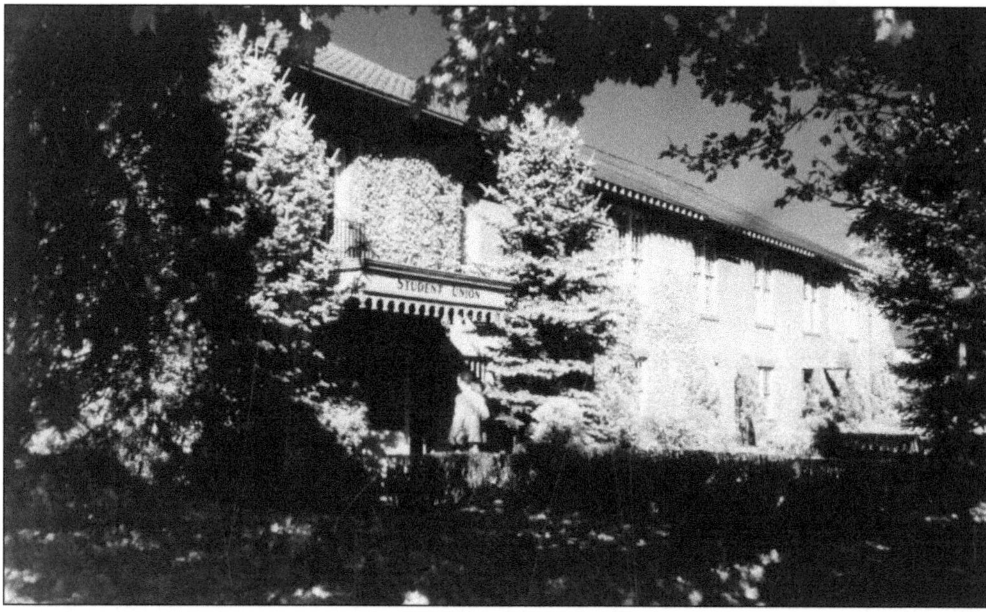

Dean of Women Permeal French opened the Blue Bucket Inn to provide a recreation and dining center for students. It included a ballroom on the second floor and a tea room and restaurant on the first. It was remodeled and opened as the Student Union Building in 1937. It housed ASUI offices, publication offices, the bookstore, a "coke shop," and the popular Bucket Lounge. (SPEC, PG 2-143-11.)

The Co-Op Bookstore (pictured in 1939) became the popular campus hangout called the Perch when the bookstore moved to the Student Union Building. Longtime Perch owner Madge sold ice cream cones using the pronouns "she" (vanilla); "he" (chocolate); and "it" (swirl). A new campus bookstore was completed in the fall of 1990 and now includes a Starbucks and a VandalStore. A Boise branch is located on Idaho Street. (SPEC, PG 92-2973.)

The Student Union Building is pictured with an illuminated Joe Vandal on the side around 1963. Three additions to the old Blue Bucket Building made way for the new Student Union in the 1960s. It was the center for most Idaho student activities and included a bowling alley and Borah Theater. Two major remodeling projects refurbished the International Ballroom and created the Vandal Ballroom—both locations for numerous campus and community activities. (SPEC, PG 2-143-36.)

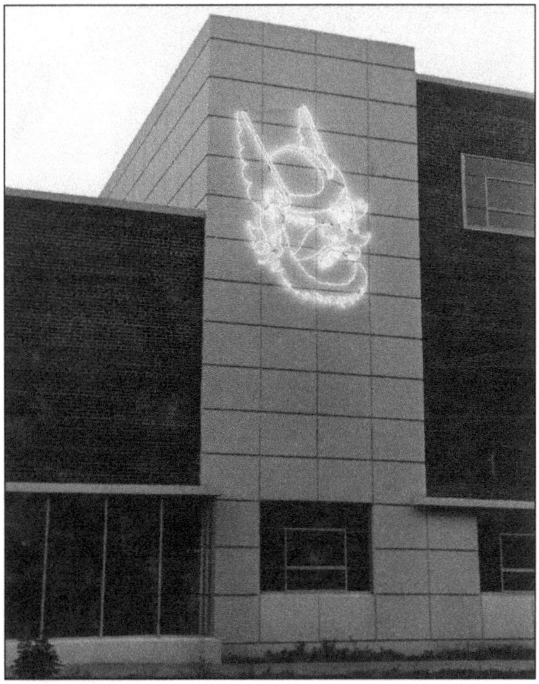

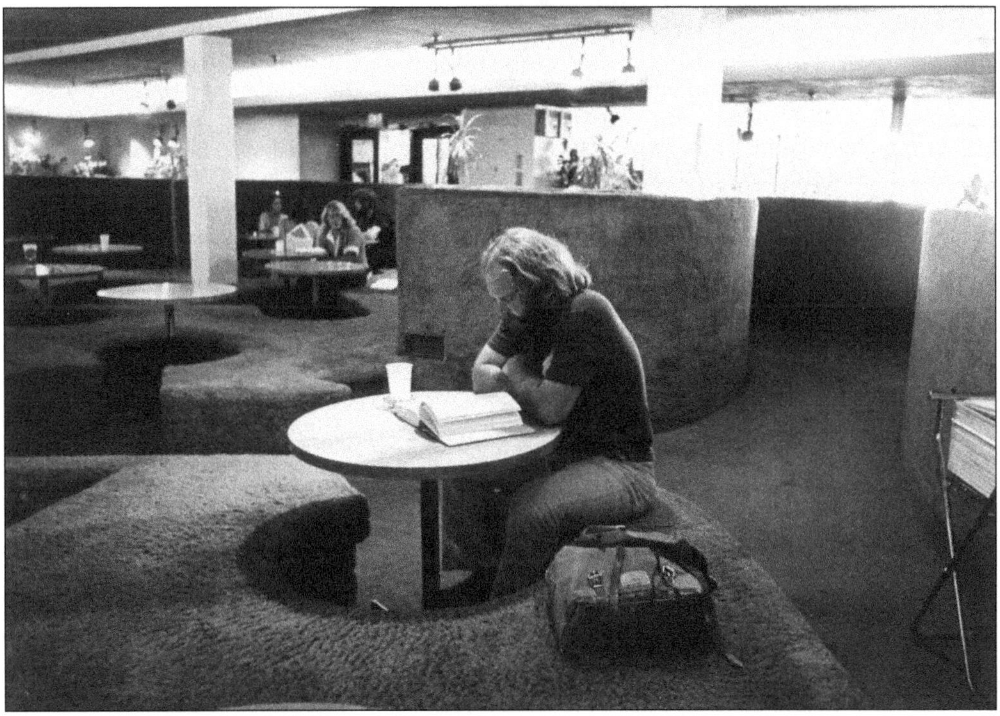

In the early 1970s, a student-led effort resulted in a redesigned Student Union Building dining area. Bright blue shag carpet covered specially built alcoves and sitting areas to provide cozy spaces for individual studying or group conversations. Administrators found it difficult to provide oversight in the space, and while avant-garde at first, the design soon became outdated. (SPEC, UA 1991-040.)

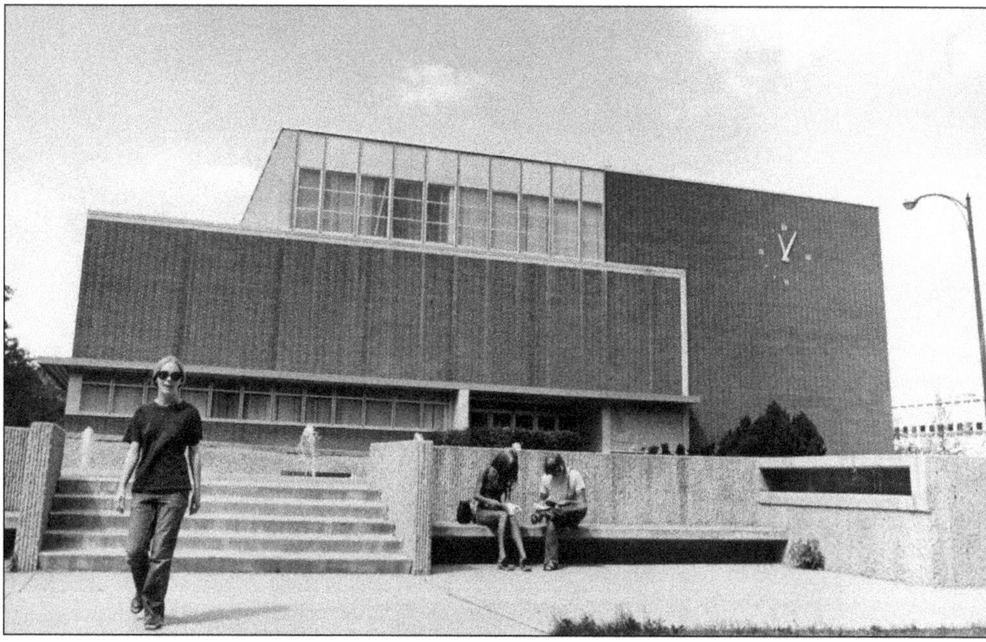

The University of Idaho Library was first housed in the Administration Building and lost most of its collection in the 1906 fire. Head Librarian M. Belle Sweet rebuilt the collection over her 43-year career. The Library remained in the new Administration Building until 1957, when the first separate Library Building opened and included specialized collections for graduate study and government documents. It also housed the University of Idaho branch of the US Post Office from 1957 to 1990; UI was assigned its own zip code in 1992. A 1993 addition included an 84-foot clock tower that has become a familiar campus site. In 2016, a complete first-floor renovation included space for the Making, Innovation, and Learning Laboratory, a new Special Collections Reading Room, and enhanced collaborative learning spaces for students. (Above, SPEC, UA 2001-001; below, UI Photo Services.)

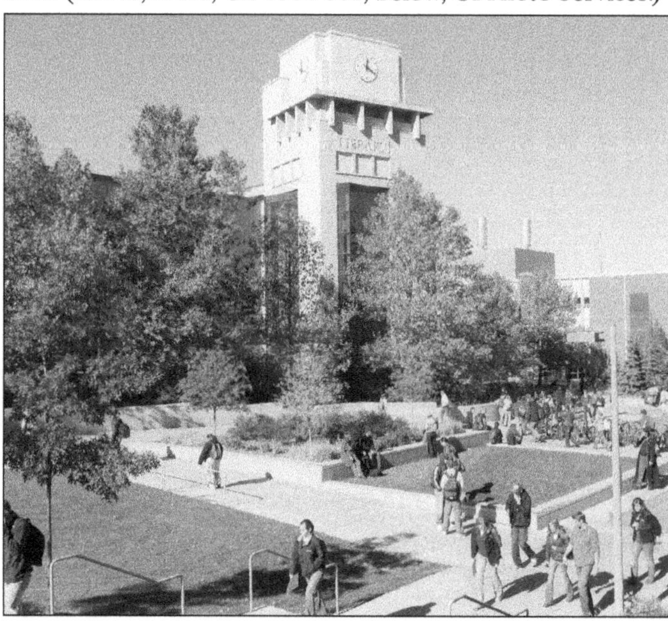

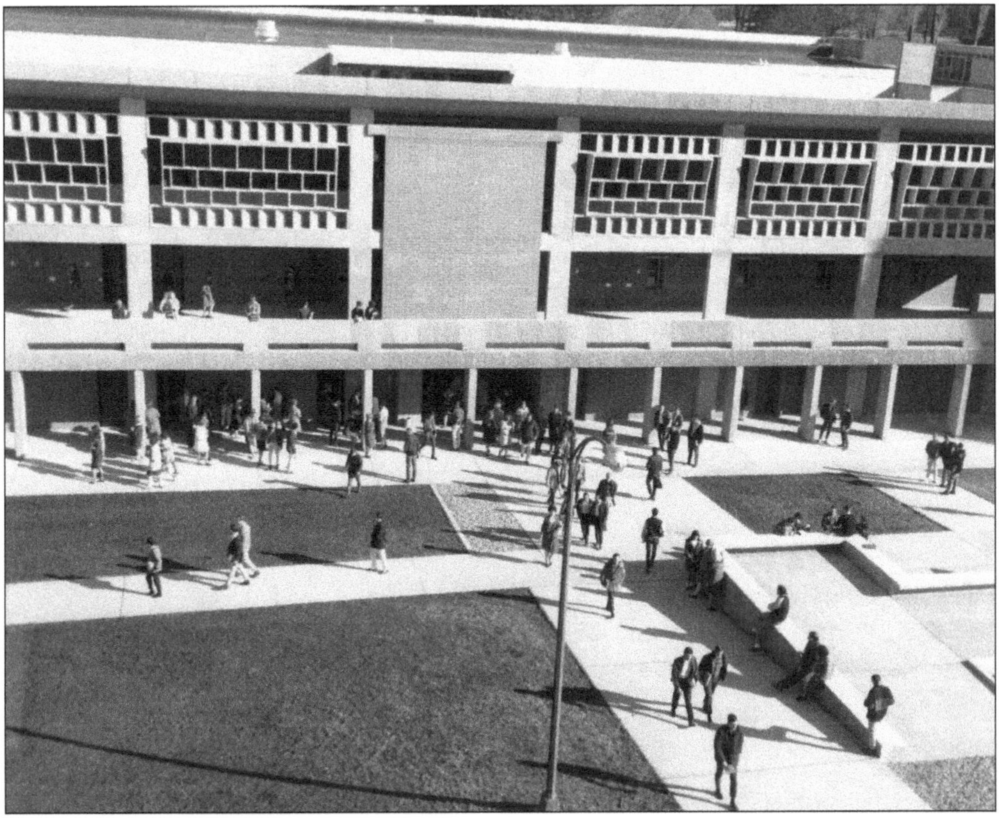

University Classroom Center was a state-of-the-art teaching facility when it opened in 1964. Located on the academic mall, it housed the media center, student support offices, and classrooms. A hidden hallway extended behind each classroom where instructors could place slides and other audiovisuals that were projected on screens in the rooms. Each classroom featured outside doors. The building was torn down, except for its skeleton, in 2003. (SPEC, PG 1-128-15.)

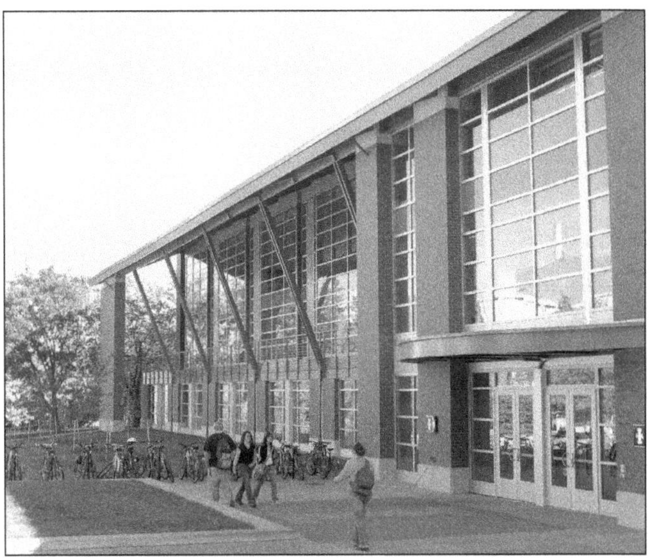

Since 2005, students have been able to move easily from the connected Idaho Commons to the Teaching and Learning Center. Built utilizing the University Classroom Center's skeleton, the TLC includes 29 classrooms featuring teaching podiums that provide instructors with multimedia and internet access. The Commons houses many student services, dining options, a small art gallery, and meeting rooms. (UI Photo Services.)

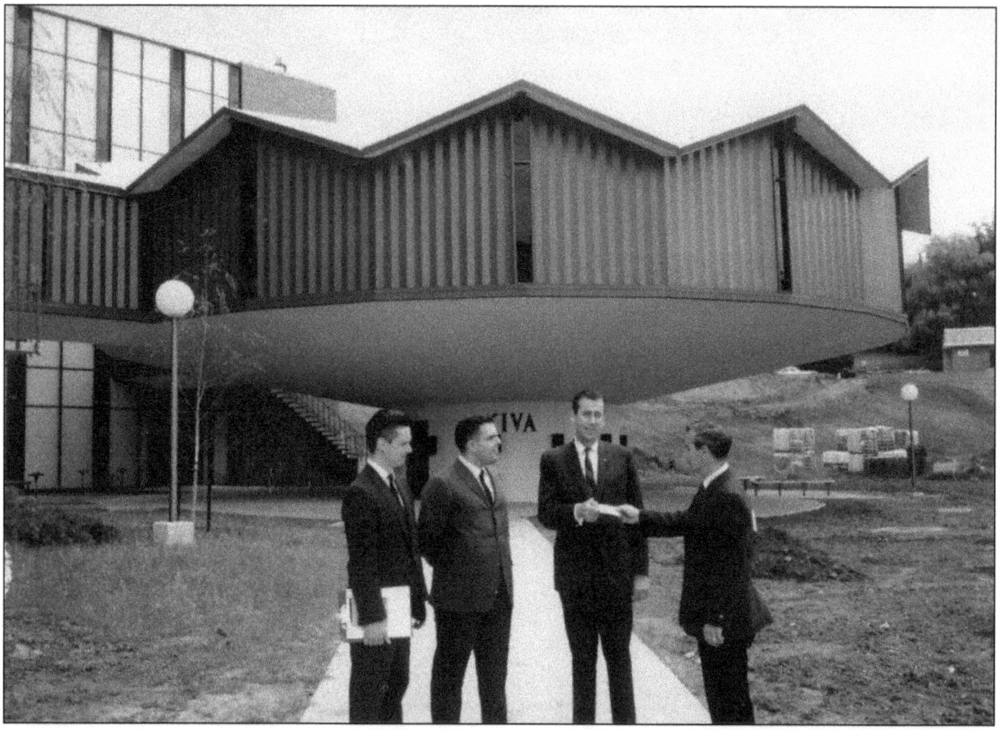

Built in 1967, the Education Building featured the architecturally interesting Kiva, a fluted-sided building atop a pedestal that was proposed as a place where people could engage in collaborative learning. It was designed to provide the flexibility to accommodate large group lectures, professional meetings, team teaching, and even theatrical performances. At the 1969 dedication are, from left to right, unidentified, Forrest E. Sears, Dean Everett Samuelson, and Edmund Chavez. The Kiva was demolished in 2014 as part of a renovation of the Education Building. A combination of appropriated funds, bonding, and private donations facilitated the design and construction of an education facility for the 21st century. Faculty can model up-to-date pedagogical methodology, and students enjoy amenities designed to encourage socializing and group study. The new Education Building opened in the fall of 2016. (Above, SPEC, PG 1-139-1; below, courtesy of Kristin Becker.)

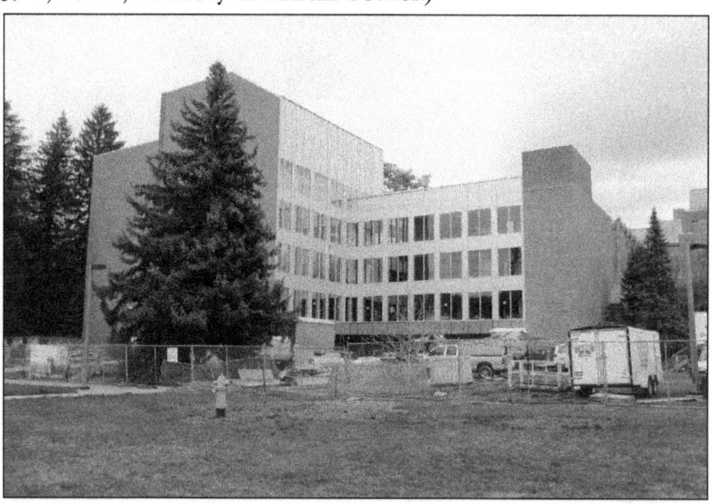

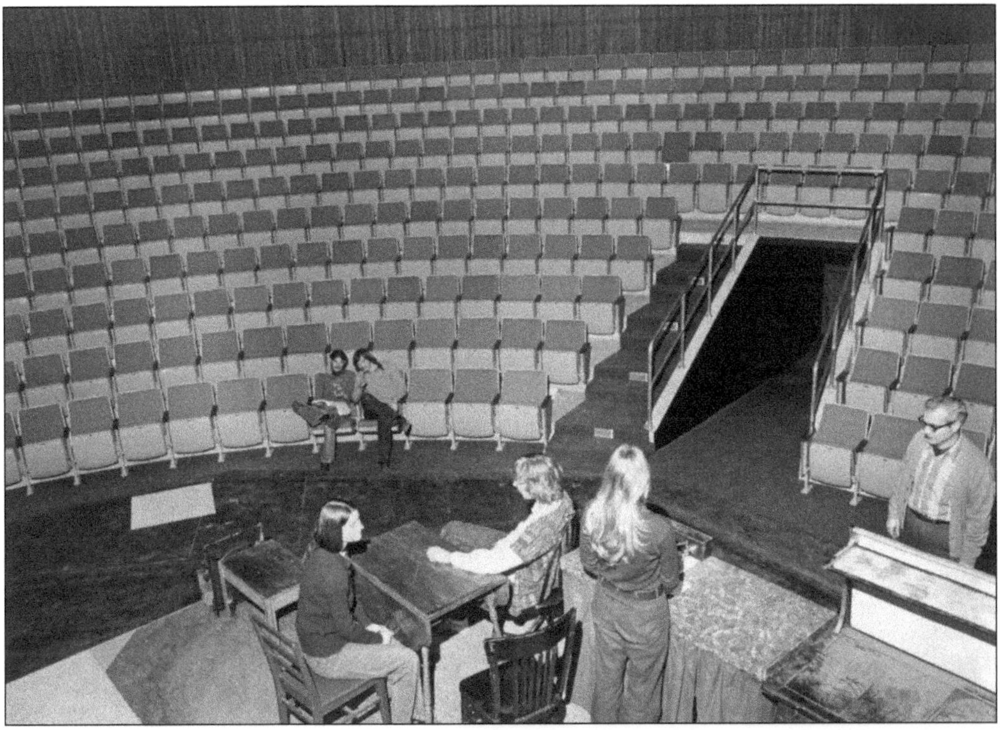

The Performing Arts Center opened in 1974 and was renamed Hartung Theater in honor of Pres. Ernest Hartung. Bill Fagerbakke is just one celebrated Theatre Department graduate. After a knee injury ended his UI football career, he turned to acting. Fagerbakke is best known for his role as Dauber in *Coach* and as the voice of Patrick Star in *SpongeBob SquarePants*. Pictured are students rehearsing in 1975. (SPEC, PG 1-45-15a.)

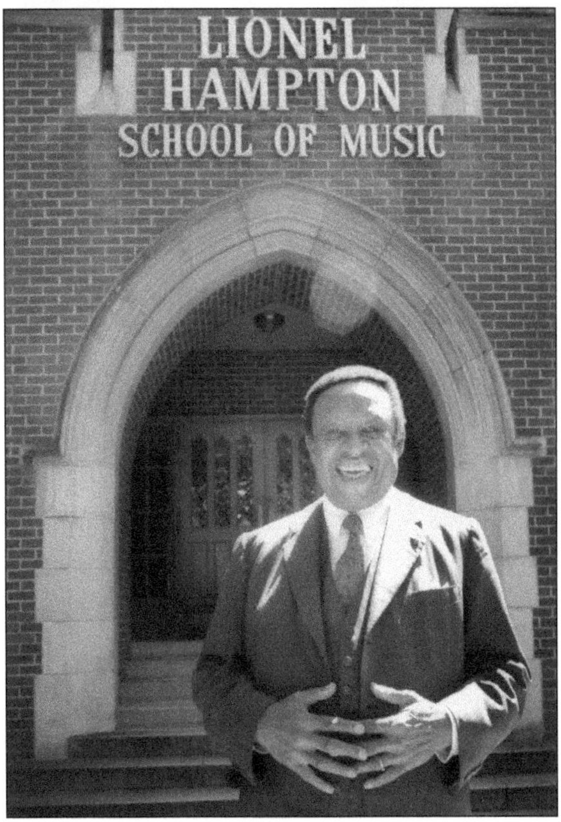

The School of Music building was dedicated in 1952 and named for legendary vibraphonist and band leader Lionel Hampton in 1987. It is the first school of music named for a jazz musician in the United States. In 2010, the recital hall was renamed the Haddock Performance Hall. Its cast iron seats were restored to their original splendor, making it a timeless space for performing and learning. (SPEC, UA 1998-003.)

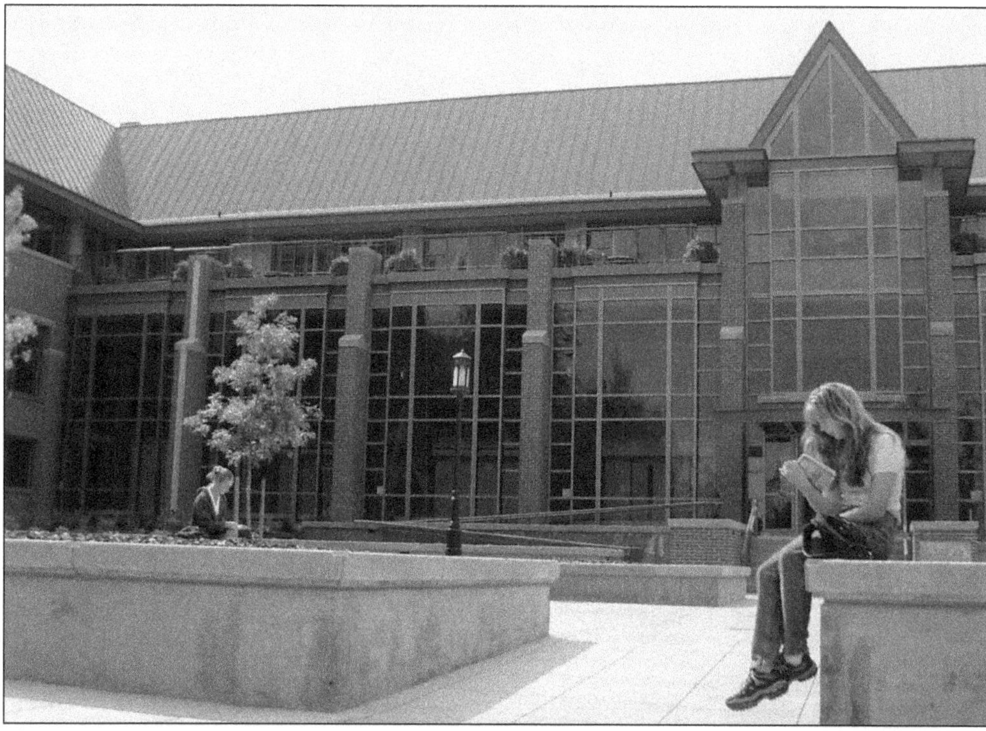

Dedicated in 2002, the Albertson Building houses the College of Business and Economics and was the first academic building on campus funded entirely by donations. Among the building's state-of-the-art features is the US Bank Trading Room, which includes 22 trading stations and a Bloomberg terminal for real-time market analysis to facilitate students' hands-on security trading. A 20-foot ticker display keeps students apprised of market conditions. (UI Photo Services.)

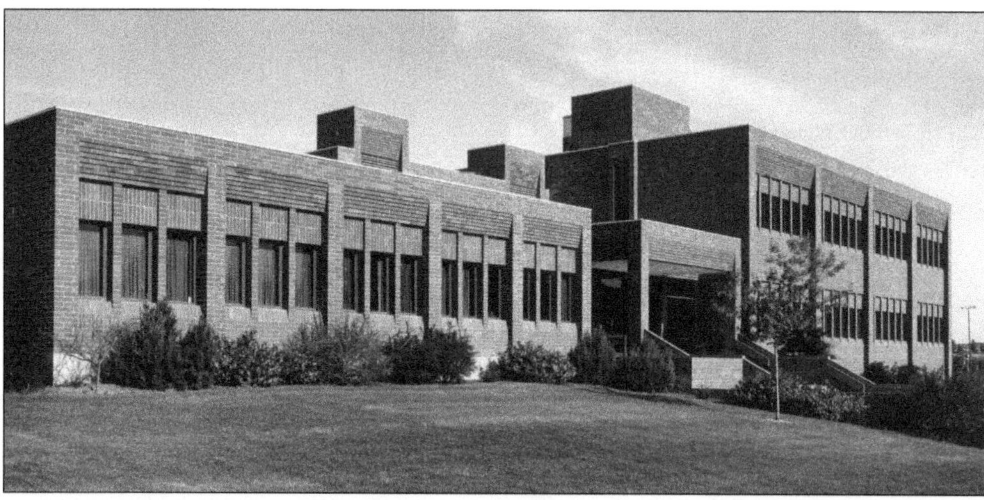

Menard Law Building is pictured in 1974. The College of Law was established in 1909 and is the only public accredited law school in Idaho. Students may study in Moscow or in Boise at the Idaho Law and Justice Center (the old Ada County Courthouse). In 1984, the building was named in honor of Dean Albert Menard and is the university's first building designed for legal education. (SPEC, UA 2001-001.)

The forestry program is one of the nation's oldest and most respected. "The Snag" is an ancient white bark pine snag taken from near Clarkia on 6,000-foot Freezout Ridge in the summer of 1970. In 1972, the new College of Forestry, Wildlife, and Range Sciences building was installed around the tree. Reflecting the changing discipline, in 2000, the unit became the College of Natural Resources. (SPEC, UA 2001-01.)

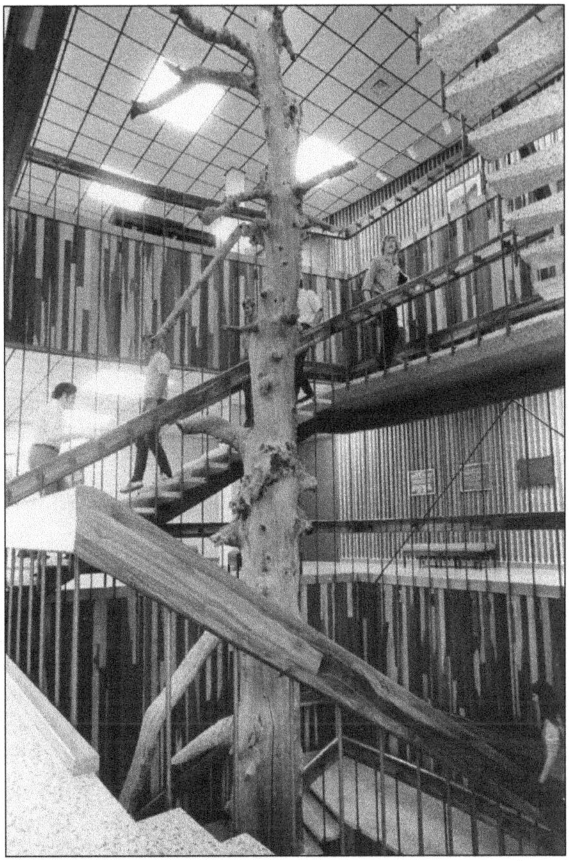

The College of Agricultural and Life Sciences operates 860 acres of farms in the Moscow area used for both teaching and research. The Dairy Barn, pictured in 1962, was constructed during the 1930s, when the college boasted that five UI cows produced more than 30,000 pounds of milk a year. For years, UI had fistulated cows (with an interior hole for scientific research) known as "holey cows." (SPEC, UA 1989-61.)

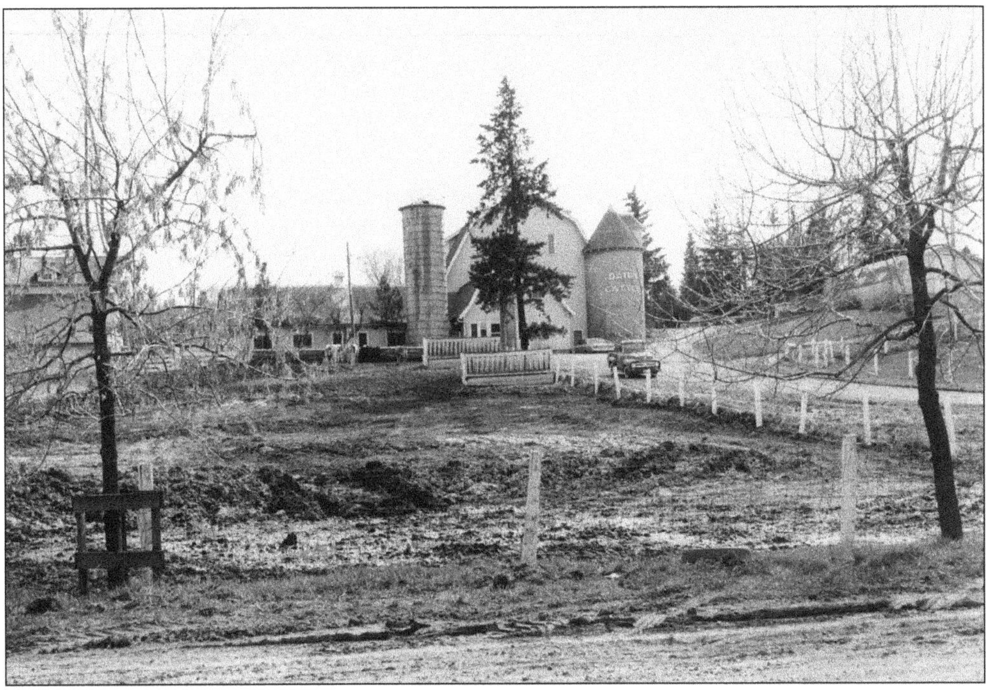

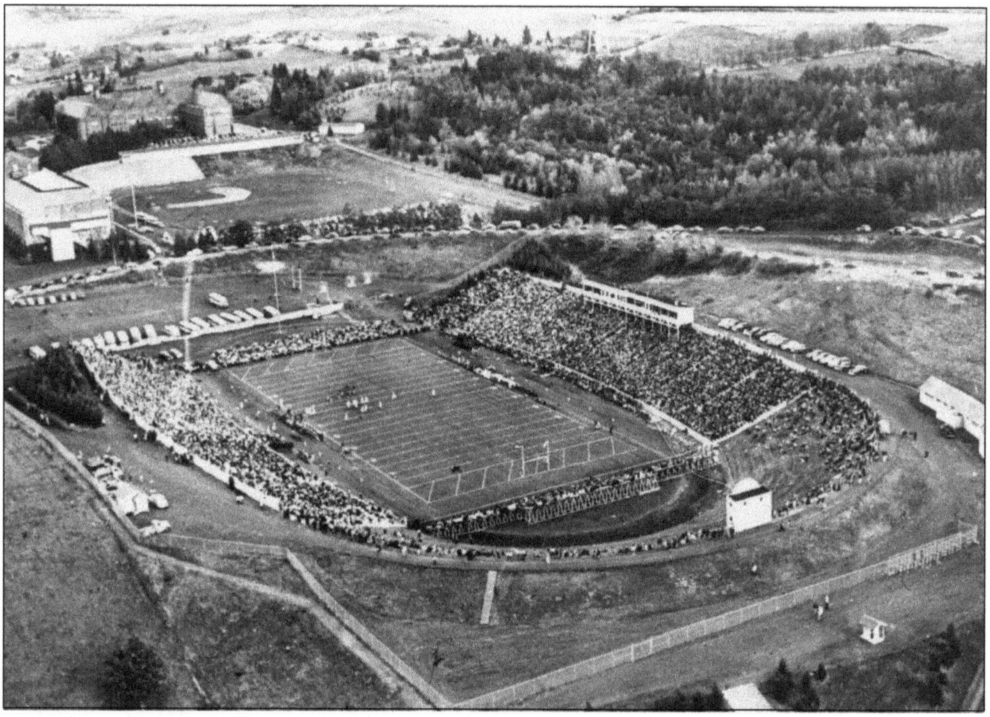

University of Idaho men and women played baseball at MacLean Field from 1895 to 1966. Also the site of women's field hockey and other sports, it was named in honor of university president James MacLean. The Education Building currently occupies this location. Neale Stadium (in the foreground), named for Pres. Mervin Neale, was the site of intercollegiate football games from 1936 to 1969. It partially burned in a 1969 arson fire. (SPEC, PG 1-85-9.)

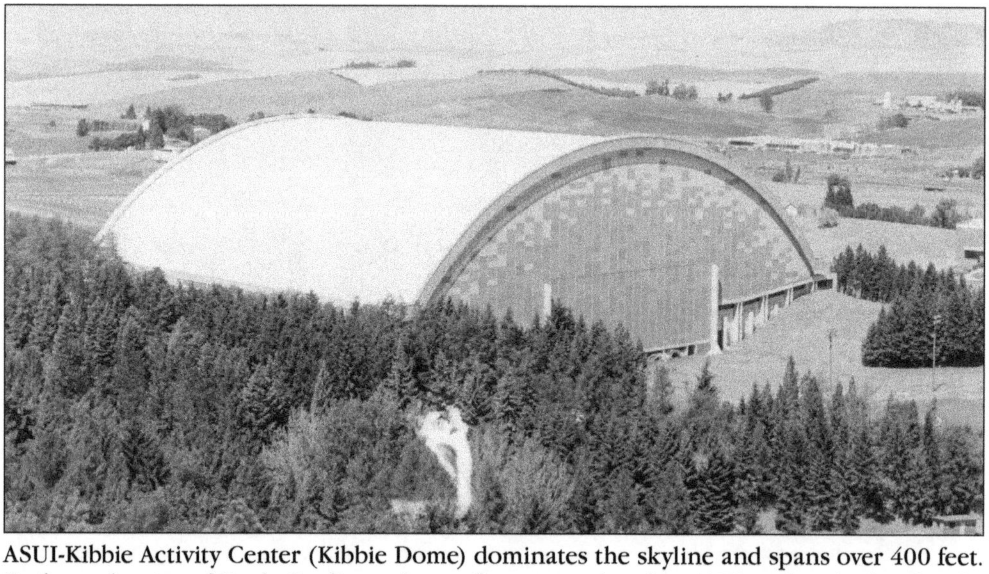

ASUI-Kibbie Activity Center (Kibbie Dome) dominates the skyline and spans over 400 feet. Built on the site of Neale Stadium, the roof was completed in 1975 and is the height of a 12-story building. Renovations have included training rooms, offices, and premium seating. The Kibbie Dome is home to Vandal football, indoor track and field, tennis, and basketball. In 2001, the Cowan Spectrum basketball venue debuted. (SPEC, UA2001-01.)

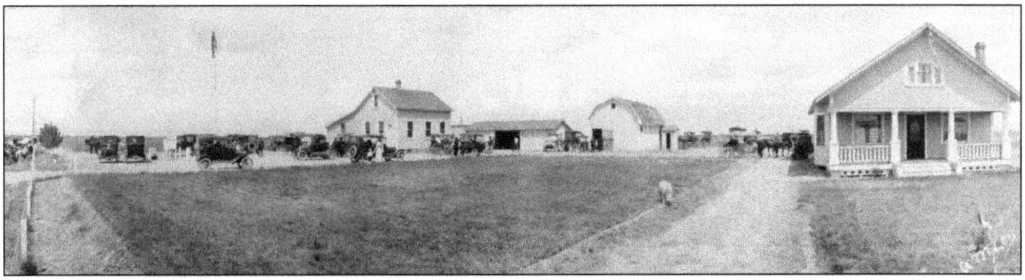

The Aberdeen Research and Extension Center was established in 1911 to serve dryland and irrigated farms in eastern and southern Idaho. Irrigation presented farmers with a new set of challenges that required educational efforts from the university. The University of Idaho purchased the land in 1925; Aberdeen holdings now include 440 acres with world-class potato research. Pictured is a 1916 Farmers' Night, now the Aberdeen Twilight Tour. (Courtesy of Bill Loftus.)

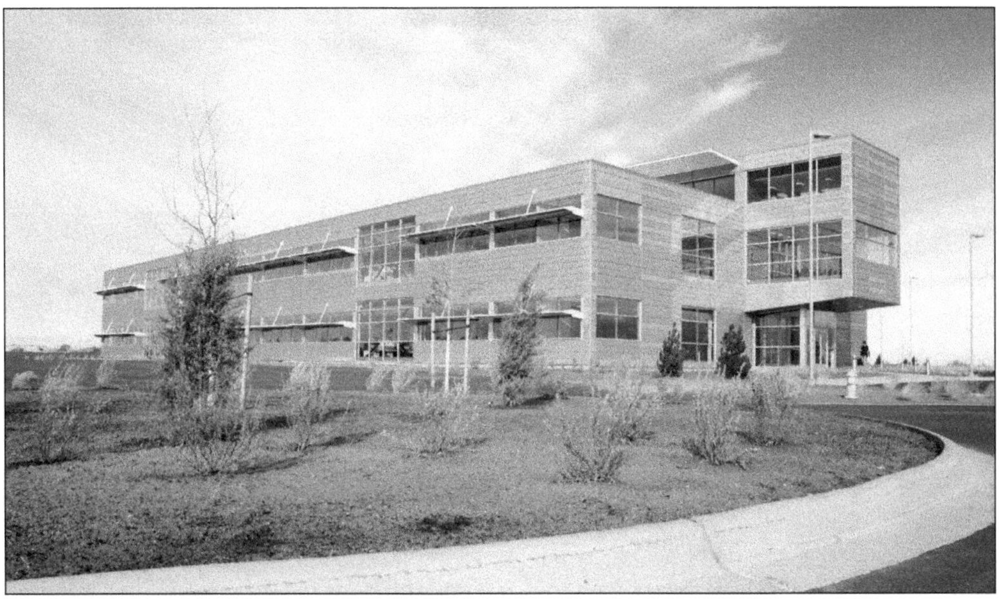

In southeastern Idaho, the University of Idaho carries out an ambitious research agenda in partnership with the Idaho National Laboratory and others. Located in Idaho Falls, the Center for Advanced Energy Studies building was dedicated in 2009 and is a unique Idaho Falls facility where UI is a leader among four institutions promoting research that seeks solutions for renewable energy. (UI Photo Services.)

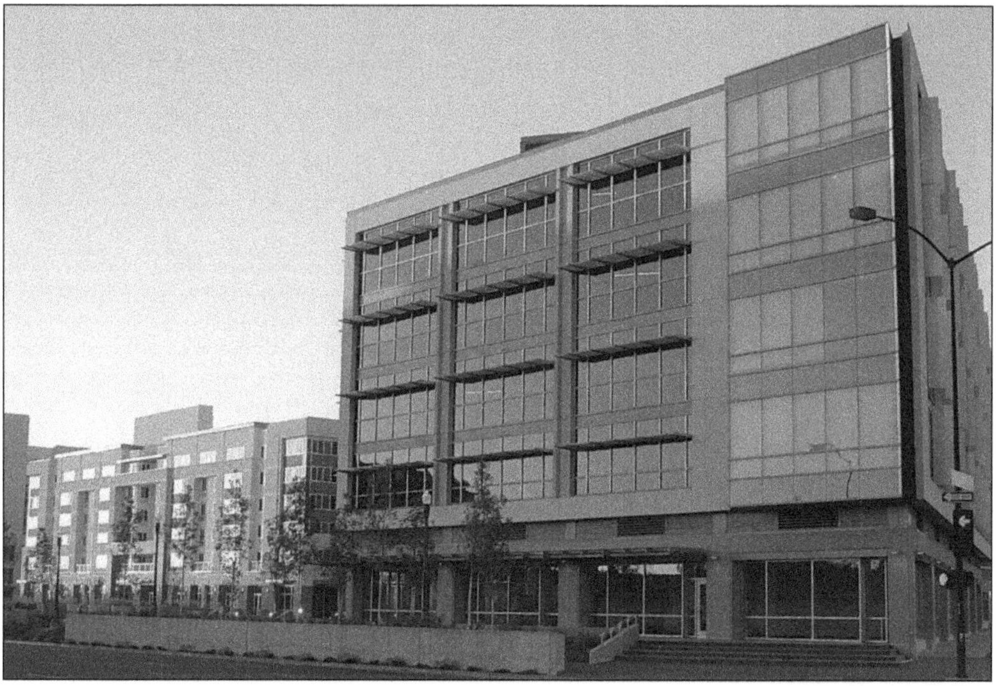

UI-Boise Center provides educational opportunities for students at all stages. The university has served southwestern Idaho since it opened an extension office there in 1910. The UI Water Center (shown here) features one of the few water flumes in the world used for Center of Ecohydraulics research, the James A. and Louise McClure Center for Public Policy Research, and the College of Art and Architecture's Integrated Design Laboratory. (UI Photo Services.)

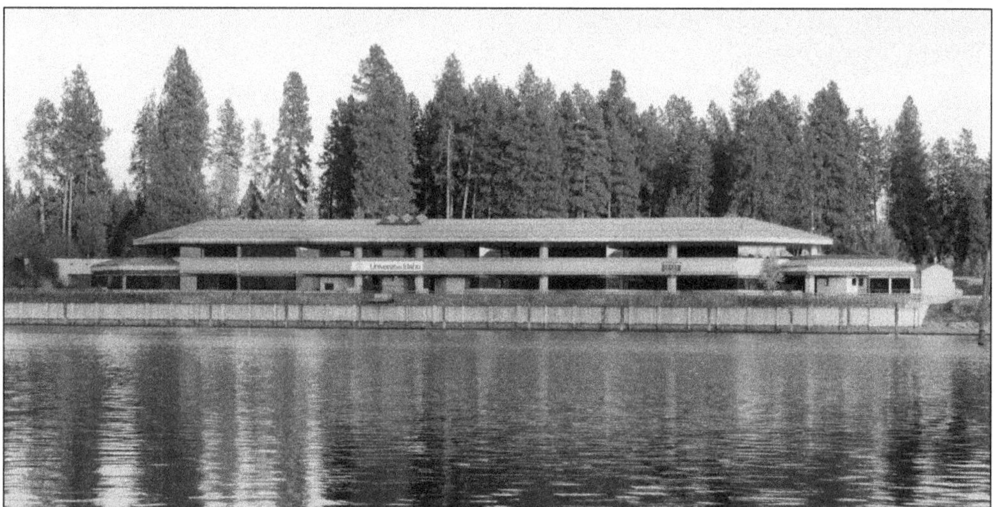

The Coeur d'Alene Center, located on the banks of the Spokane River, offers outstanding educational experiences, including certificate options and bachelor's, master's, and doctoral degrees. The UI executive master's in business administration program is located there. The Post Falls Research Park is an emerging business incubator and provides another dimension to the Coeur d'Alene Center's entrepreneurial emphasis. The Coeur d'Alene Center promotes technology for young people through its "Dig'n IT" program. (UI Photo Services.)

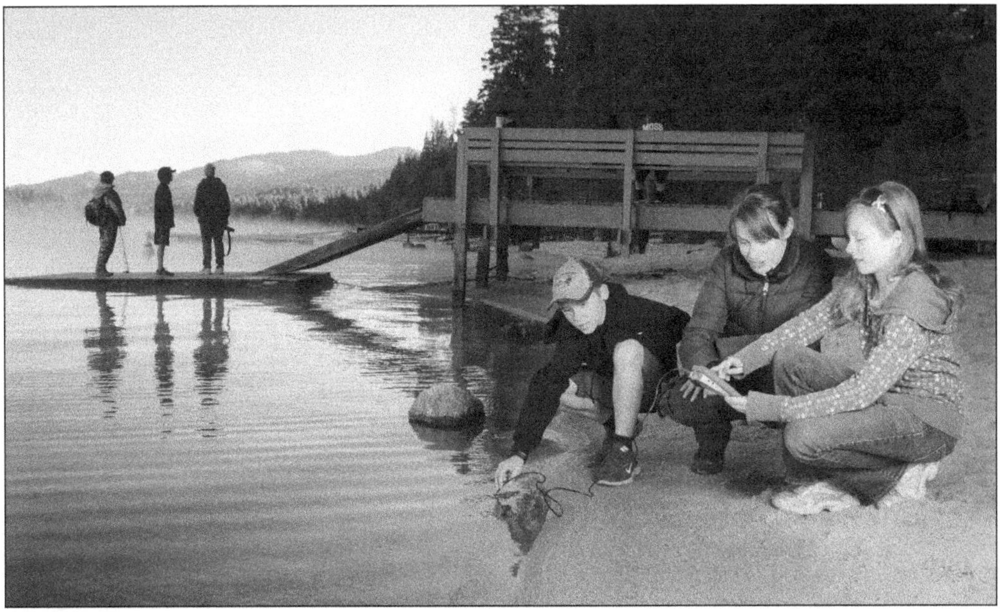

The McCall Field Campus, on the banks of Payette Lake, has been operated by the University of Idaho for more than 75 years. Originally the site of a field school for forestry students, the McCall Field Campus evolved into a multi-use facility. The McCall Outdoor Science School focuses on science, technology, engineering, and mathematics opportunities for thousands of K-12 students each year. (Courtesy of College of Natural Resources.)

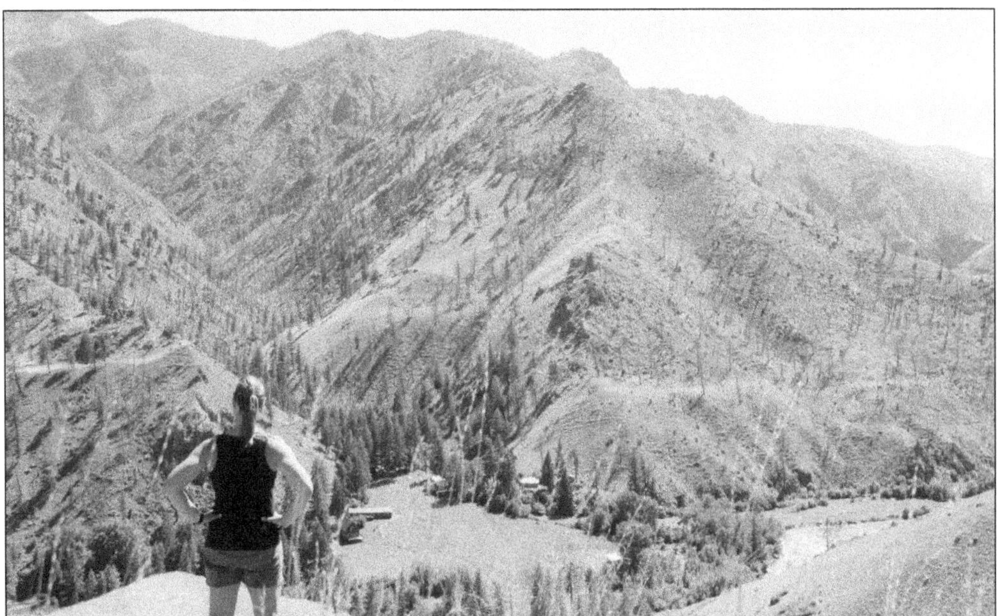

Taylor Ranch Station in the Frank Church River of No Return Wilderness is surrounded by four million acres of wilderness in central Idaho. Originally an Idaho homestead, Taylor Ranch has operated as a UI research facility since 1970. Its remote location provides unique research opportunities for federal and state projects. The Semester in the Wild program offers students an interdisciplinary educational opportunity in this beautiful location. (UI Photo Services.)

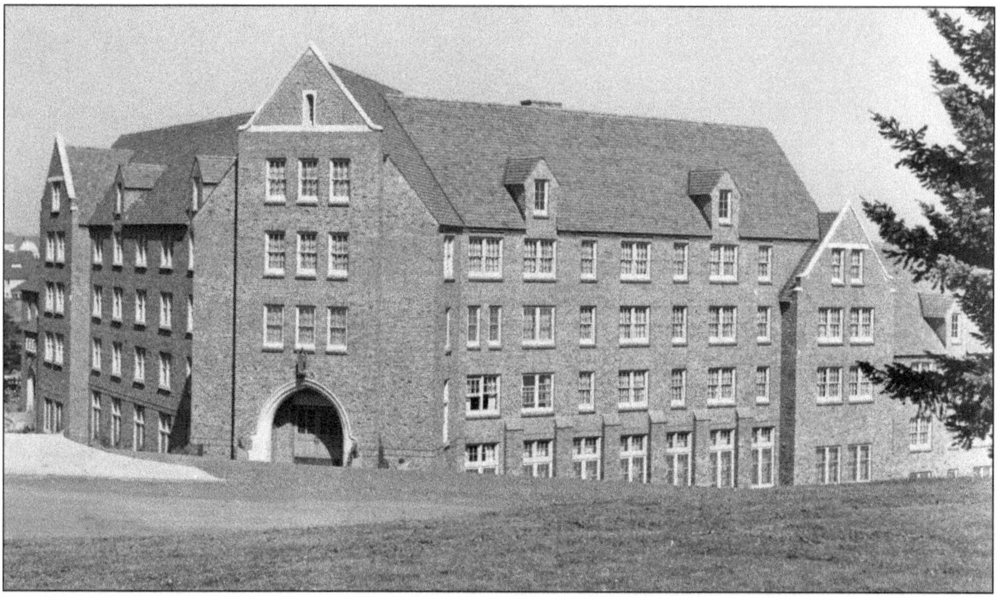

Originally built as a men's dormitory, Willis Sweet Hall (named for UI founder and early board of regents member), this 1936 building was renamed in 1982 to honor Moscow native Carol Ryrie Brink (honorary doctorate, 1965), 1936 Newbery Medal winner for *Caddie Woodlawn*. Brink Hall is home to the Departments of English and Mathematics. Interior design students created plans for the new Faculty-Staff Lounge, dedicated in 2014. (SPEC, PG 1-75-01.)

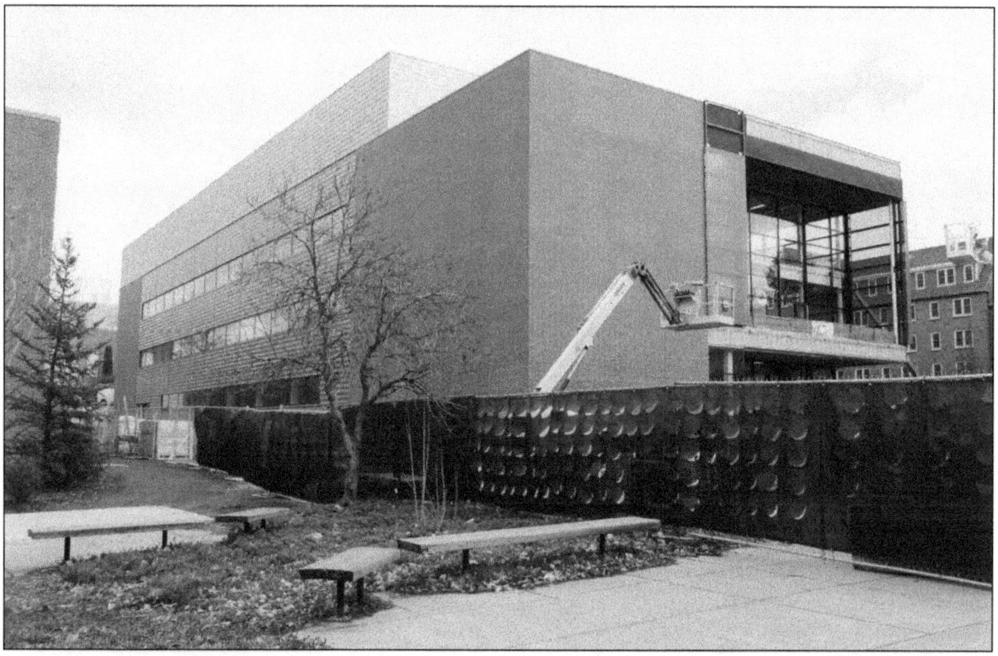

The University of Idaho's newest research building, the Integrated Research and Innovation Center, supports multidisciplinary researchers by providing new, collaborative, state-of-the-art laboratories, meeting rooms, and other learning spaces constructed with maximum flexibility to allow for changing needs over the next 25 to 50 years. The IRIC building opened in the fall of 2016. (Courtesy of Kristin Becker.)

Two

Degrees and Departments

Academics have been the foundation and purpose of the University of Idaho since its beginning in 1889. The institution offers 85 undergraduate, 63 master's, 31 doctoral, and 2 specialist degrees. More than 100,000 individuals have earned a University of Idaho degree since 1896.

In 1901, Pres. James MacLean organized the College of Letters and Science, the College of Agriculture, and the School of Applied Science (later Engineering). The regents established the College of Law in 1909 and the School of Mines and the School of Forestry in 1917. The School of Education started in 1920. Architecture was a mandated program in Idaho's constitution; the College of Art and Architecture dates from 1981. In 2004, the College of Letters and Science evolved into two separate colleges—Letters, Arts, and Social Sciences, and Science. These two colleges share primary responsibility for students' fulfillment of general education requirements. Graduate programs are housed in the College of Graduate Studies since its beginning in 1925.

The university takes great pride in the hands-on experiences it offers to students in every discipline. As part of the State Board of Education's Complete College Idaho program, starting in 2014, the university has added career counselors and internship coordinators to all of its colleges. The College of Business and Economics sponsors an annual Business Plan Competition, while the College of Engineering's Design Expo features senior capstone projects and is the Northwest's longest running interdisciplinary event of its kind. At the UI Innovation Showcase, undergraduate and graduate students in every discipline have an opportunity to display their research and creative activity successes.

In recognition of its high academic standards, the University of Idaho is home to the first Phi Beta Kappa (scholastic honorary society) chapter in the state. Idaho Alpha Chapter was established in 1925. High achieving students belong to honor societies in their various disciplines. Undergraduate students can also study under the Honors Program, established in 1983.

The Carnegie Foundation has designated the University of Idaho as a "higher research activity" institution. The university engages in nearly $100 million of funded research annually, including leading nine institutions in the Idea Network of Biomedical and Research Excellence, the largest biomedical research project in Idaho history. It also plays a leading role in a $20-million project to understanding climate change in the Pacific Northwest, sponsored by the US Department of Agriculture's National Institute of Food and Agriculture.

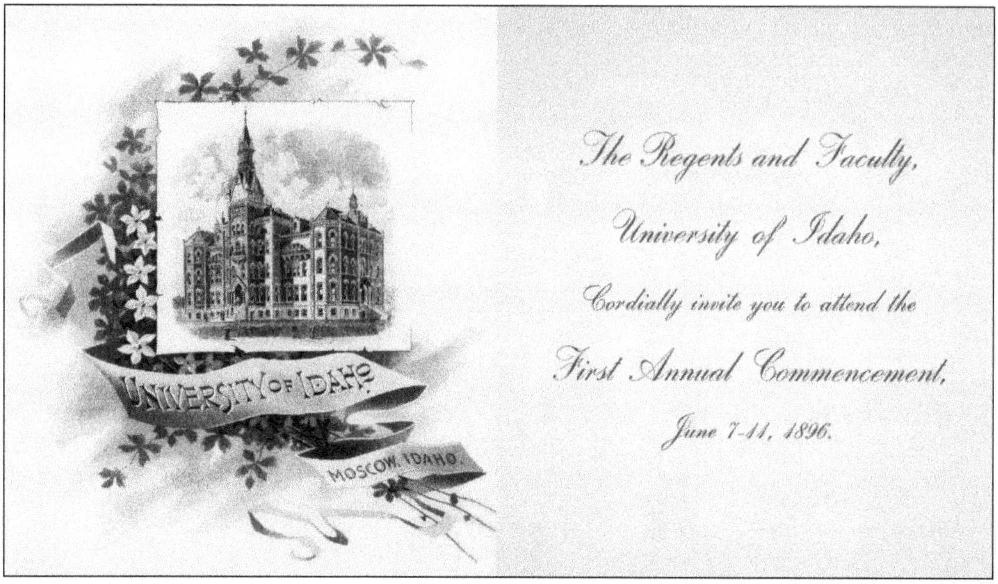

The first class to graduate from the University of Idaho in 1896 included four students, three from Idaho and one from the state of Washington. The composition of the class illustrates the democratizing aspect of the land-grant experiment, as the university welcomed women since the beginning. In the early years, most students were not able to qualify for full admission; they enrolled in the University of Idaho's preparatory department, which closed in 1913 after operating for 21 years. Annual academic fees were $15. The cover of the first commencement program in 1896 included an illustration of the original Administration Building. Pictured below are, from left to right, Stella Maude Allen, Florence May Corbett, Charles Luther Kirtley, and Arthur Prentis Adair. (Above, SPEC, PG 1-51-48a; below, SPEC, PG 2-122-8.)

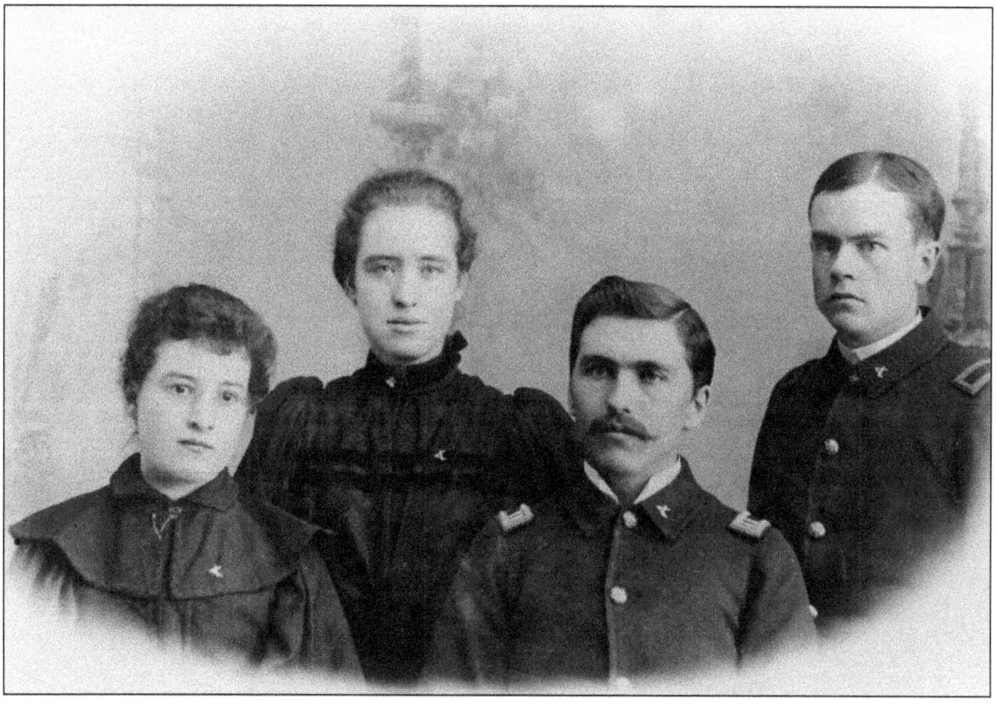

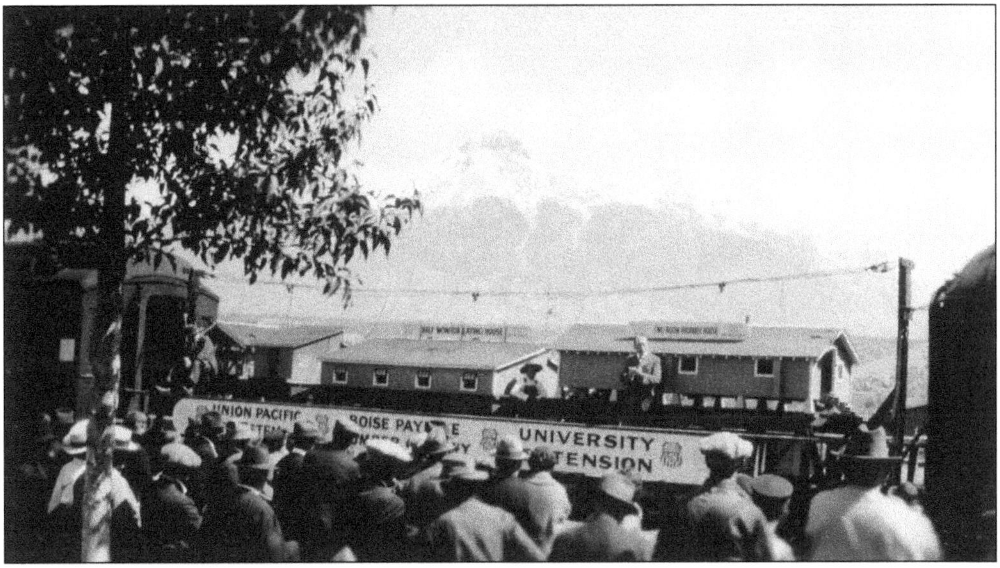

The University of Idaho began offering "farmers' institutes" throughout the state in 1898; over the years, they reached thousands of Idahoans. The College of Agriculture leased railcars, called demonstration trains, to transport equipment and faculty around the state. The trains' visits to Idaho towns were opportunities for farmers to socialize while getting up-to-date information that affected their production. The institute was later named the "Movable School." (SPEC, UA 1989-061.)

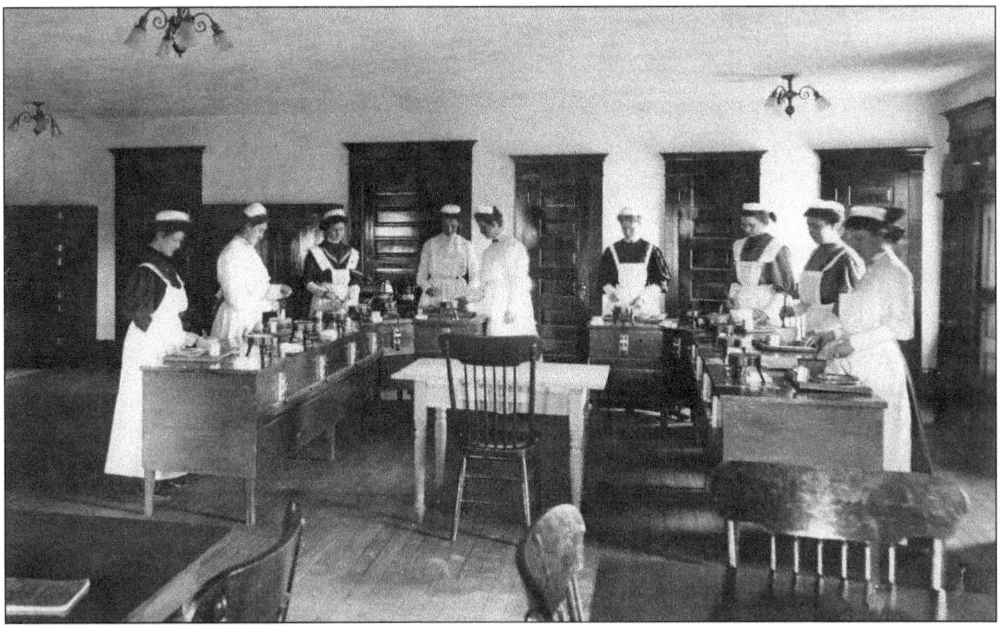

In 1902, the University of Idaho became the first school in the Pacific Northwest to establish a department of domestic science, the same year these women participated in a cooking class in Ridenbaugh Hall. The department was renamed Home Economics in 1911; it officially became the Margaret Richie School of Family and Consumer Science in 1993. (SPEC, PG 1-221-17.)

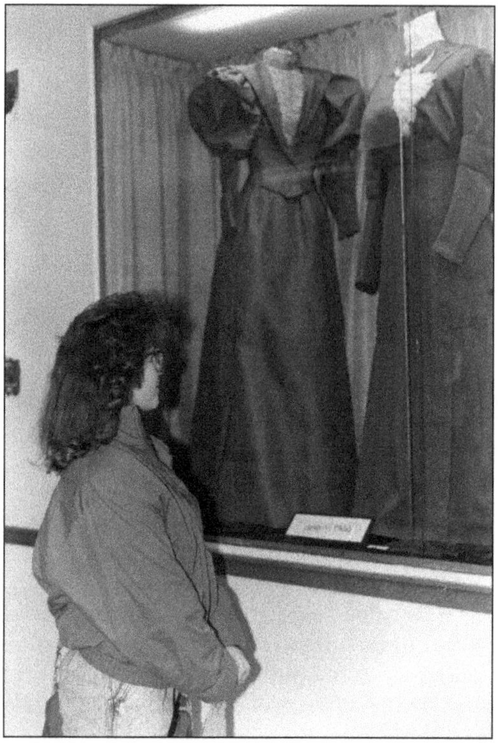

Student Jeanette Slichter views dresses on display from the Leila Old Historic Costume Collection, officially named in 1981 and currently housed in Hays Hall. The collection includes over 10,000 textile and clothing items, all connected to Idaho or the university. Professor Old started the collection to provide teaching and learning opportunities for students in Home Economics. Soon, virtual displays will allow wider access to the collection. (SPEC, UA 2008-015.)

Home Economics students participate in an upholstery class around 1945. In 1952, Home Economics moved to its new building, Niccolls Hall. A building renovation in 2014 included the Carmelita Spencer Food Laboratory and a state-of-the-art Child Development Laboratory. The School of Family and Consumer Science joined the College of Agriculture in 1983 and was renamed after Margaret Richie in 1993. (SPEC, PG 1-221-19.)

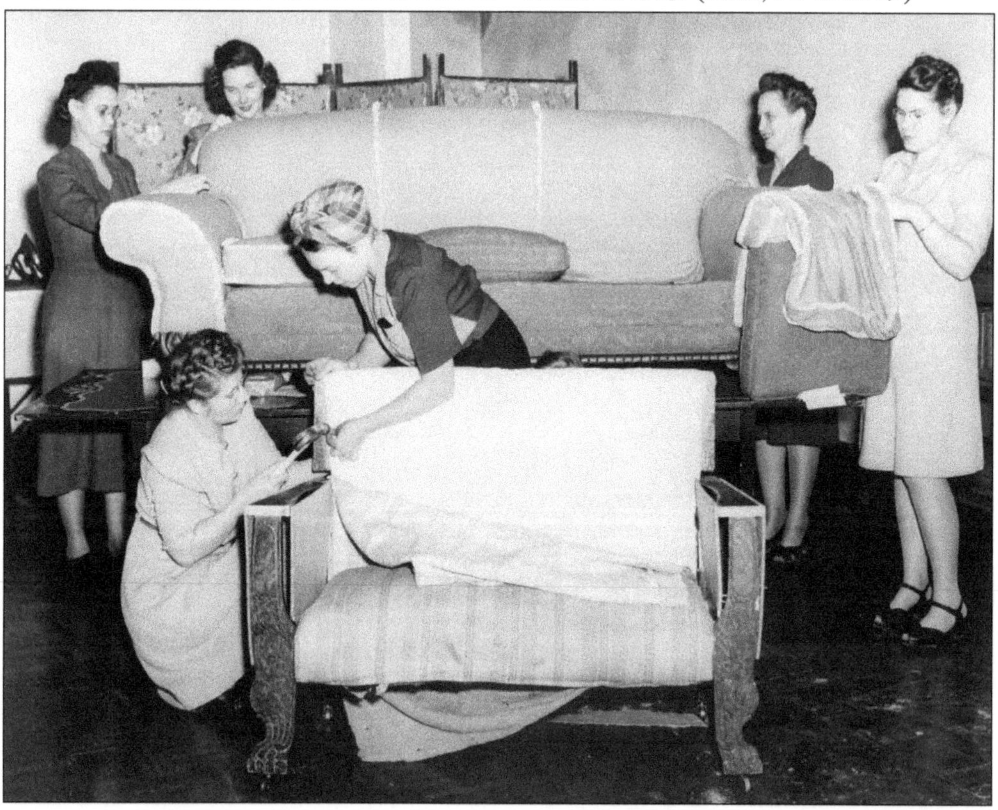

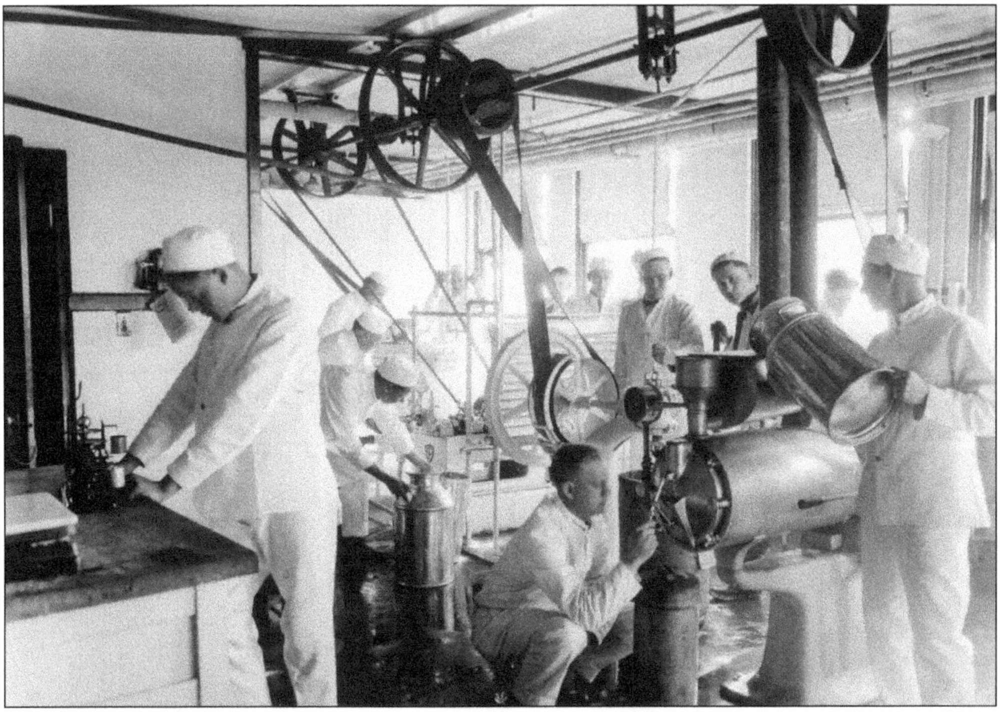

Students work in the ice cream laboratory around 1925. Dairy science continues to be at the forefront of teaching and research in the College of Agricultural and Life Sciences. Nearly 100 head of Holstein cattle are part of a program dedicated to the efficient production of high quality dairy products. The new livestock, dairy, and the environment initiative will expand the university's research in this area. (SPEC, PG 1-205-17.)

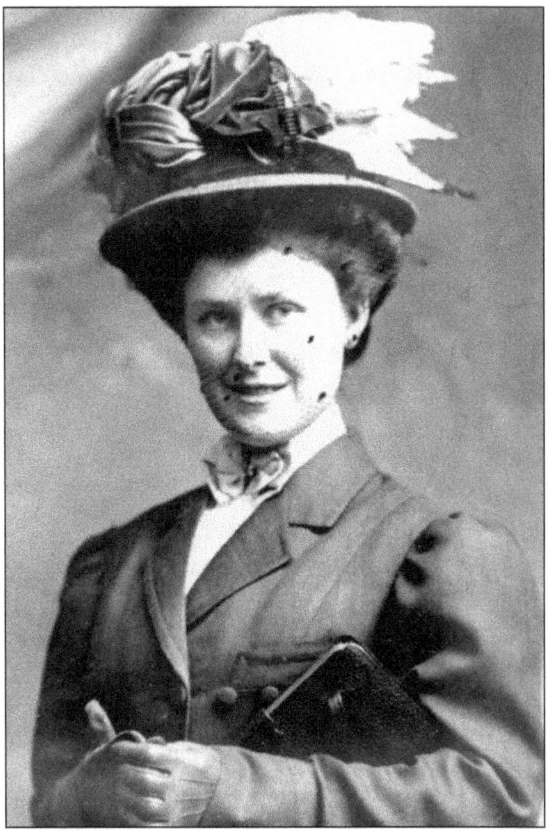

Mary Hall Niccolls (1908, domestic science), always remembered how a scholarship she received greatly aided her pursuit of her degree. Upon her death, she left $433,034 to create the Mary Hall Niccolls Scholarship Fund, which has provided support for over 500 students in the Margaret Richie School of Family and Consumer Science. Niccolls Hall, long referred to as the Home Economics Building, was named in her honor. (SPEC, PG 3-501a.)

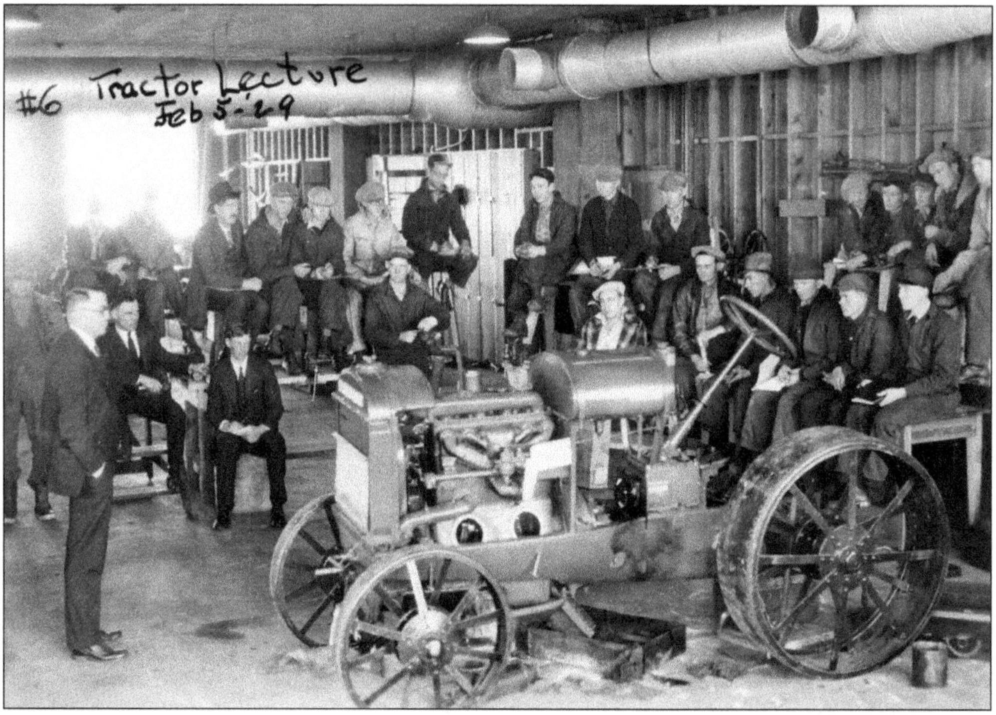

An agricultural engineering tractor lecture is pictured on February 5, 1929. As tractors replaced horses, UI experts taught farmers how to repair and maintain them. This knowledge was vital for Idaho agriculturalists. Because of their often remote locations, farmers and ranchers had to rely on their own ability to keep tractors in the field. (SPEC, PG 1-217-2.)

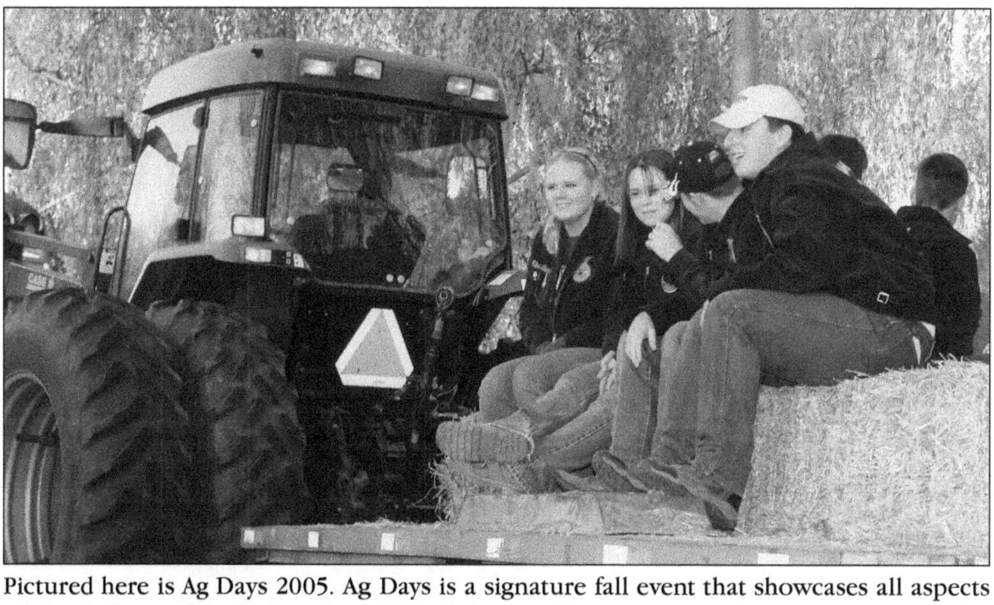

Pictured here is Ag Days 2005. Ag Days is a signature fall event that showcases all aspects of the College of Agricultural and Life Sciences. The event provides an opportunity for prospective students to experience the college and also welcomes alumni back to campus. Ag Days takes place on a home football weekend, and events include Idaho-grown meals, educational panels, and workshops. (UI Photo Services.)

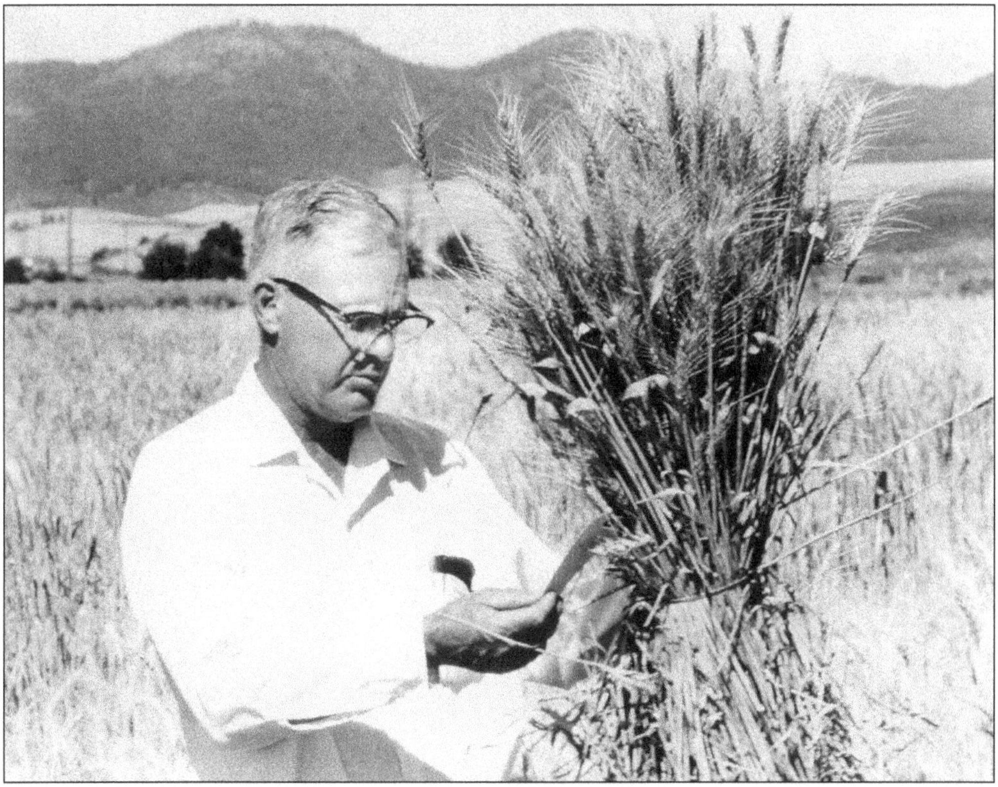

The University of Idaho's Agricultural Experiment Stations assist farmers around the state in the development of new crop varieties and research. Pictured here is agronomist Warren K. Pope, who developed the hard red winter wheat Tendoy in 1966. The Agricultural Experiment Stations have published research bulletins and publications under different names since 1892. (SPEC, UA 91-40.)

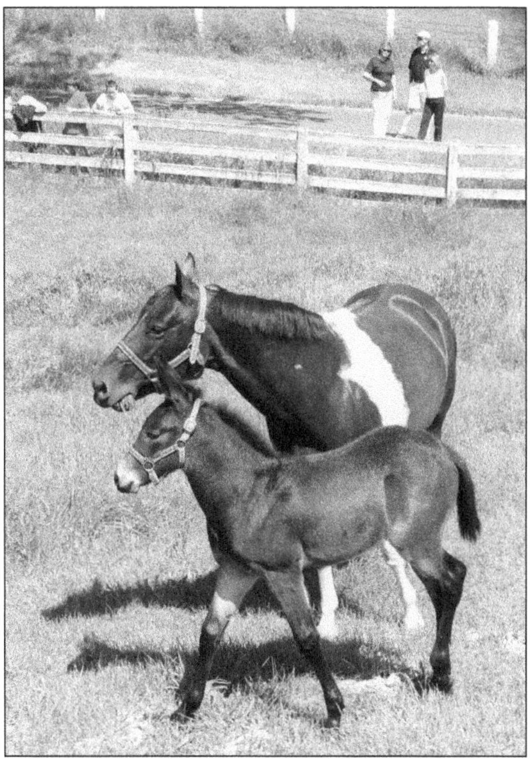

Idaho Gem (born on May 4, 2003) was the first cloned member of the equine family born as a result of fetal cell culture established at the Northwest Equine Reproduction Laboratory at the University of Idaho, under the direction of Dr. Gordon Wood and Dr. Dirk Vanderwall. Idaho Gem was an identical genetic copy of his brother, champion racing mule Taz. (UI Photo Services.)

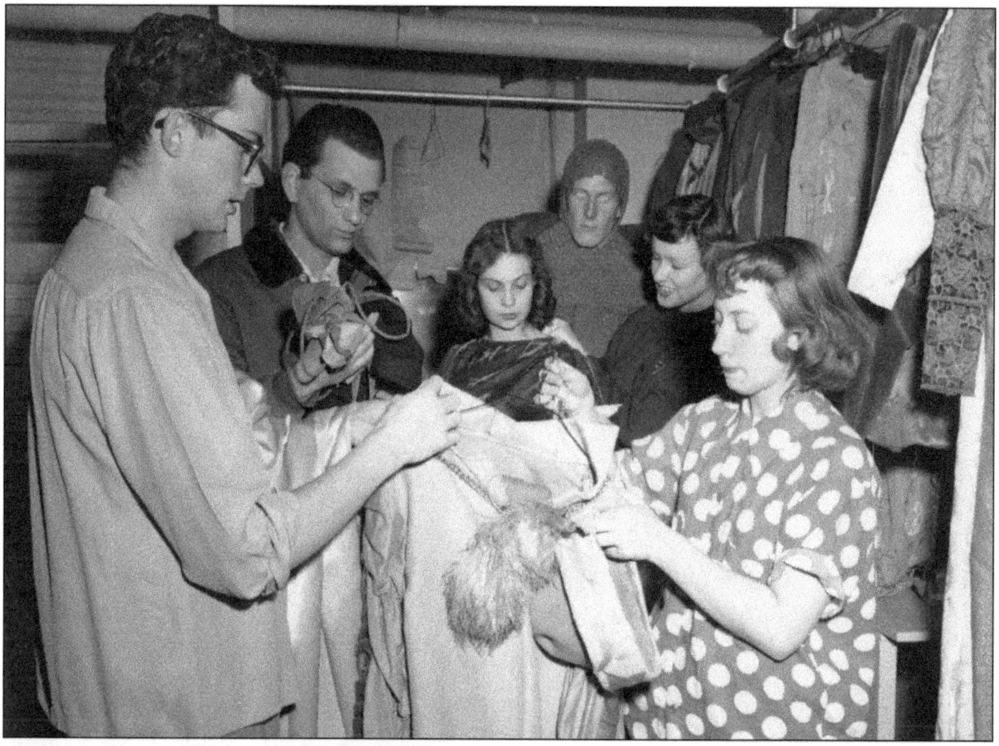

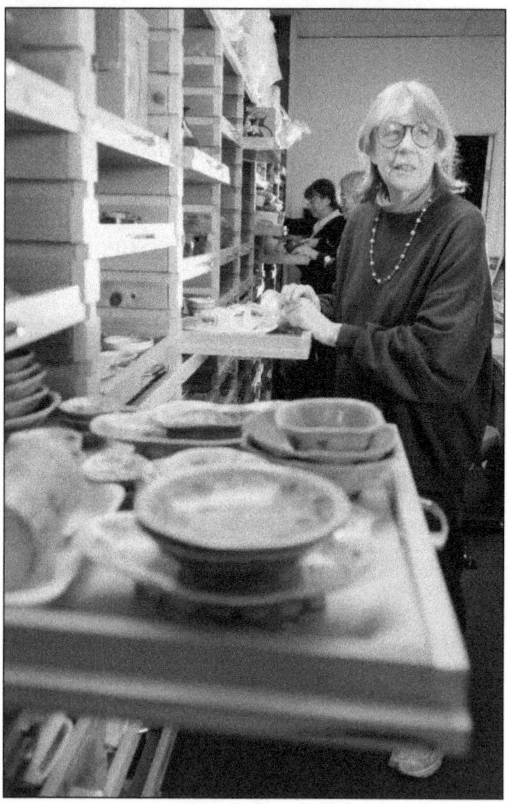

Pictured is backstage costume selection for the 1952 production of *Hamlet*. The Theatre Department maintains an extensive costume inventory that provides student opportunities and rental options for area schools and groups. Since 1973, the Hartung Theater has been home to performances and productions, and its various underground rooms contain costumes and numerous props. From left to right are Clyde Winters, Mort Grinker, Jo Magee, Rex Hill, Doris Moore, and Joan Coble. (SPEC, PG 2-141-1h.)

The Alfred W. Bowers Laboratory of Anthropology, named for its 1949 founder, provides hands-on experiences in anthropology and historical archaeology. In 1969, the board of regents designated the laboratory as an official research organization; it was named the northern Idaho repository for the Idaho Archaeological Survey in 1992. The Asian American Comparative Collection (curator Dr. Priscilla Wegars shown here) is acclaimed throughout the region. (UI Photo Services.)

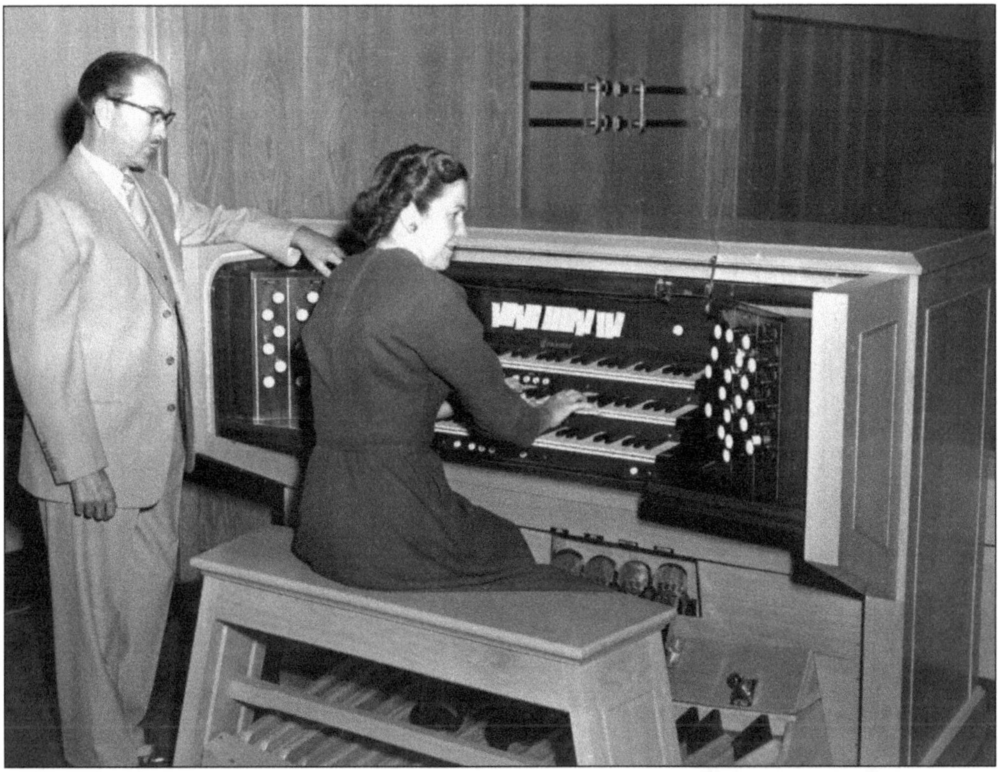

Music faculty Hall Macklin (left) and Marion Frykman test a new pipe organ in 1953. A gift from George and Mary Frederick Jewett, the memorial organ was named in honor of George Jewett's mother, Margaret Weyerhaeuser Jewett, and is housed in the Haddock Performance Hall. Alumni and friends purchased Marion Frykman's studio piano, which sat in the president's living room for years. (SPEC, PG 1-400-21.)

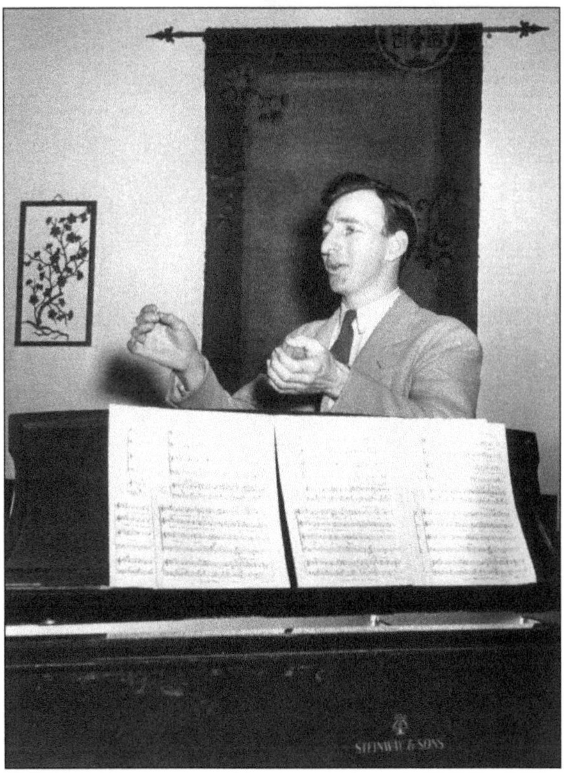

Under the direction of Glenn Lockery, the University of Idaho Vandaleers (first appearing in 1930) gained prominence on campus and across the state. Lockery joined the UI faculty in 1947 after having been a member of the first Robert Shaw Chorale. He conducted the Vandaleers in performances that ranged from Brahms, Handel, and Bach to the perennial favorite "Blue Tick Fly." Lockery retired in 1981. (SPEC, PG 3-452a.)

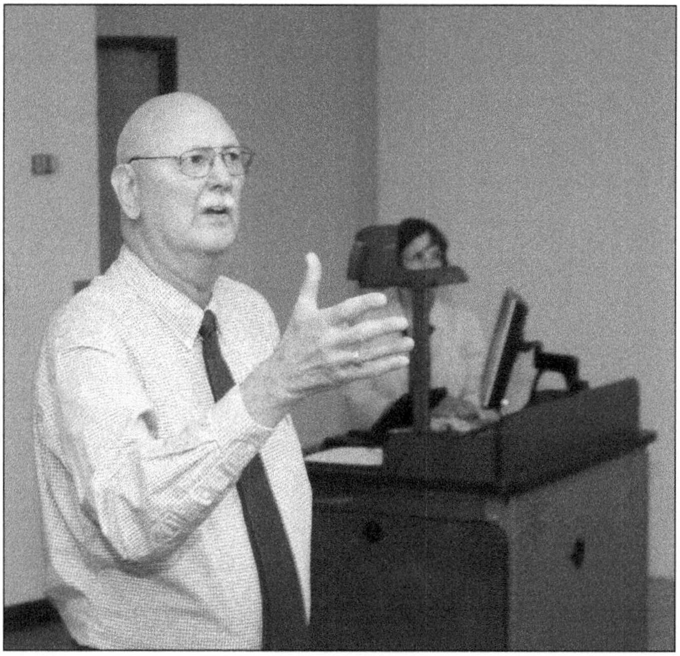

Education professor Terry Armstrong was a cofounder of the UI Found Money Fund in 1981, which started with a balance of 3¢. Countless Vandals have contributed change picked up around campus; the fund now exceeds $340,000. Use of the fund will begin with the bicentennial in 2089. President Gibb appointed Armstrong special assistant to the president, a position he held for 12 years. (Courtesy of College of Education.)

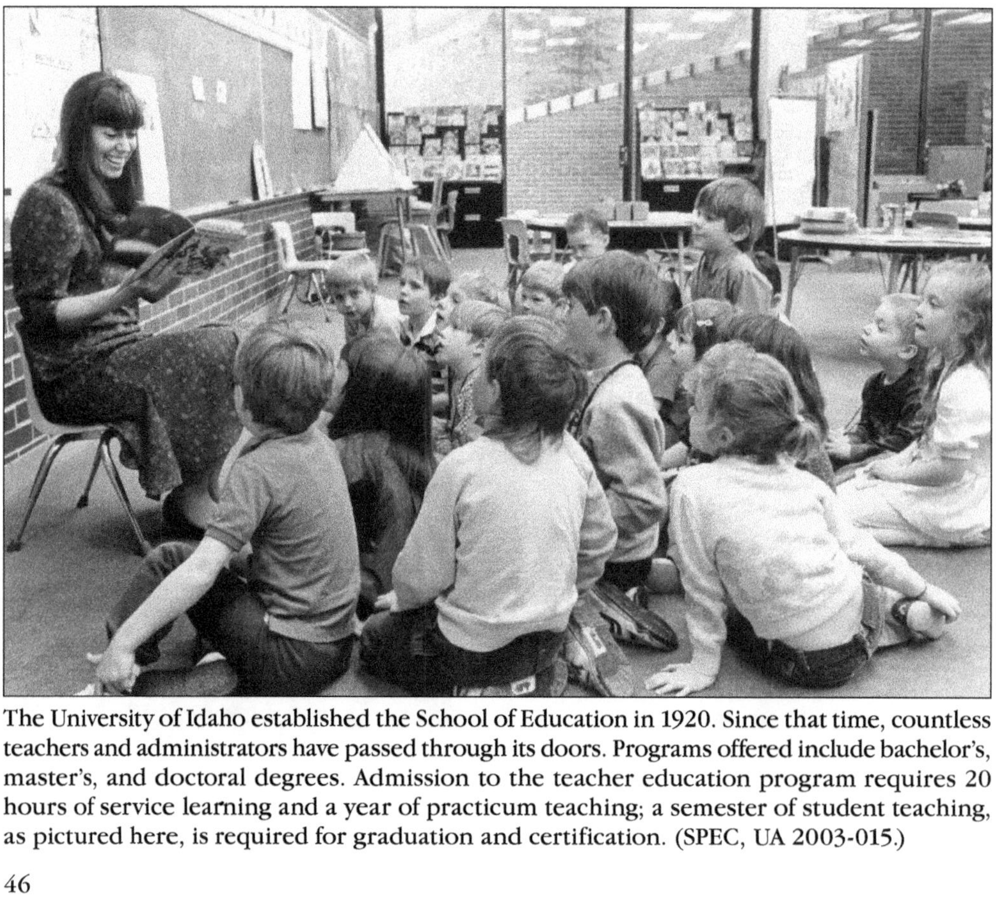

The University of Idaho established the School of Education in 1920. Since that time, countless teachers and administrators have passed through its doors. Programs offered include bachelor's, master's, and doctoral degrees. Admission to the teacher education program requires 20 hours of service learning and a year of practicum teaching; a semester of student teaching, as pictured here, is required for graduation and certification. (SPEC, UA 2003-015.)

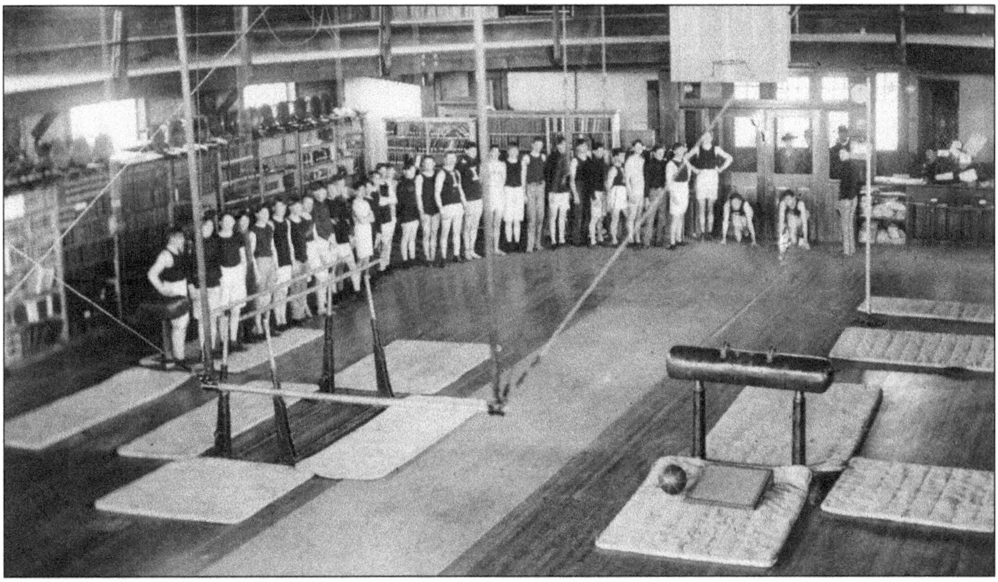

Students line up in their gym uniforms for a class in the old gymnasium in 1909. Bookshelves filled with books line the edge of the gymnasium in the background due to the building being used as a combination classroom and library after the 1906 fire. According to Rafe Gibbs in *Beacon for Mountain and Plain*, "When basketball games were played at night, both players and ball bounced against the shelves and books tumbled out." (SPEC, PG 1-54-6.)

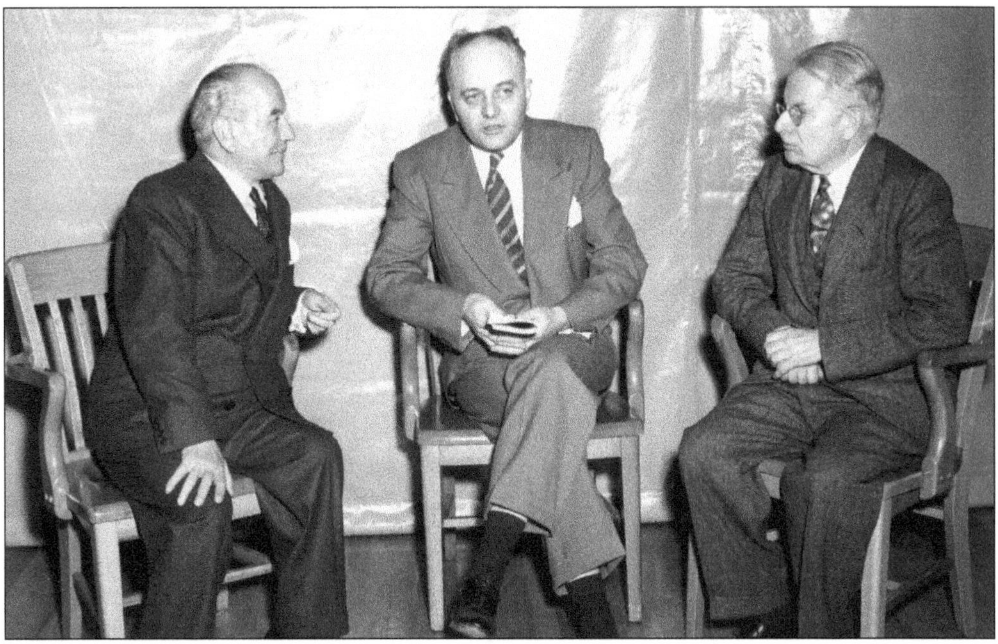

Salmon Levinson provided funds to establish the William E. Borah Foundation for the Outlawry of War, which supports the Borah Symposium. Pictured in 1955 from left to right are Dr. Carlos Davila, US-Chilean ambassador; Dr. Boyd Martin; and Dr. Quincy Wright. In 1979, Martin and his wife, Grace, endowed the Martin Institute—home of the undergraduate degree in international studies and a variety of programs highlighting international relations. (SPEC, PG 4-5-11.)

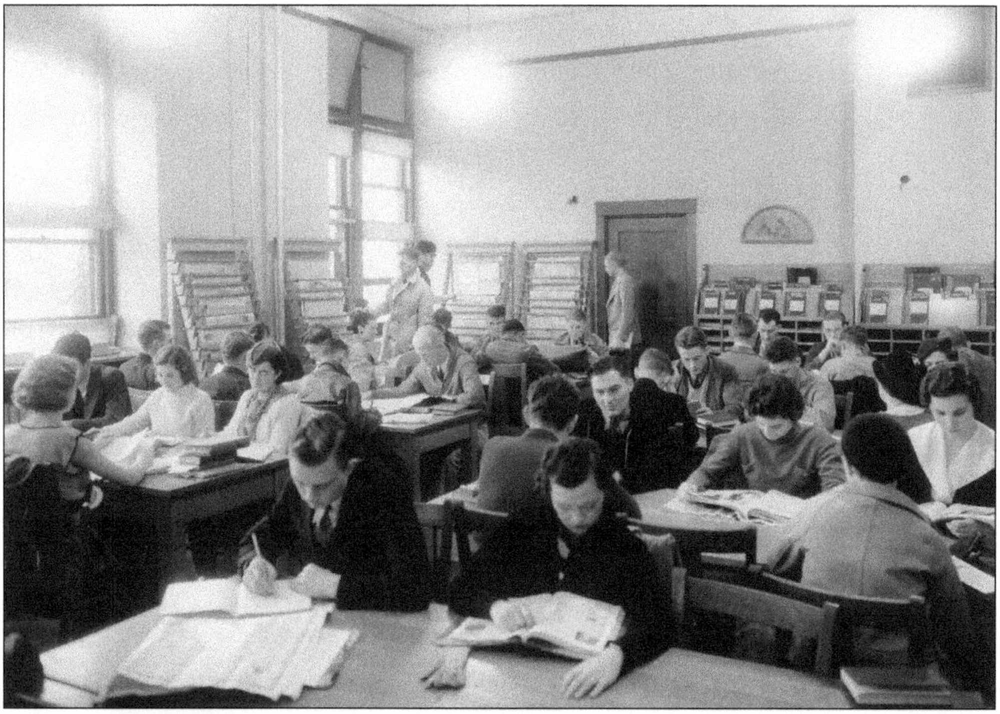

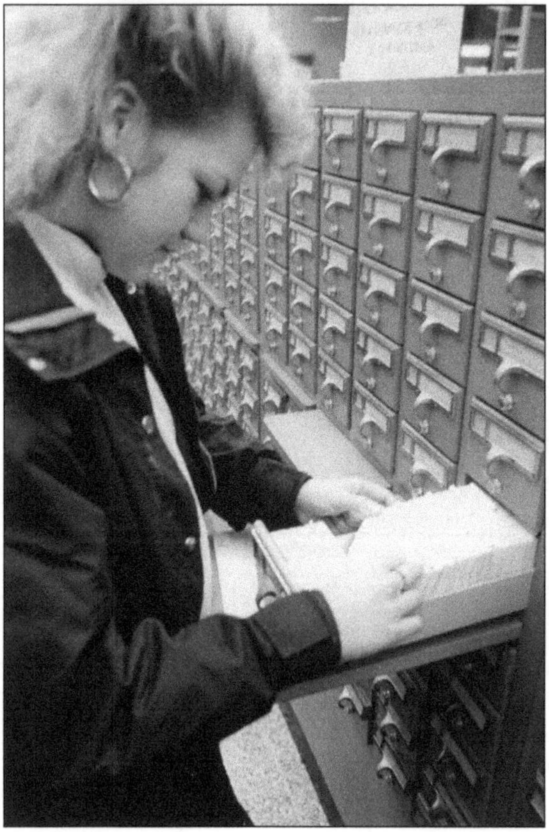

After the 1906 fire, the Library rebuilt its collections to support the academic needs of campus. The periodicals reading room (pictured) helped Idaho students stay connected with their hometowns through subscriptions to newspapers around the state. The Library continues to subscribe to local and rural newspapers throughout Idaho both in print and online. Large spaces still exist in the Library, including individual and group study. (SPEC, PG 1-201-7.)

Sports sciences student Kelly Costello checks the Library's card catalog for sources in 1988. For years, Idaho researchers used this method to locate library resources. Idaho's card catalog was replaced by computer generated microfiche in 1979, preceding an online catalog in 1990. Membership in consortia such as the Orbis Cascade Alliance provides access throughout the Northwest region and the world through interlibrary loan services. (SPEC, UA 2001-002.)

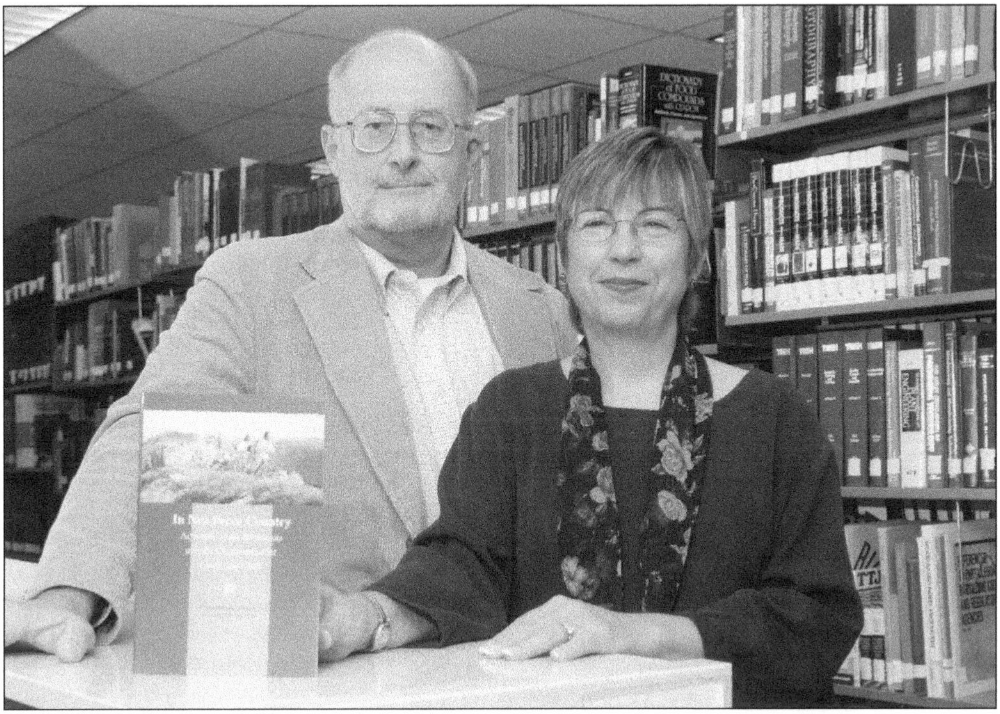

Library faculty Dennis Baird and Lynn Baird (named dean of university libraries in 2007) pose with their book *In Nez Perce Country*. The University of Idaho has an established commitment to preserving Nez Perce tribal history and traditions. University faculty regularly publish scholarly articles, creative works, reports, and books that have a direct impact on the state, nation, and the world. (UI Photo Services.)

Students purchase textbooks at the Student Union Building Bookstore in 1965. For years, the ritual of buying textbooks accompanied the start of each semester. The VandalStore now provides students with comparative prices from various vendors, and students can order their books online in physical or electronic formats. A book rental program and free open source course materials offer an alternative to textbook purchases. (SPEC, PG 101-3444.)

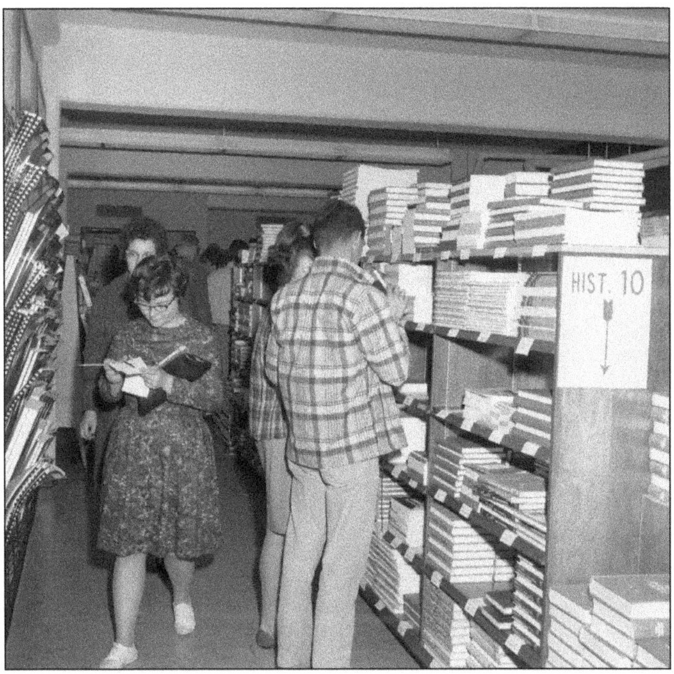

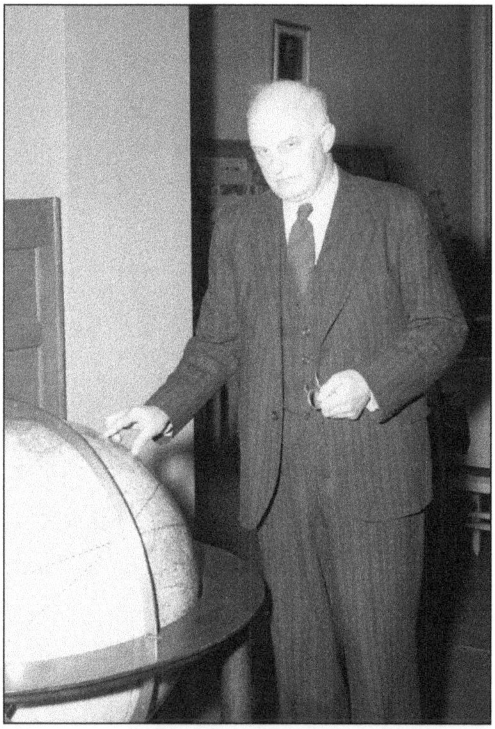

Prof. Erwin Graue was a demanding teacher known for not allowing his economics students to chew gum in class. He is especially remembered for his correspondence with nearly 90 former students serving in the armed forces during World War II, communications the men in uniform cherished. The Graue Scholar Program through the College of Business and Economics honors this dedicated scholar and teacher. (SPEC, PG 40-ING38.)

For 50 years, station KUID has been an integral part of Idaho Public Television, serving people around the state. Students learn how to run expensive equipment, develop program ideas, and produce regular and specialty programming such as documentaries. Broadcasting is part of the School of Journalism and Mass Media, the only Council on Education in Journalism and Mass Communications–accredited school in the state. (SPEC, PG 24-228.)

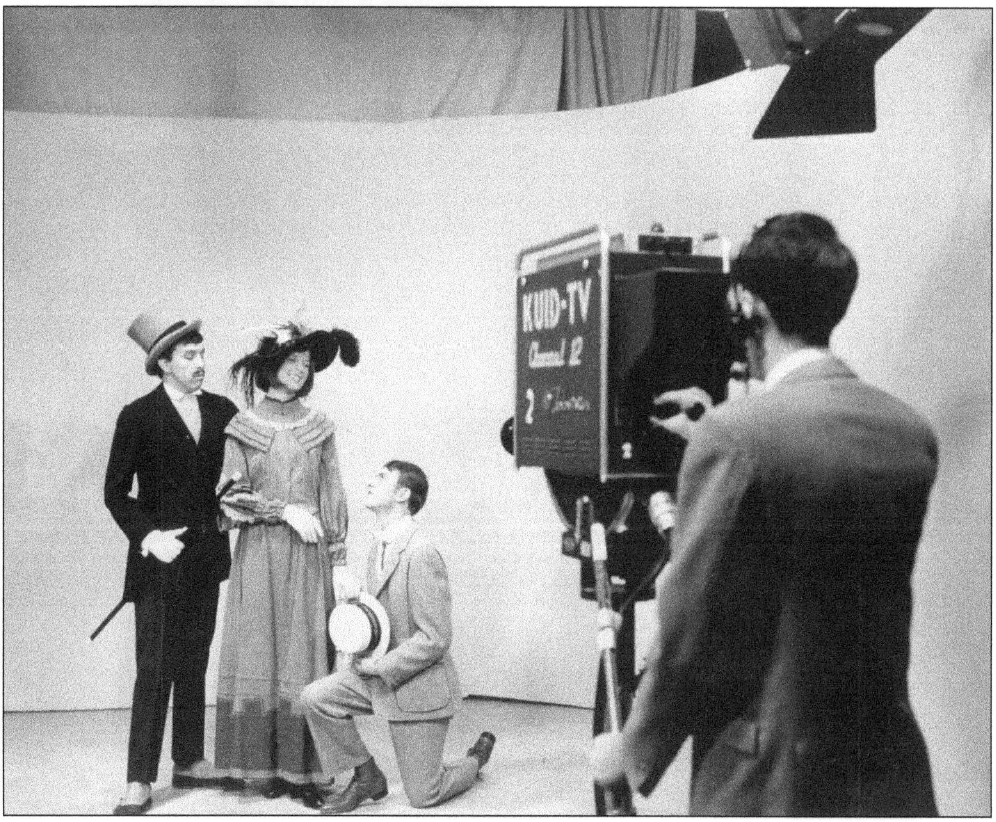

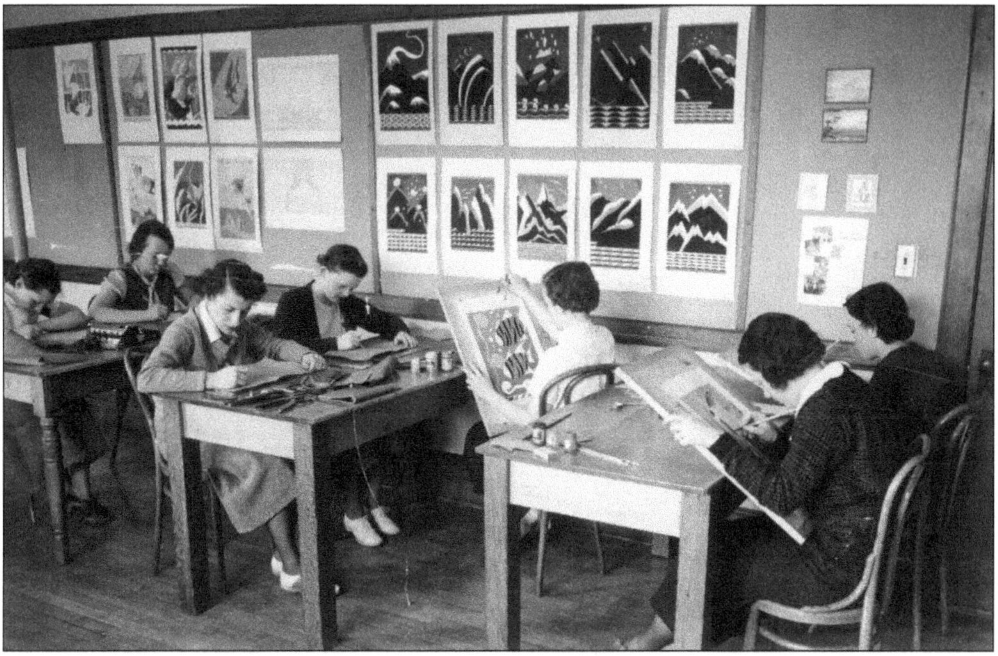

The College of Art and Architecture, founded in 1981, promotes integrated concepts of art, design, and technology with a focus on environmental stewardship. Programs include architecture; bioregional planning and community design; landscape architecture; interior design; art & design; and gaming, simulation and virtual design. Pictured above are students drawing at tables during an art design class in 1938; below, a student builds an architectural model around 1990. (Above, SPEC, PG 1-241-2; below, SPEC, PG 52-241.)

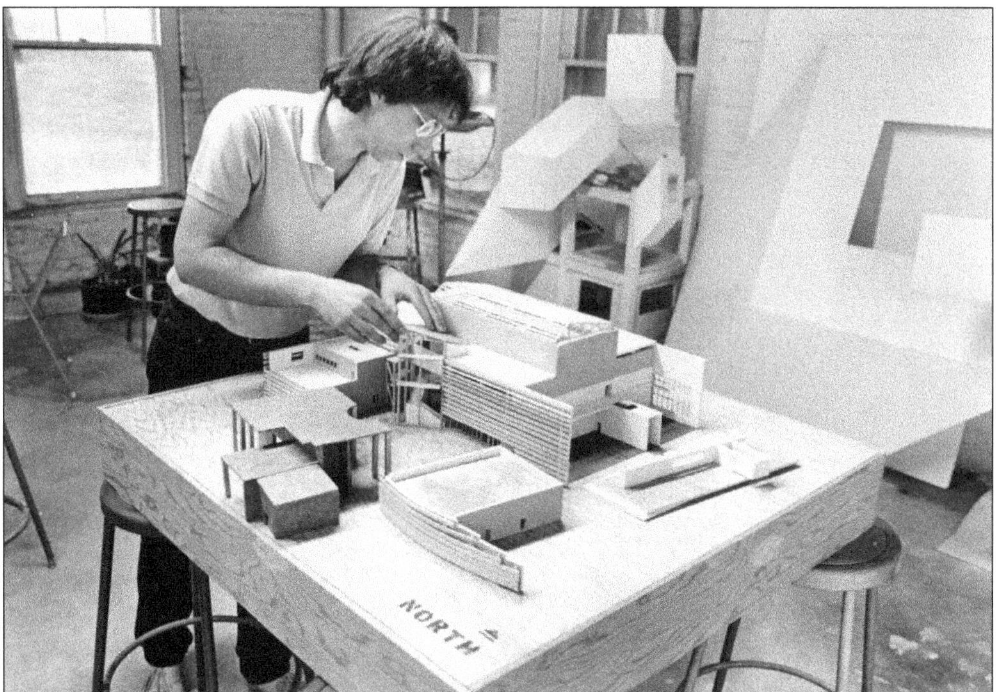

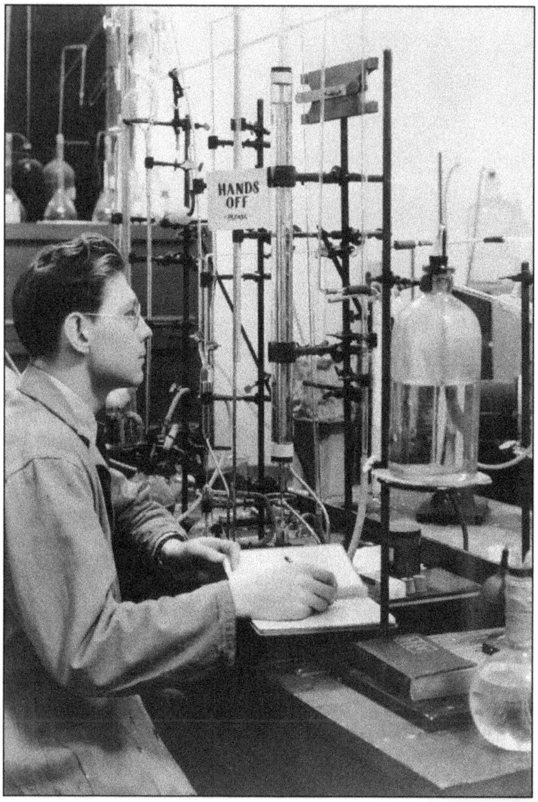

Chemistry fellow Louis Schroer Keyser uses equipment in his laboratory in 1934. Graduate students such as Keyser experience nationally competitive academic and research opportunities. The University of Idaho has awarded advanced degrees since 1898. The Graduate School dates from 1925 and formally became the College of Graduate Studies in 1988. (SPEC, PG 1-211-5.)

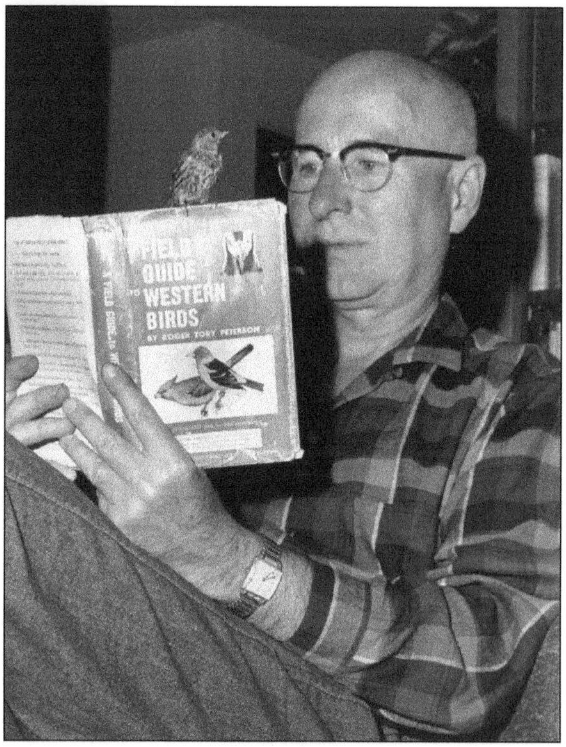

Potlatch, Idaho, native Malcom Renfrew graduated from the University of Idaho in 1932. Renfrew was part of a DuPont group whose work resulted in Teflon. He returned to UI to head physical sciences in 1959 and received an honorary doctorate in 1976. Renfrew Hall was named in his honor in 1985. He and Carol Campbell Renfrew (1935; honorary doctorate, 2006) were fixtures at Idaho events. (SPEC, PG 3-766a.)

Since arriving in 1961, Jean'ne Shreeve has established a reputation as a world authority on fluorine chemistry. She has published more than 500 scholarly journal articles and was named a fellow of the American Chemical Society in 2010. Professor Shreeve served as chair of chemistry from 1973 to 1987 and vice president for research from 1987 to 1999, the only woman to have occupied that position. She is a University Distinguished Professor. (SPEC, VF Personnel.)

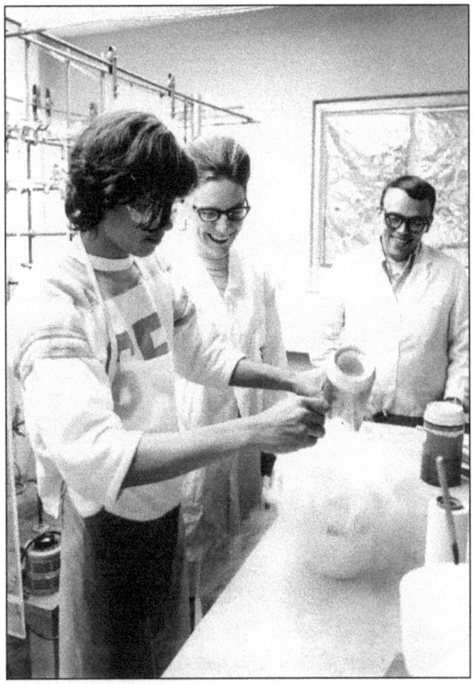

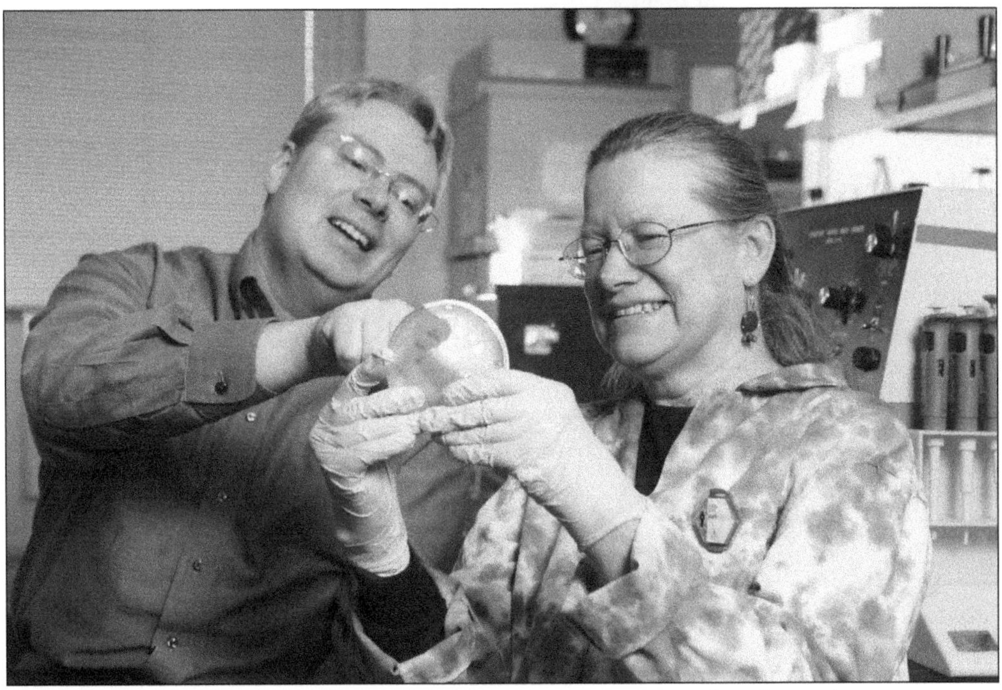

Prof. Paul Joyce (named College of Science dean in 2013) and Prof. Holly Wichman represent the bioinformatics and computational biology degree program, which includes faculty from nine different departments. The related Institute for Bioinformatics and Evolutionary Studies and Center for Modeling Complex Interaction are home to interdisciplinary research projects. Wichman was named a University Distinguished Professor in 2012; Joyce in 2016. (UI Photo Services.)

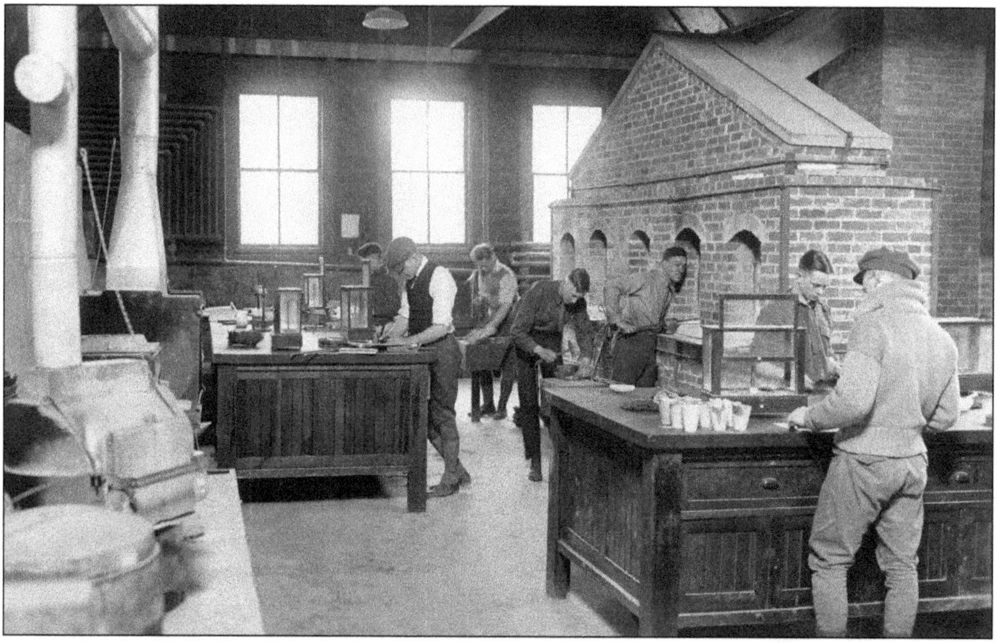

A School of Mines fire assaying class is pictured in 1923. University of Idaho–trained mining professionals took positions in mines around the world. The university closed the College of Mines and Earth Sciences in 2002, when courses moved to the College of Engineering and the College of Science. The Assay Building (1906) was demolished in 1984 to make way for Life Sciences North, renamed for Pres. Richard Gibb in 1993. (SPEC, PG 1-223-6.)

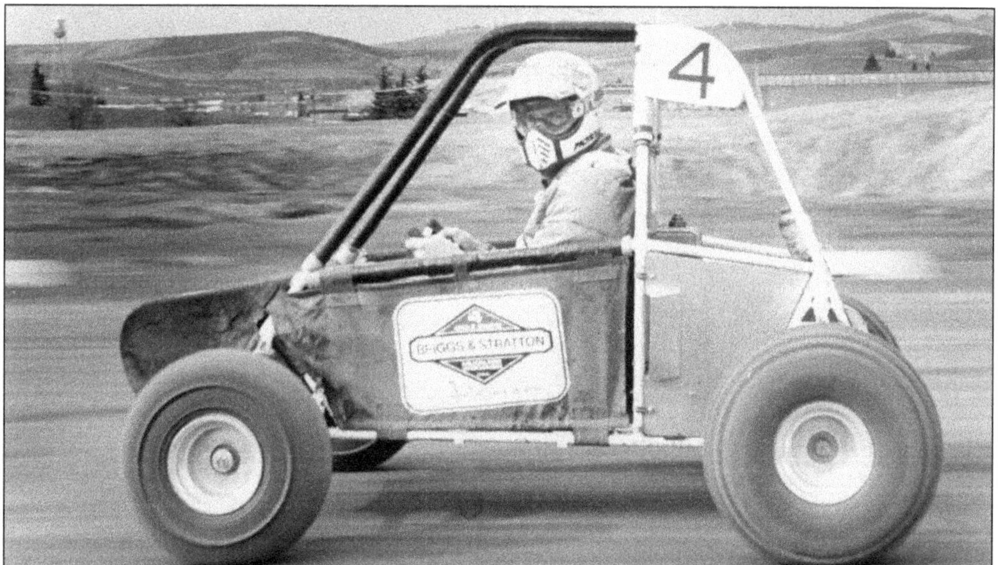

Transportation efficiency and safety are subjects of inquiry in the College of Engineering's National Institute for Advanced Transportation Technology, which works closely with the Idaho Transportation Department and the Federal Highway Administration on numerous research projects. The college prides itself on providing hands-on experiences for students including its widely attended Engineering Expo held every spring. Pictured here is an experimental high efficiency vehicle. (SPEC, PG 52-229.)

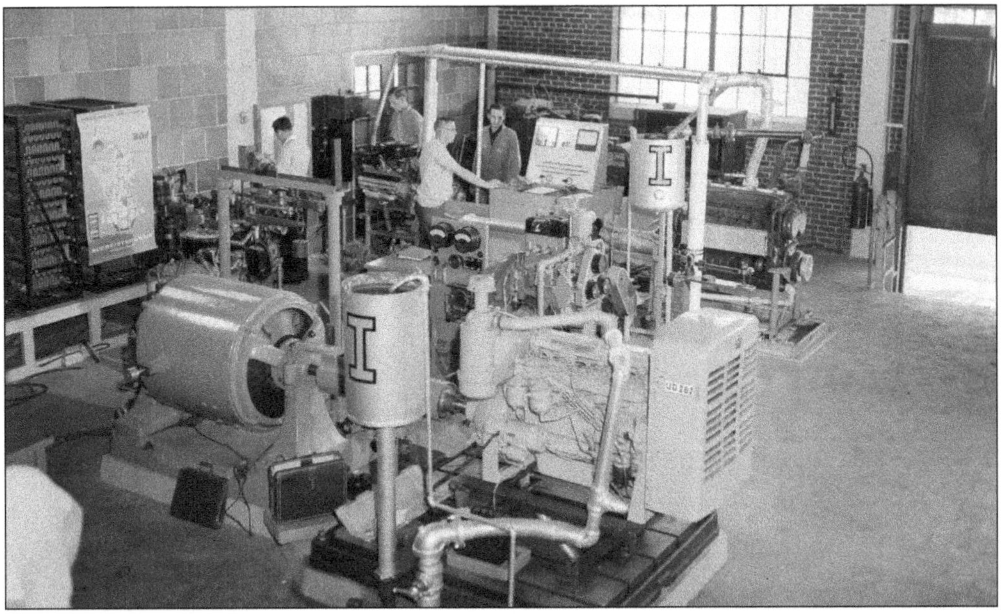

A College of Engineering laboratory is pictured here in 1960. The university has featured leading engineering programs for more than 125 years. The college offers degrees in biological, chemical, civil, computer, electrical, materials science, nuclear, technology management, and mechanical engineering. The engineering senior capstone project has been named one of the top 10 in the nation, and provides students with design and research opportunities. (SPEC, PG 101-2058.)

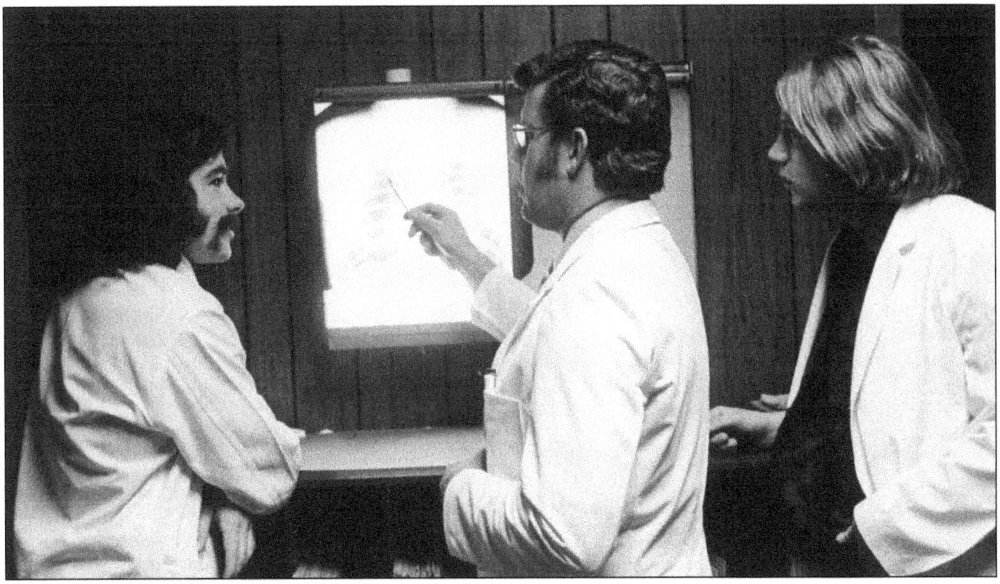

The University of Idaho is a partner with the University of Washington School of Medicine in the Washington, Wyoming, Alaska, Montana, Idaho (WWAMI) medical education program. Idaho students receive the medical doctor degree from the nationally ranked University of Washington in primary care, family medicine, rural medicine, and research. More than 50 percent of Idaho WWAMI graduates return to the state to practice, helping to address Idaho's physician shortage. (SPEC, UA 91-040.)

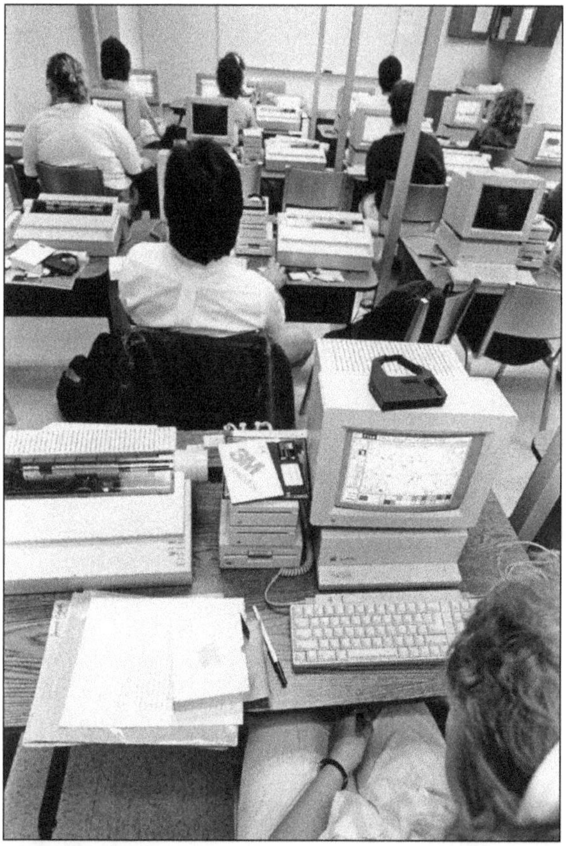

Student usage of computers has expanded exponentially since their introduction at the University of Idaho in the mid-1960s. The university's first computers were reserved for researchers and experts, but soon they became standardized. The university established the Computer Science Department in 1978; it continues to offer undergraduate and graduate degrees. (SPEC, UA 2003-015.)

Prof. Linda Morris speaks about Vandal Innovation and Enterprise Works (VIEW), a campus-wide initiative to catalyze entrepreneurial thinking at the University of Idaho. Since 2008, interest in entrepreneurship on campus has experienced tremendous growth, and VIEW has been rebranded as Idaho Entrepreneurs. Morris also served as interim provost—the first woman to hold that position at the University of Idaho. (UI Photo Services.)

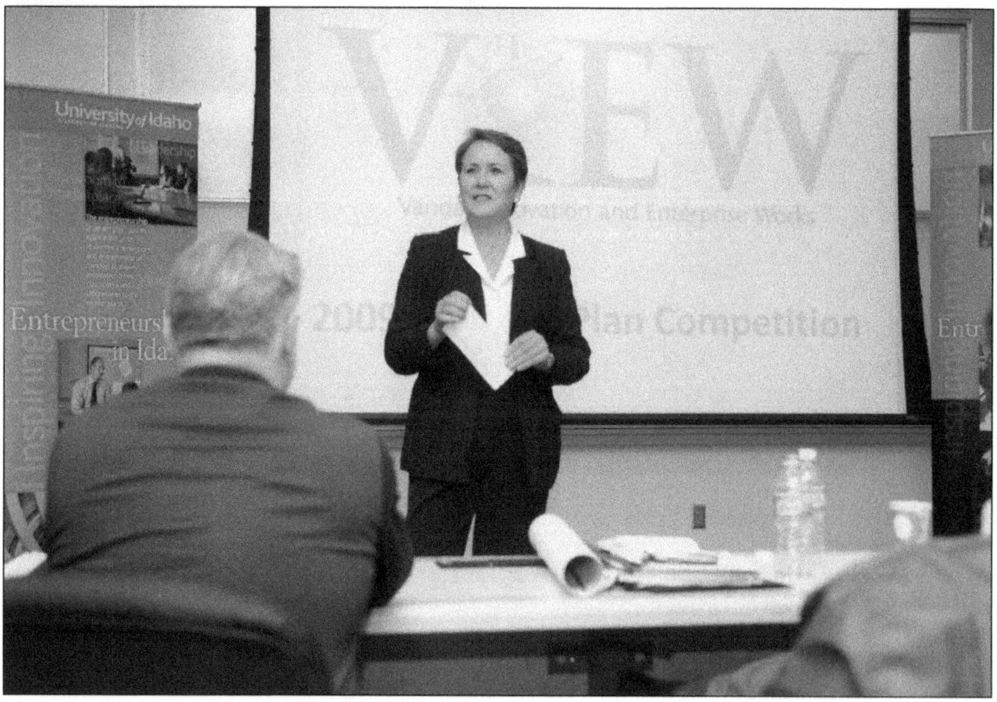

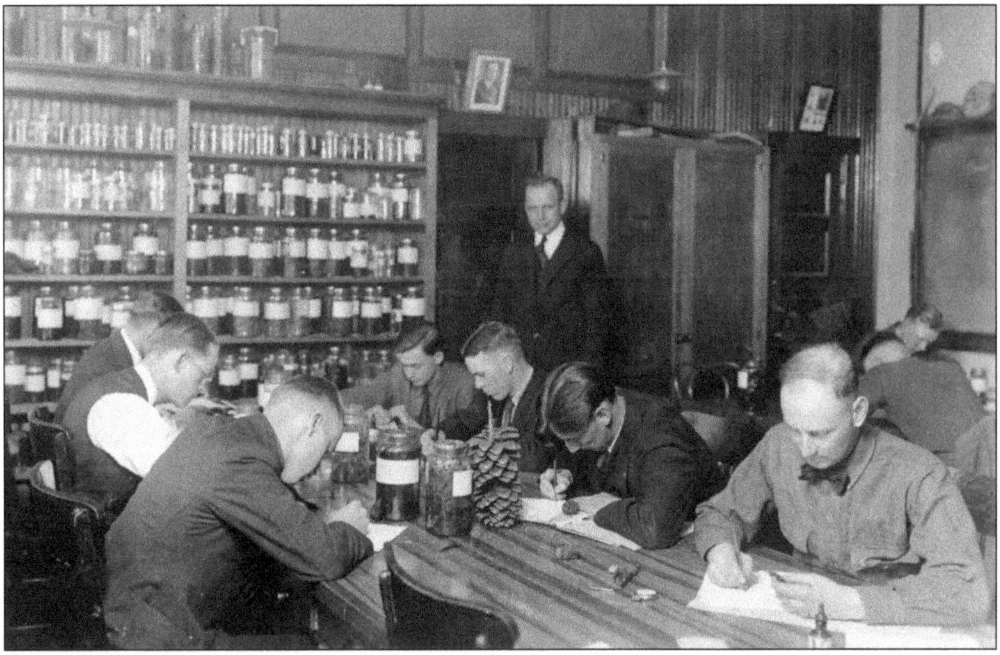

This forestry lab was under the direction of C.W. Watson in 1923. Clarence Watson came to the University of Idaho in 1921, having graduated from the nation's first school of forestry at Yale. He served as faculty advisor for *The Idaho Forester*, a student-edited journal published from 1917 to 1997. (SPEC, PG 1-218-6.)

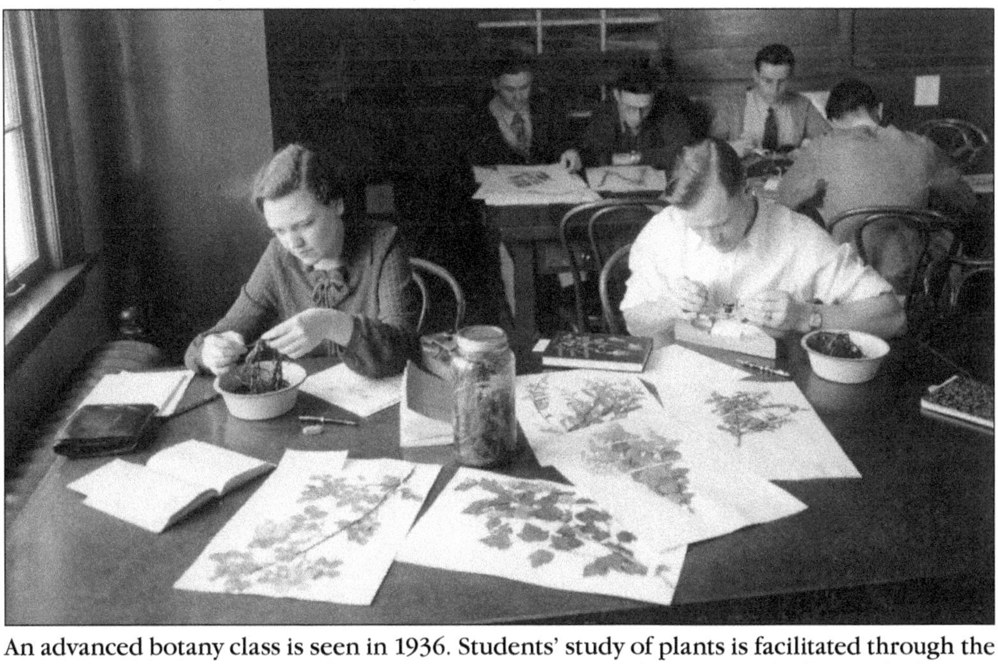

An advanced botany class is seen in 1936. Students' study of plants is facilitated through the Stillinger Herbarium. Established in 1892 by Louis F. Henderson, it is the largest herbarium in Idaho and functions as the official state repository. While most of the original collection was lost in the 1906 fire, the herbarium collections today include more than 200,000 plant and fungal specimens. (SPEC, PG 1-215-6.)

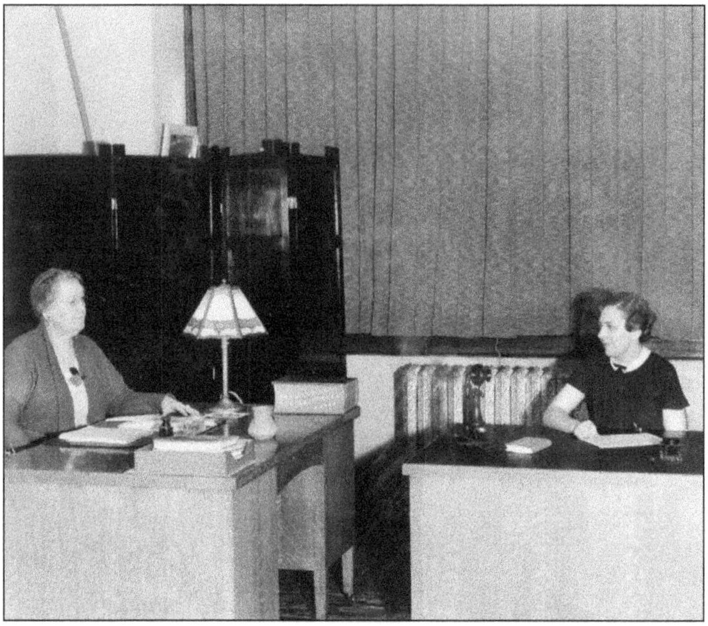

The unflappable Permeal French (left, shown here with her secretary) became UI's first dean of women after serving as Idaho's state superintendent of schools. She later founded the Blue Bucket Inn. She was a formidable force on campus throughout her tenure from 1908 to 1936 and personified her sobriquet "the Dowager of Discipline." Her portrait, presented to the university in 1938, hangs in the Bruce M. Pitman Center. (SPEC, PG 3-6c.)

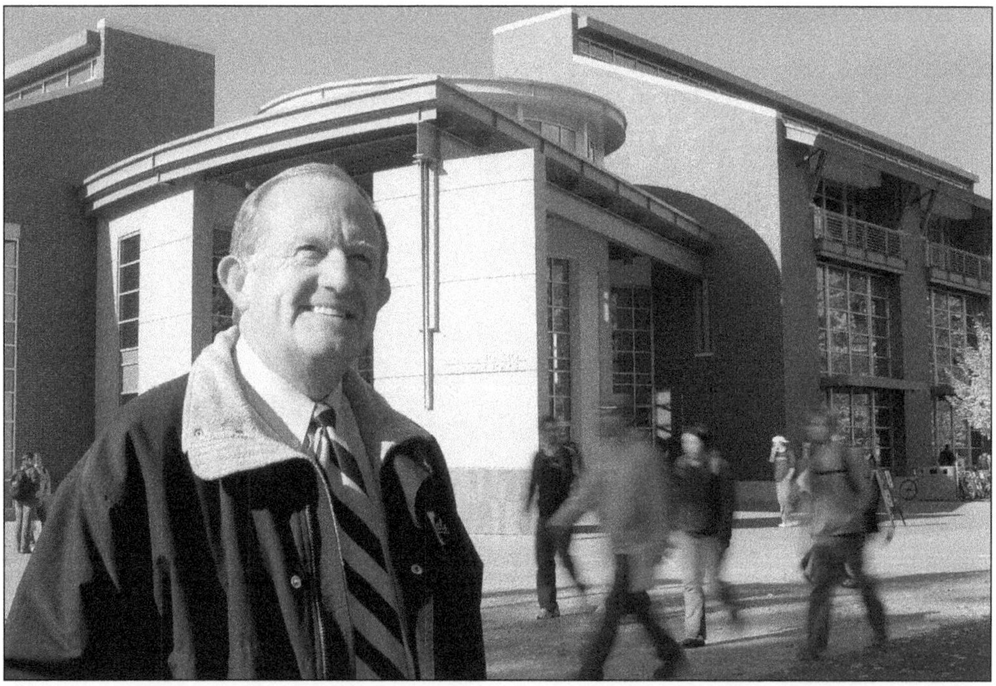

Pictured in front of Idaho Commons, Bruce M. Pitman served students for over 40 years. As dean of students, he fostered a campus climate where cocurricular activities complemented academics and emphasized service. The Bruce M. Pitman Center (formerly the Student Union Building) was named following his retirement in 2015. Enrollment services, the registrar, financial aid, and the Doceo Center (technology innovations for K-12 education) are housed there. (UI Photo Services.)

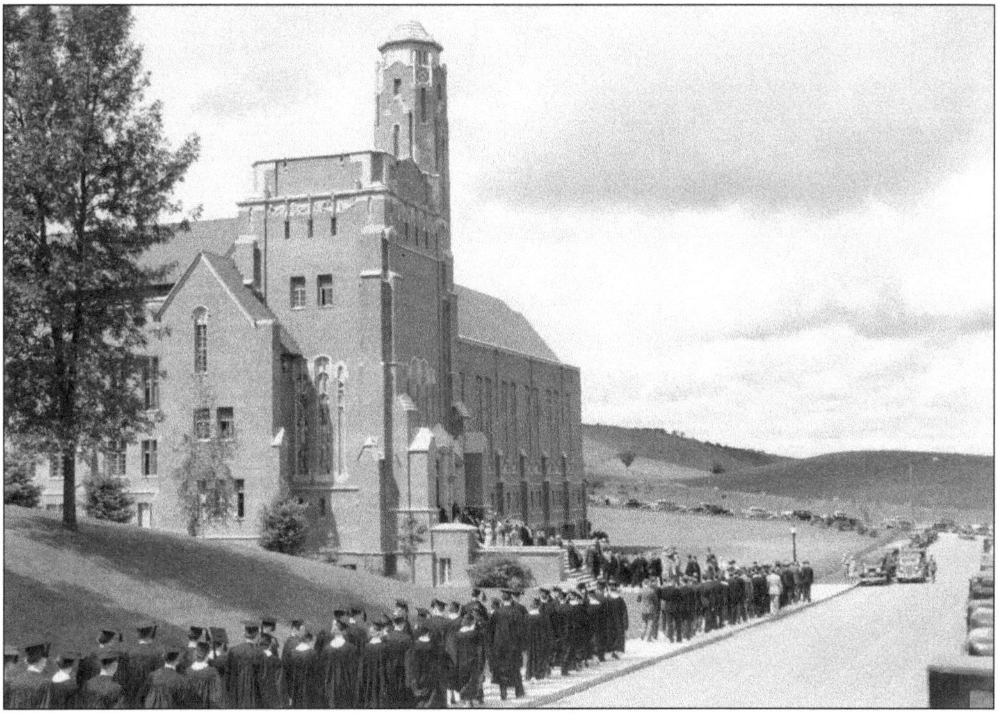

Dedicated to the memory of students killed during World War I, Memorial Gymnasium opened in 1929, constructed with private money and student fees. It was designed by University of Idaho Department of Architecture head David C. Long with assistance from Prof. Theodore Prichard. The building's Tudor Gothic design features colored glass windows, a tall octagonal tower, and gargoyle-like figures of football players. Known as "Mem Gym," it has served as a sports arena and physical education venue. First Lady Eleanor Roosevelt gave a 1938 lecture here, one of many reasons that the building was listed in the National Register of Historic Places. Memorial Gym was also the site of commencement exercises. State of Idaho officials are often present at commencement. Below, from left to right, are Gov. Cecil Andrus, Sen. Frank Church, and Pres. Ernest Hartung in 1972. (Above, SPEC, PG 1-61-11; below, SPEC, PG 2-109-172.)

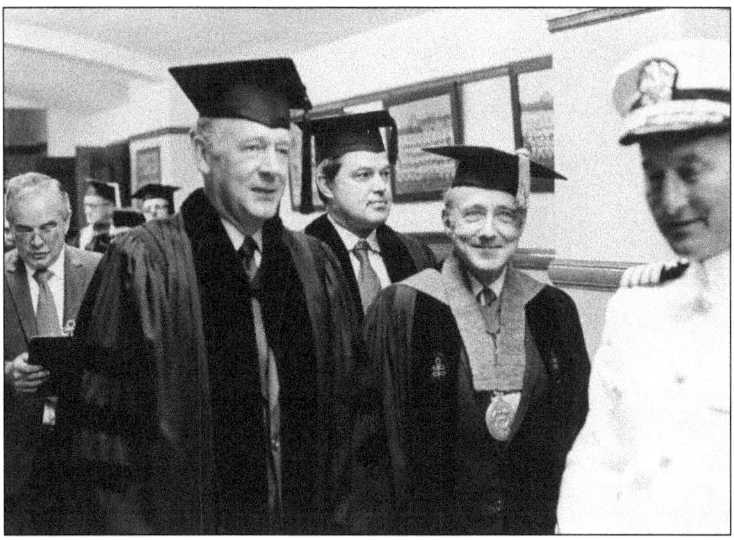

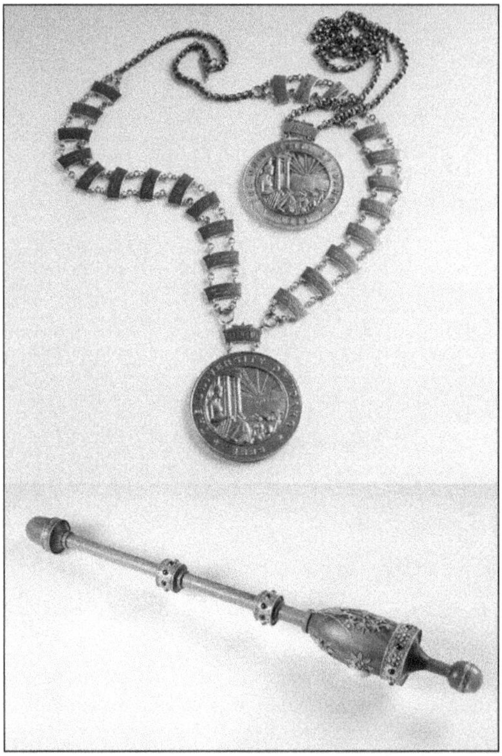

The University of Idaho mace, designed by Prof. Edmund Chavez with metal work by Idaho artist Ray Goodner, was first used in the 1989 centennial commencement. It is 32 inches long, made of walnut, and encircled with bands of Idaho gold and silver with garnets and opals. The head is embellished with silver and gold representations of camas plants and syringa flowers. The President's and Regents' Medallions were commissioned in 2004. The President's Medallion base is a gold-leafed university seal and is worn suspended by a chain with gold-leaf charms, each one representing a president who served the institution. It is a tradition for graduates to process from Memorial Gymnasium to the Kibbie Dome, site of modern commencement exercises. The processional symbolizes the passage from student status to alumni. Below, bagpipers lead marchers in 2002. (Both, UI Photo Services.)

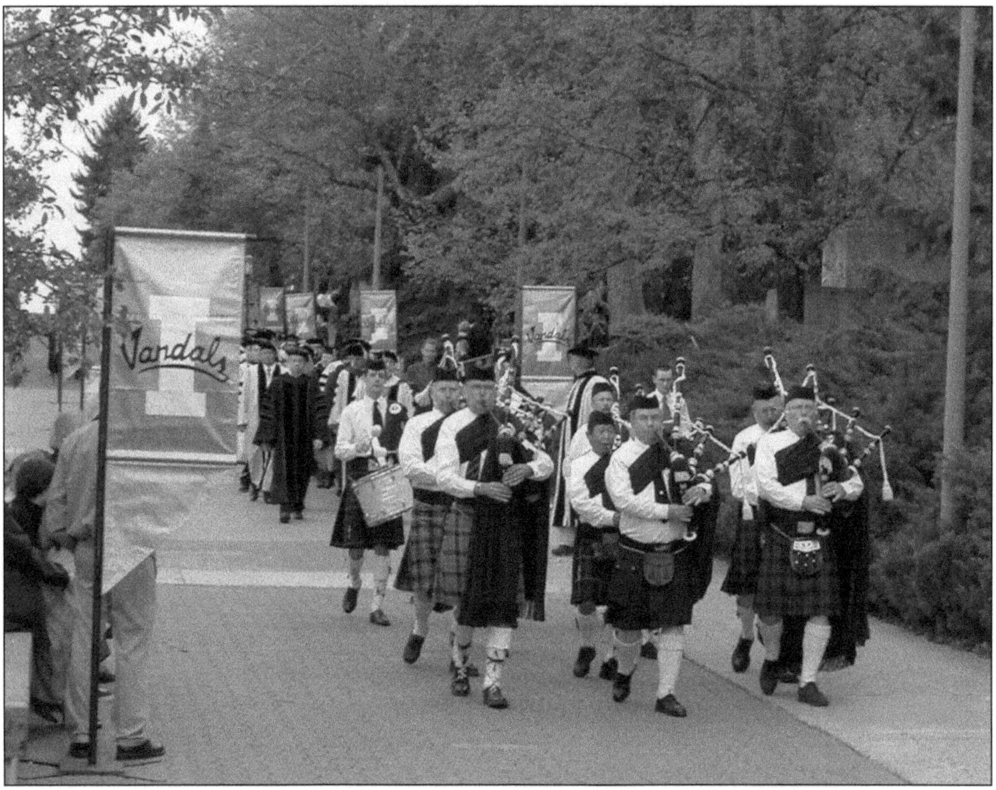

Three

Athletics

As early as 1893, when students from neighboring Washington Agricultural College came to the Moscow campus to compete in various track and field events, athletics has been a colorful and often exciting part of University of Idaho life. Vandal athletics have provided student athletes, the student body, alumni, and countless supporters and fans with thrills, entertainment, and a shared identity.

Legendary basketball coach Hec Edmondson prided himself on ferocious defensive teams that sportswriters claimed "vandalized" their opponents. Referring to this frenzied defense, a writer for the *Argonaut*, Harry Lloyd "Jazz" McCarty, referred to the basketball team as "Vandals" in a 1917 pre-game column, and the moniker stuck. By 1921, all University of Idaho teams officially adopted the nickname. Joe Vandal, the university's mascot, first appeared in the late 1950s, and through several iterations remains a revered Idaho symbol.

Beginning in the 1920s, University of Idaho rooters and players started singing the fight song after athletic contests. "Oh, Idaho" was sung to the tune of "On, Wisconsin." The Associated Students of the University of Idaho (ASUI) sponsored a contest in 1930 to identify an original song for the university, and J.M. "Morey" O'Donnell (1936) won with "Go, Vandals, Go," sung far and wide ever since.

Argonaut sportswriter Bill McGowan instigated a tradition that lasted for about 30 years when he began the "Loser's Walk," a nine-mile trek the losing side undertook following the University of Idaho–Washington State College (later Washington State University) football game. Vandal fans still reminisce about 1954, when Idaho defeated Washington State by a score of 10-0 and Cougar supporters hiked the distance for the first time in 29 years.

While major sports have been a focus since Idaho's first intercollegiate football game in 1894, Vandals have excelled in other sports as well. Idaho boxers enjoyed tremendous success during the 1930s and 1940s, including three national championships. University student-athletes have competed in skiing, men's swimming, gymnastics, soccer, water polo, and rodeo, to name a few sports.

In 1922, the National Women's Athletic Association adopted a constitution and committed to encouraging women's interest in sports. In the early 1970s, in compliance with Title IX, Idaho began awarding athletic scholarships to women, and women's sports became firmly entrenched. The University of Idaho added women's soccer to its array of intercollegiate sports in 2000 and women's swimming in 2004. Currently, Vandals compete in 16 men's and women's Division I sports.

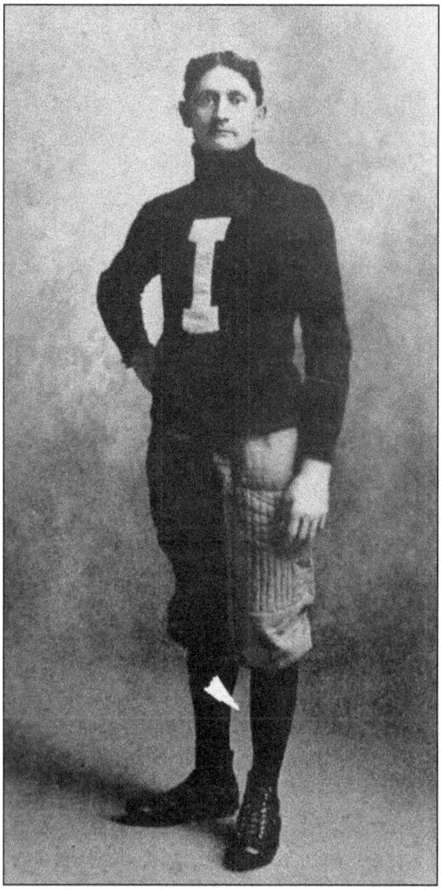

John R. Middleton (known as "Mid" to his teammates) quarterbacked Idaho teams from 1903 to 1905 and then became a successful coach at his alma mater (assistant football coach 1906–1907; head football coach 1907–1909). His "Idaho Spread" represented the origins of the shotgun formation, widely used today at both the collegiate and professional levels. (SPEC, PG 3-537d.)

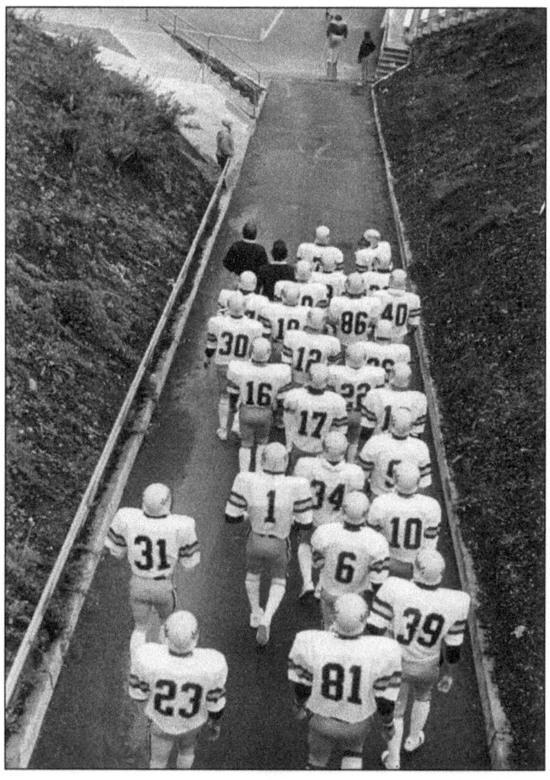

Built in 1936, Neale Stadium did not include locker rooms, offices, or weight rooms. Vandal players and their opponents dressed in the Memorial Gymnasium facilities and walked across to Neale Stadium. Pictured are Vandal football players led by head coach Dennis Erickson preparing to enter Washington State University's Martin Stadium in 1982. (SPEC, UA 1989-27.)

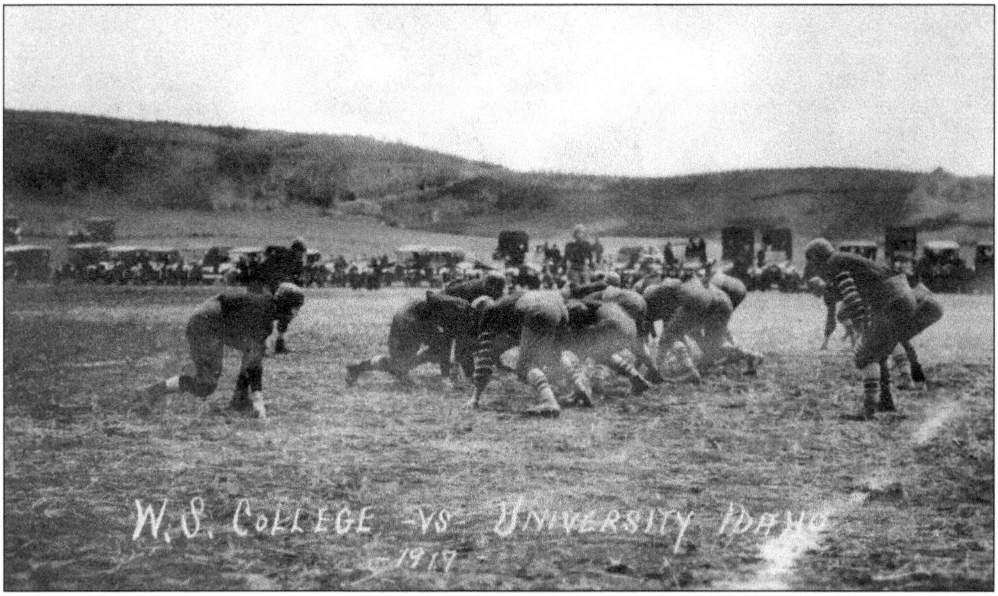

This postcard of the 1917 University of Idaho vs. Washington State College football game was found in a student scrapbook. Football players wore leather helmets and little protective padding at the time. Even the spectators enjoyed few amenities, but the rivalry endured. (SPEC, MA 2015-42.)

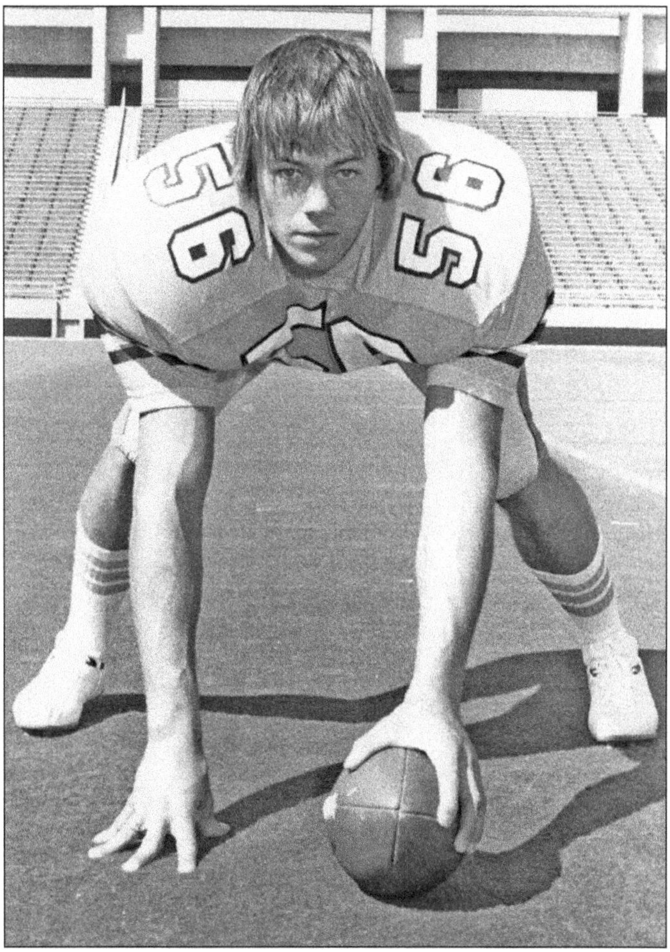

John Yarno was the first University of Idaho football player to be named an Associated Press Division I first team All-American in 1977. He played in both the Senior Bowl and the East-West Shrine Game. He was the first lineman to be named Big Sky Conference Player of the Year. His number was retired in 1977 and Moscow proclaimed January 12, 1977, as John Yarno Day. (UI Athletics.)

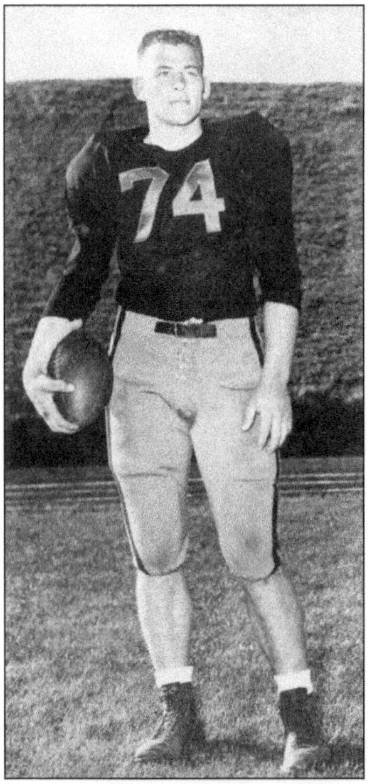

Gerald Louis "Jerry" Kramer (pictured in 1955) played for Idaho from 1955 to 1958 and was Idaho's first football All-American. He then had an 11-year career in the National Football League, where he played linebacker for Vince Lombardi and the Green Bay Packers in the 1960s. His Idaho number was retired in 1963. (SPEC, PG 3-1846b.)

Linebacker Wayne Walker (center) was Idaho Male Athlete of the Year in 1968 and 1971. He represented Idaho in the East-West Shrine Game, where he was voted Most Valuable Defensive Player. A fourth-round draft pick for the Detroit Lions, Walker made five Pro Bowl appearances. Walker had an Emmy-winning career as a sports broadcaster. He is a member of the Idaho and University of Idaho Athletics Hall of Fame. (SPEC, PG40-GRO4.)

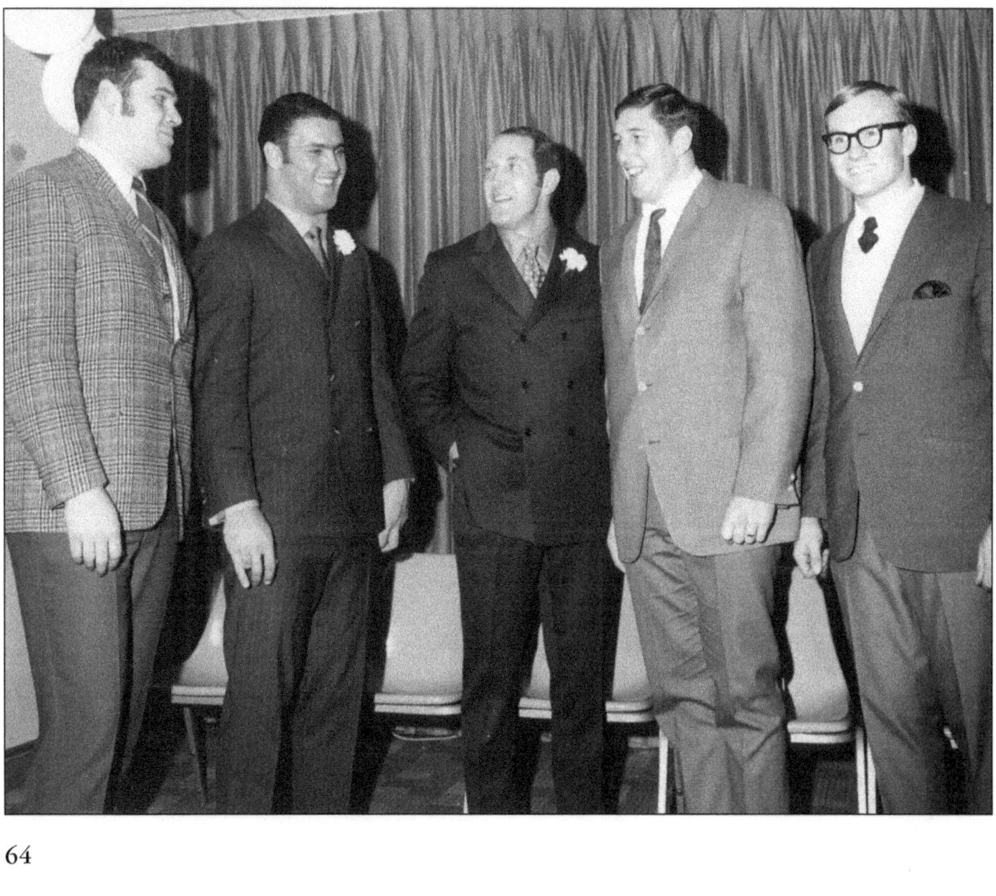

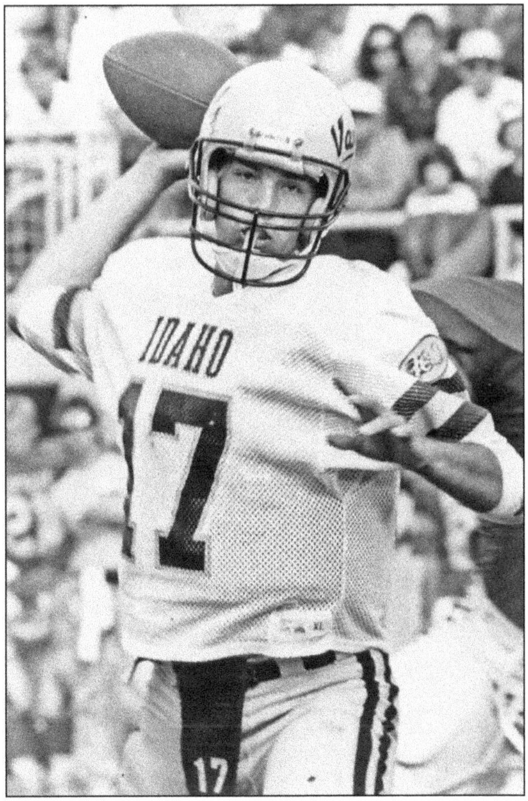

John Friesz was a prolific passer and three-time Big Sky Player of the Year. He won the 1989 Walter Payton National Player of the Year Award and first-team All-American honors twice. His number was retired in 2006, the same year he was inducted into the College Football Hall of Fame. The Vandal football MVP award is named for him. (UI Athletics.)

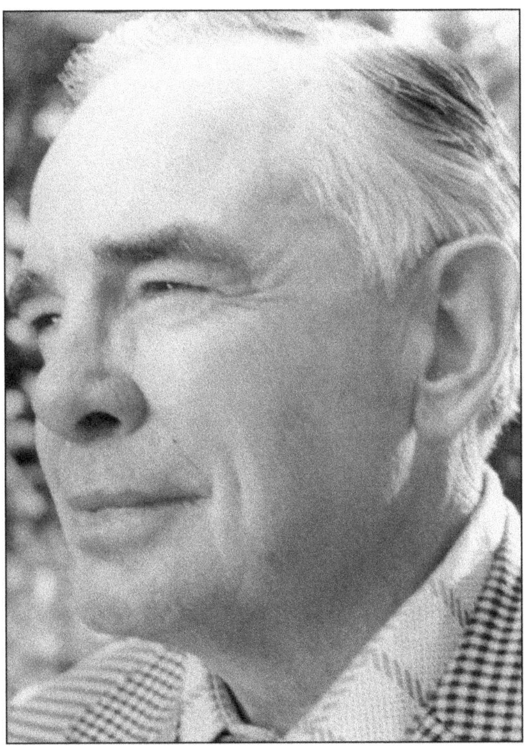

Leon Green, a member of the University of Idaho Athletics Hall of Fame, played defensive end from 1934 to 1936 on the Vandal football team. His career preceded the university keeping defensive statistics. He was a longtime UI faculty member in the physical education department. "Doc" Green advised hundreds of students and was the division director from 1953 to 1973. (Courtesy of Movement Sciences.)

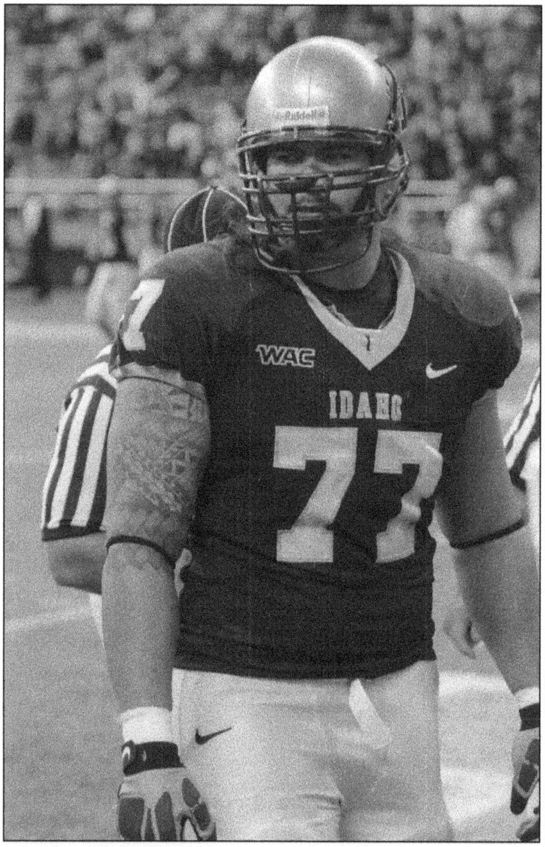

Mike Iupati, a native of American Samoa, attended the University of Idaho, where he played football from 2006 to 2009. He was named an All-American and was a leader on Idaho's Humanitarian Bowl championship team in 2009. Iupati, an offensive guard, was the San Francisco 49ers' first-round draft pick in 2010. (UI Athletics.)

In one of the most exciting bowl games ever, the University of Idaho defeated Bowling Green State University 43-42 at the 2009 Humanitarian Bowl. Behind 42-35 with 32 seconds left, the team scored with four seconds remaining on the clock. A successful two-point conversion sealed the win, and Vandal fans across the country reveled. Pictured here is the Vandal football team during their victory. (UI Photo Services.)

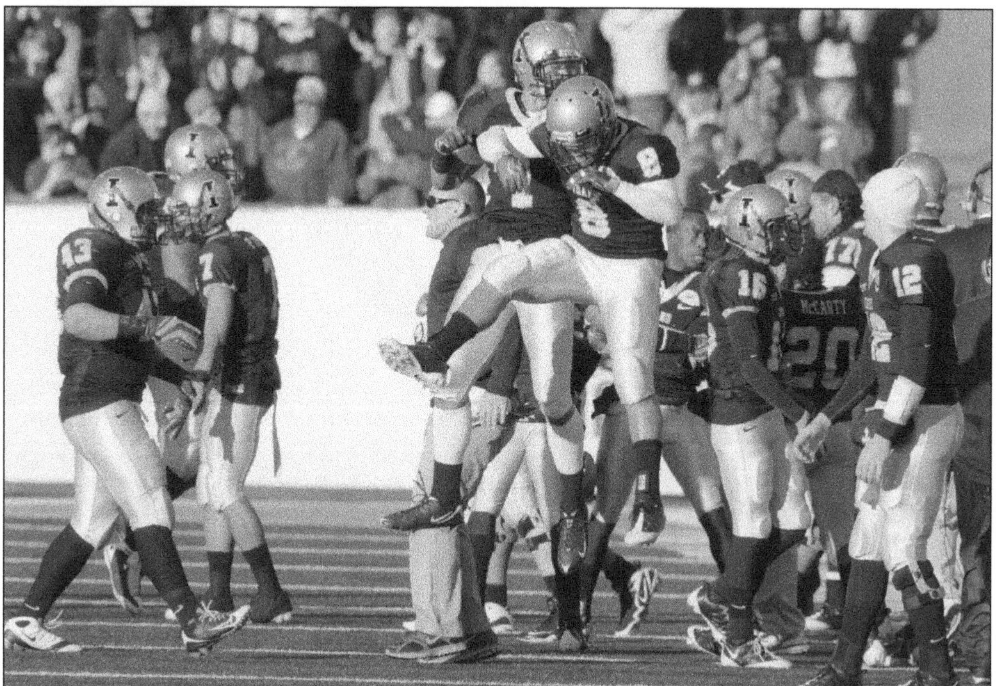

This official souvenir program cover is from the University of Idaho–Washington State College Homecoming game on Saturday, November 3, 1928, at Rogers Field in Pullman, Washington. This school rivalry, named the "Battle of the Palouse," began in 1894. The cover depicts the schools' mascots, a cougar and a vandal dressed in a Viking helmet. (SPEC, Vandal Covers Collection.)

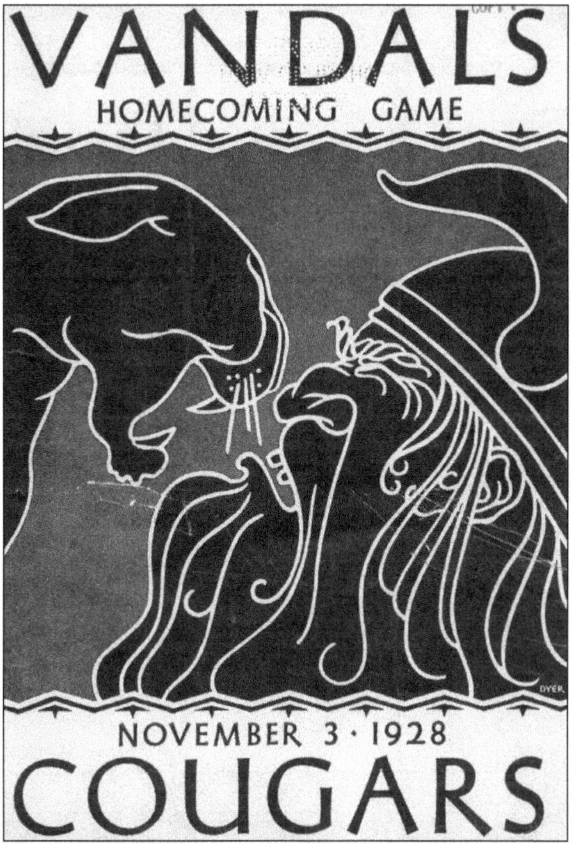

Bob Curtis, known as the "Voice of the Vandals," was a fixture in the Idaho press box for 59 years as announcer for Vandal athletic events. Curtis called 540 consecutive football games and was recognized dozens of times as the Idaho Sportscaster of the Year. In 2011, the Bob Curtis Press Box was constructed on the north side of the ASUI-Kibbie Dome and named in his honor. (UI Athletics.)

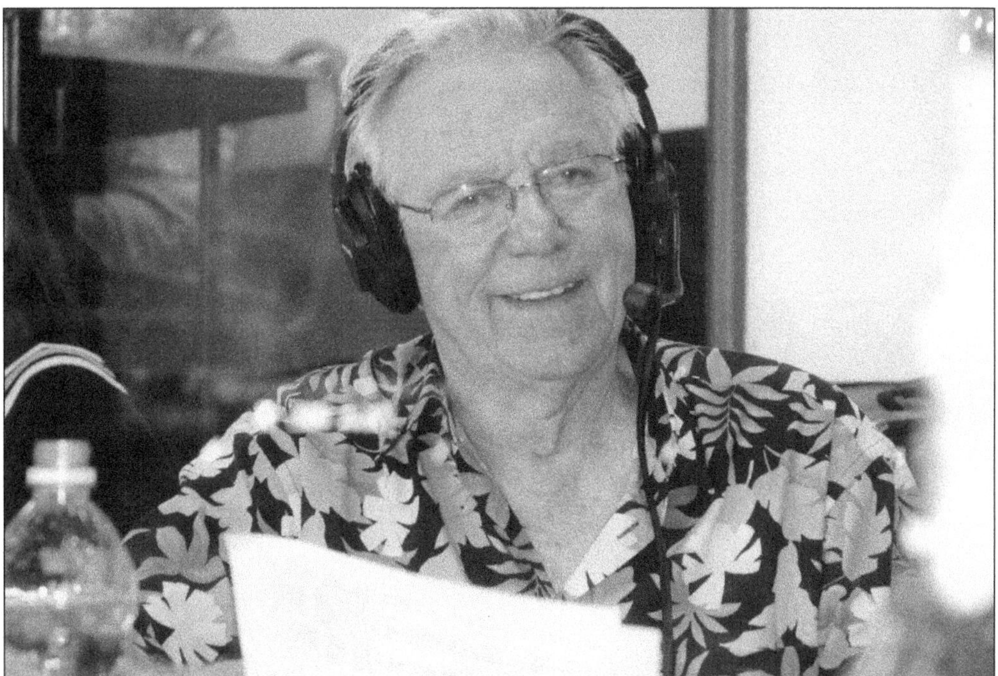

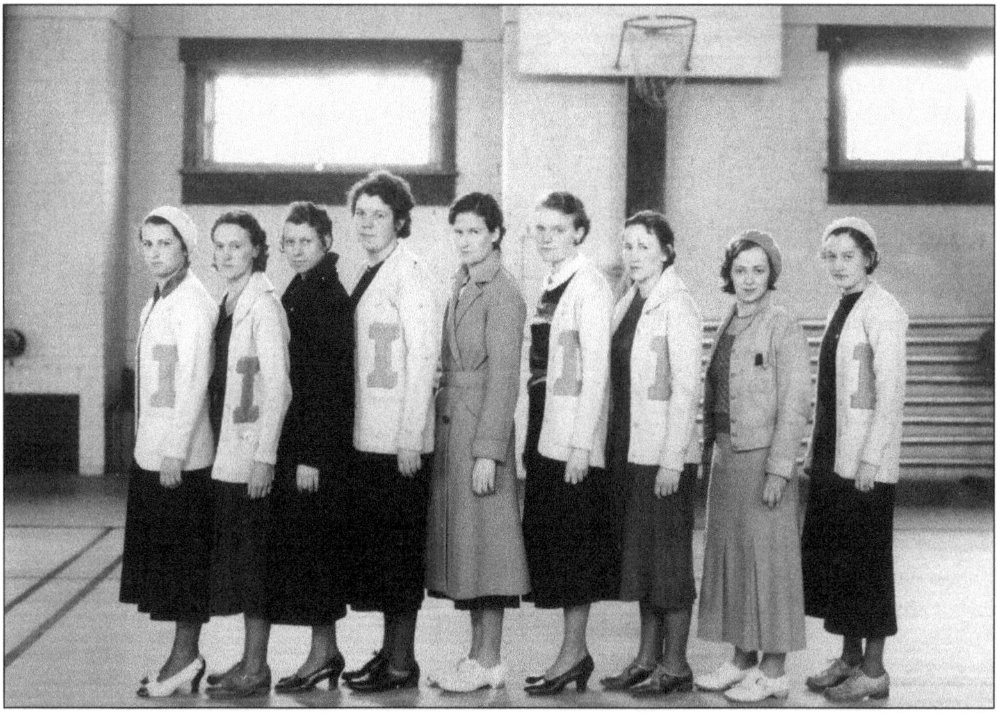

The Women's "I" Club was first formed in 1928 as an honorary club for women participating in four major intramural sports: volleyball, baseball, basketball, and rifle. The National Women's Athletic Association began in 1923, when women participated in athletics both for their health and their enjoyment before they had access to intercollegiate competition. Pictured is the 1934–1935 "I" Club wearing their letter sweaters. (SPEC, UA 1987-005.)

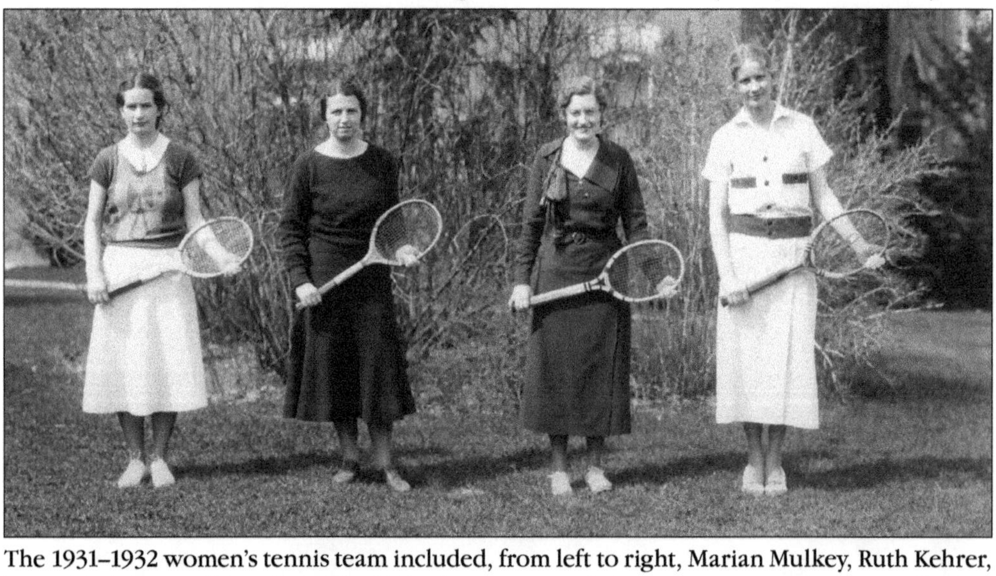

The 1931–1932 women's tennis team included, from left to right, Marian Mulkey, Ruth Kehrer, Lorna McCain, and Linn Cowgill. While these women did not compete on the intercollegiate stage, later Vandal women made a name for themselves. Three women tennis players are in the University of Idaho Athletic Hall of Fame: Barb Propst, Cathy Shanander-Law, and Patricia Shanander. (SPEC, UA 1987-005.)

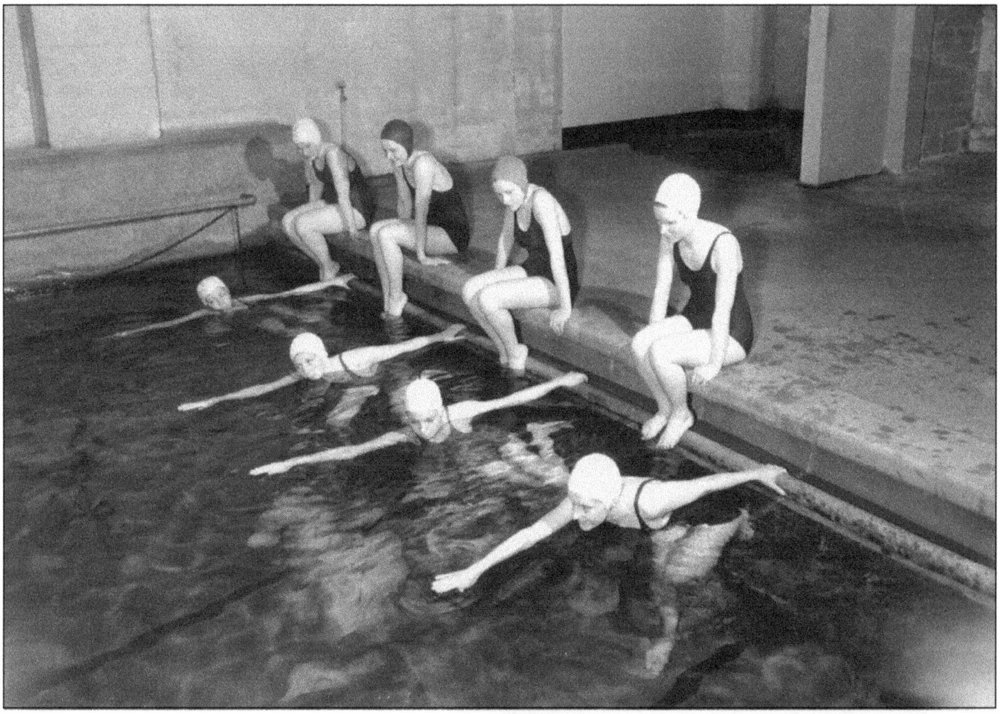

Swimming took place in the natatorium located in the basement of Memorial Gymnasium. Vandal men competed in swimming from 1928 until 1986. Gary Baker, Len Lawr, and Karl von Tagen are members of the Athletic Hall of Fame. Helldivers, a synchronized swimming team, performed there as well. Women's competitive swimming returned to the university in 2004 following an 18-year hiatus. Women swimmers follow in the path of Nancy Westermeyer, four-time Association for Intercollegiate Athletics for Women national qualifier. She was a member of the original class of women student-athletes at Idaho and earned her first scholarship in 1972. She and Nancy Bechtholdt Koch, a 24 time All-American and 1979 Idaho Female Athlete of the Year, are charter members of the University Athletic Hall of Fame. (Above, SPEC, PG 1-231-06; right, UI Photo Services.)

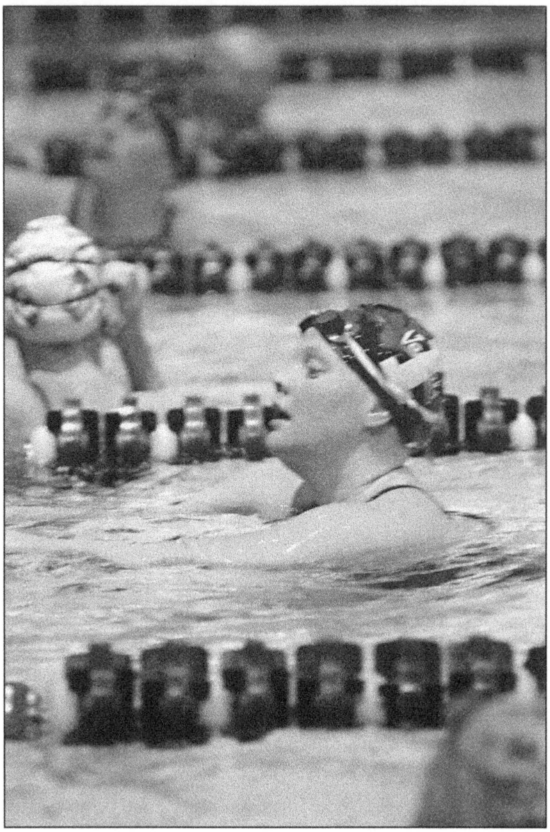

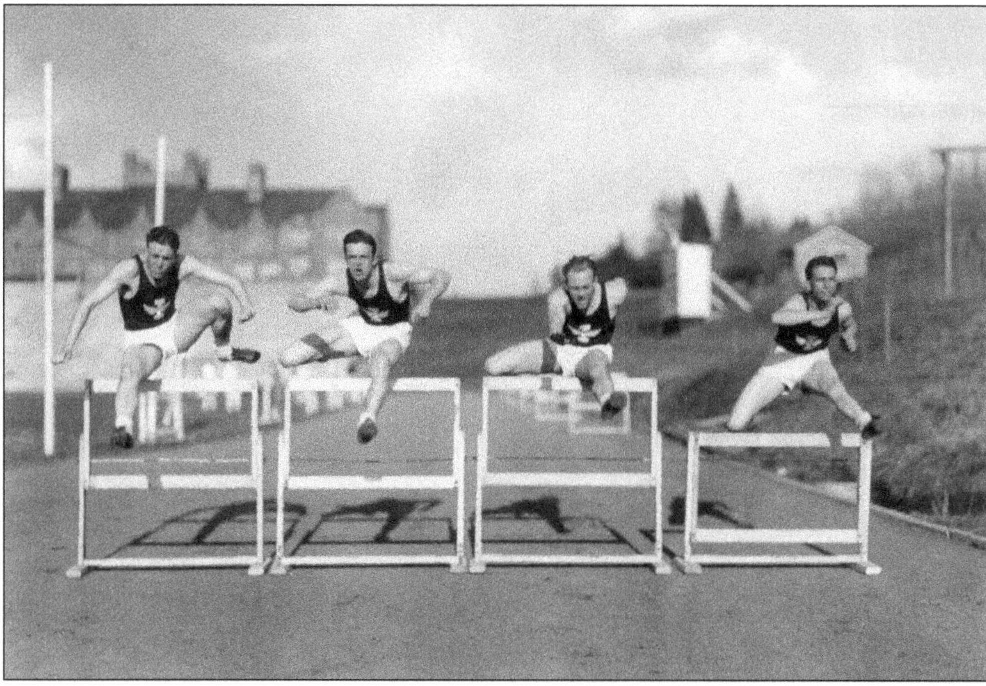

Track and field provided the University of Idaho's first intercollegiate athletics in 1893. Men's cross-country was started in 1908 by Hec Edmunson and continues, along with track and field, as both a men's and women's sport. Here, four Idaho hurdlers in wings uniforms compete in hurdles in 1933. (SPEC, PG 2-118-007.)

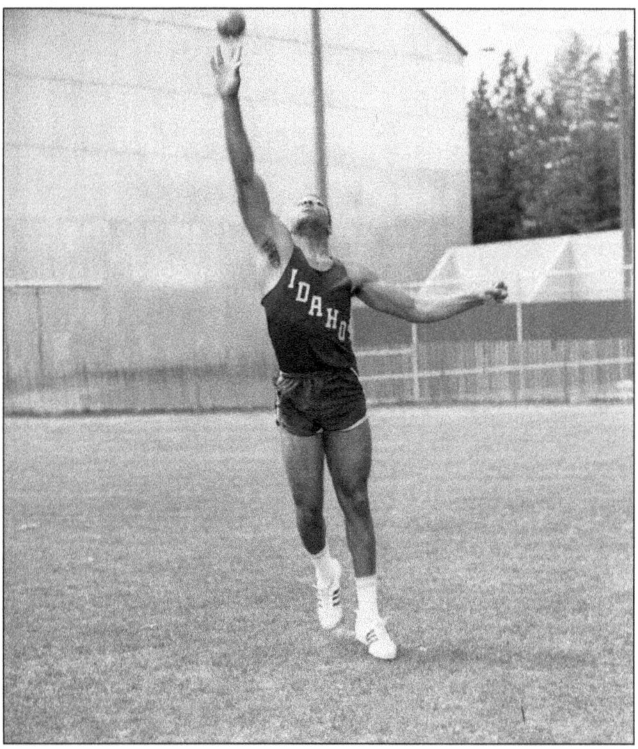

Ray "Thunder Ray" McDonald was named a football All-American in 1965 and 1966. He was a three-time Big Sky champion and two time All-American in the shot put and discus. He was taken in the first round of the 1967 NFL draft by the Washington Redskins. McDonald is a charter member of the Vandal Athletics Hall of Fame. Here, McDonald throws the shot put in 1966. (SPEC, PG 101-3560.)

Coach Doug McFarland is pictured with Idaho high jumper Steven Louis Brown. Brown made national news in 1967 when he became the first person in North America to clear seven feet. He was the NCAA high jump title holder twice. (SPEC, PG 92-1539.)

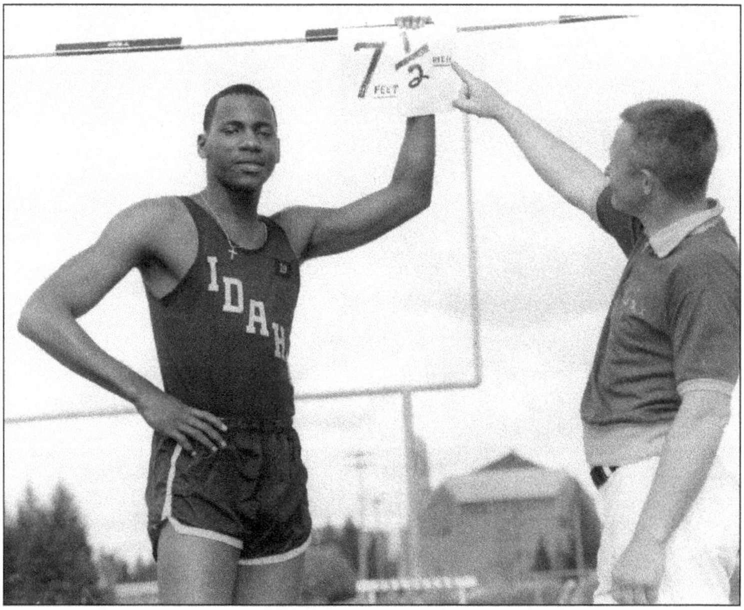

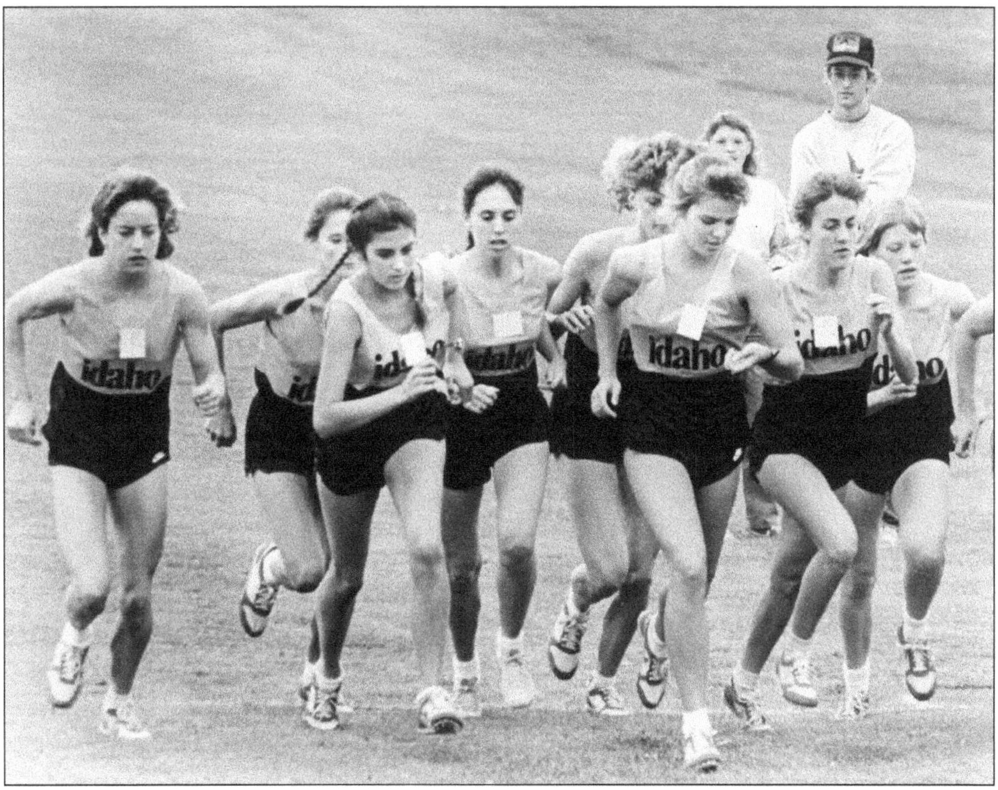

Both women's cross-country and track and field have enjoyed considerable success at the University of Idaho. Patty Sharples Scherer, the greatest woman distance runner in Idaho track history, won the 1982 national AIAW title in the 5,000 meters. She received the 1984 Broderick Sports Award as the nation's top female athlete. Katja Schreiber was Idaho's first and only female NCAA champion in the discus in 2001. (SPEC, UA 1989-027.)

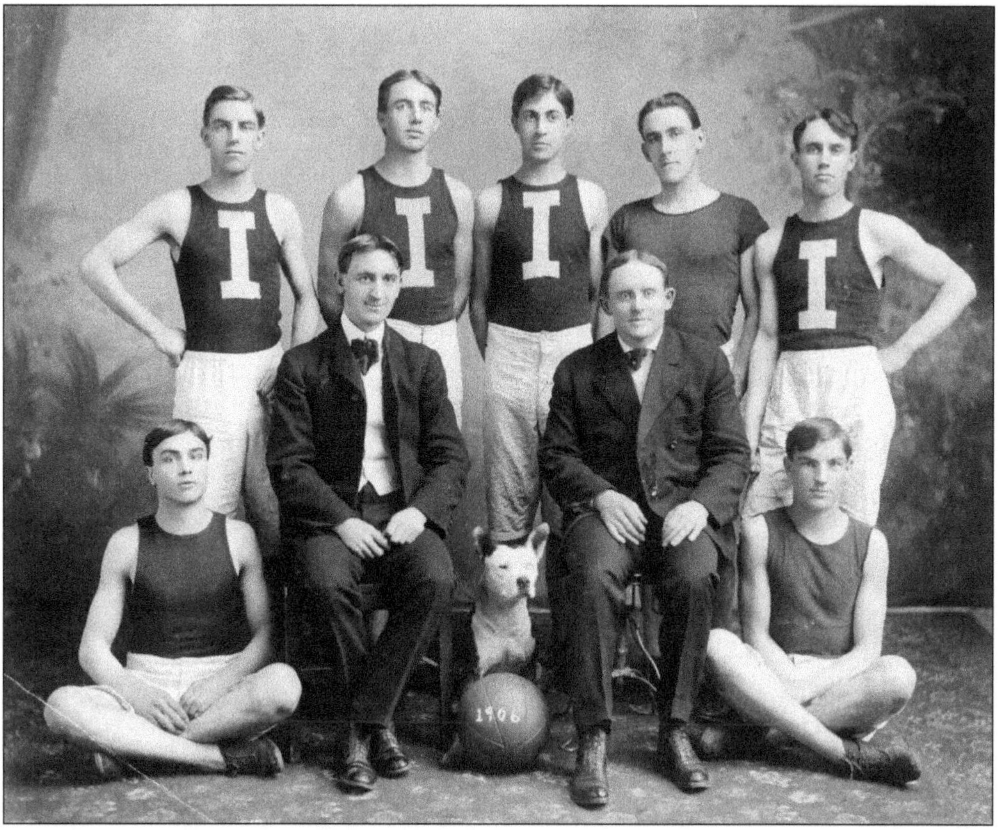

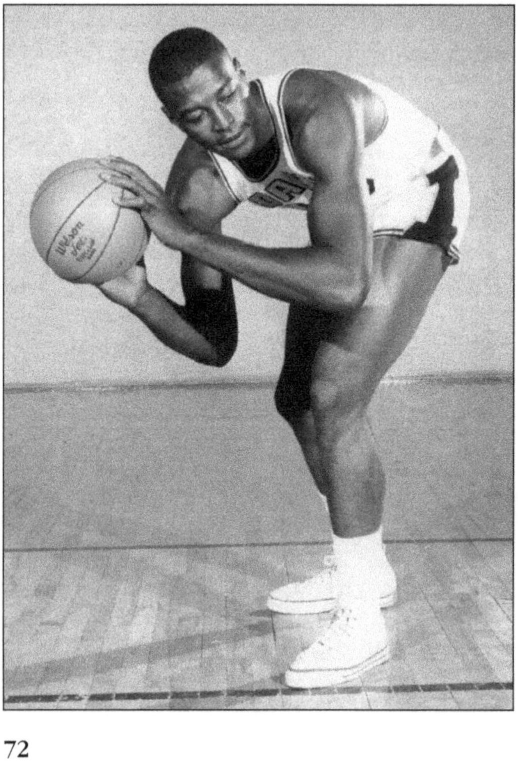

Pictured is Idaho's first men's basketball team in 1906. From left to right are (first row) manager Robert R. Horn, Edward H. Magee, dog Maje, coach John G. "Pink" Griffith, and Thomas Galloway; (second row) James W. Galloway, Rodney L. Small, George H. "Deak" Wyman Jr., Walter P. Balderston, and William E. "Bill" Robertson. (SPEC, PG 2-116-028.)

Gus Johnson was named an All-American in 1963. His number 43 was the first retired in Idaho basketball history. Johnson holds five school records, including 466 career rebounds. Large Memorial Gymnasium crowds cheered Johnson, who went on to have an 11-year NBA career. In recognition of these achievements, Idaho presents the Gus Johnson Award each year to the basketball team's top rebounder or defensive player. (SPEC, PG 3-603a.)

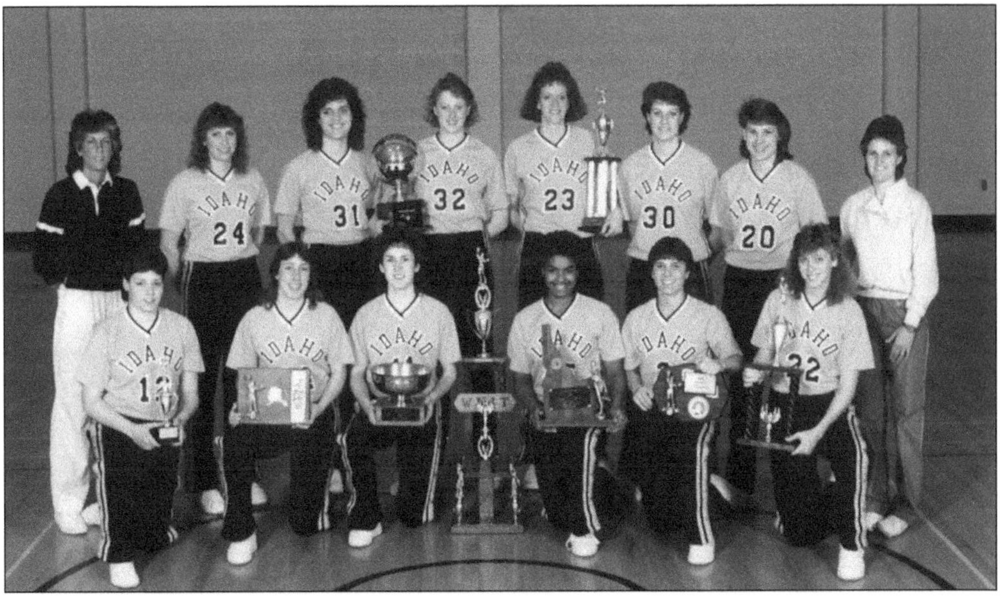

Idaho women won the National Invitational Tournament Championship in 1986, the first Vandal basketball team to win a national championship. The team is included in the University of Idaho Athletics Hall of Fame, as are coach Pat Dobratz (who had a six-year record of 142-39) and center Mary Raese. She and forward Mary Westerwelle were first-team All-Conference in the Mountain West Conference. The Vandal Women received NCAA tournament bids in 2013, 2014, and 2016. (UI Athletics.)

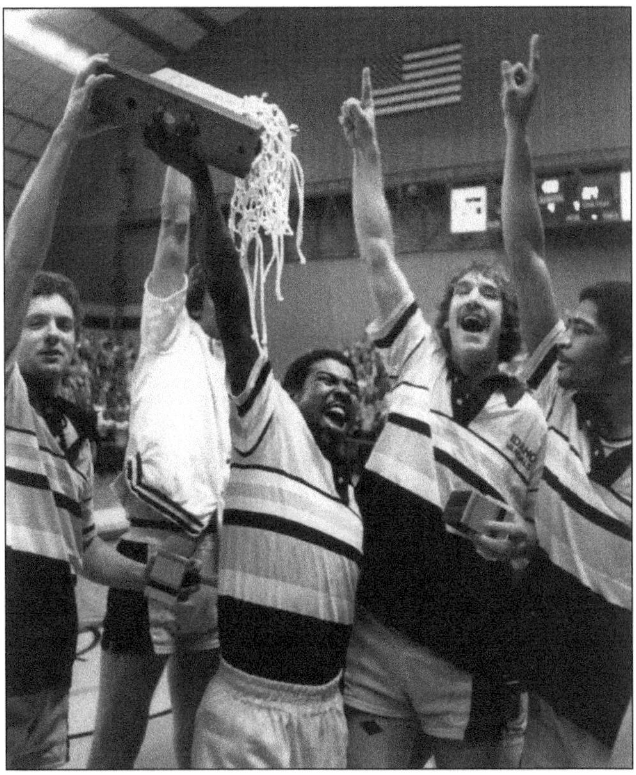

Big Sky champions in 1981 and 1982, the men's basketball team in 1982 appeared in the NCAA Sweet 16. Pictured are members of the 1980–1981 championship basketball team celebrating the after-game ritual of cutting the net. Coach Don Monson and player Brian Kellerman are members of the University of Idaho Athletics Hall of Fame. (SPEC, UA 1987-014.)

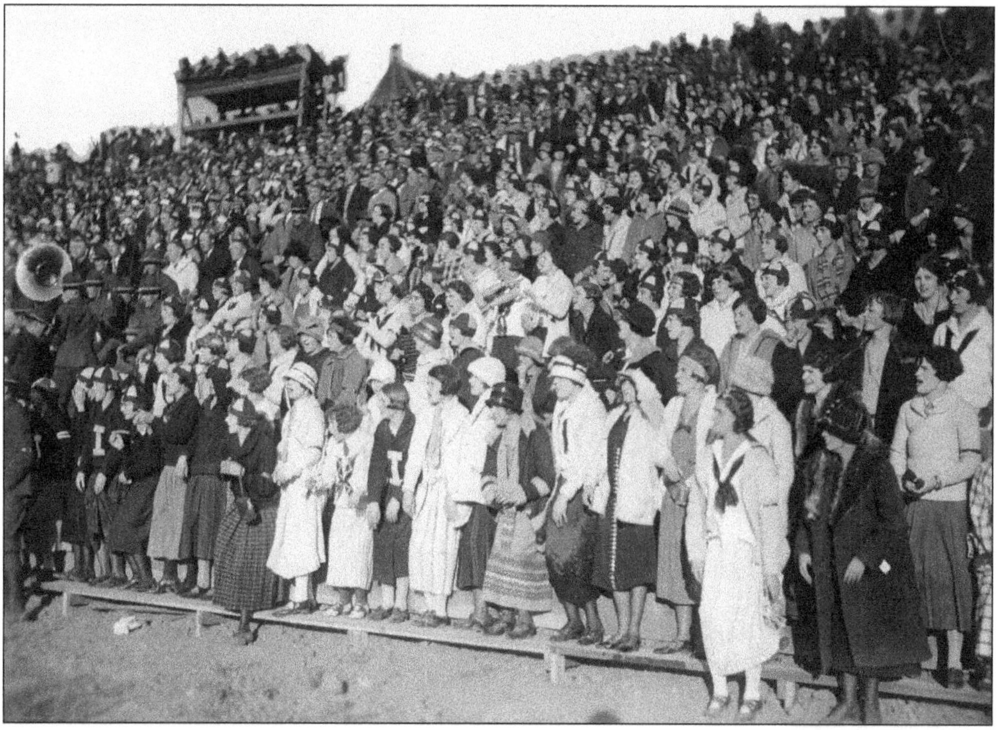

Intercollegiate athletics in general and Vandal athletics specifically are known for boisterous and passionate student fans. Above is the student cheering section at a football game in the 1920s. Football games in the Kibbie Dome guarantee that rooters spelling "Idaho" are protected from inclement weather on the Palouse. (Above, SPEC, PG 2-132-010; below, UI Photo Services.)

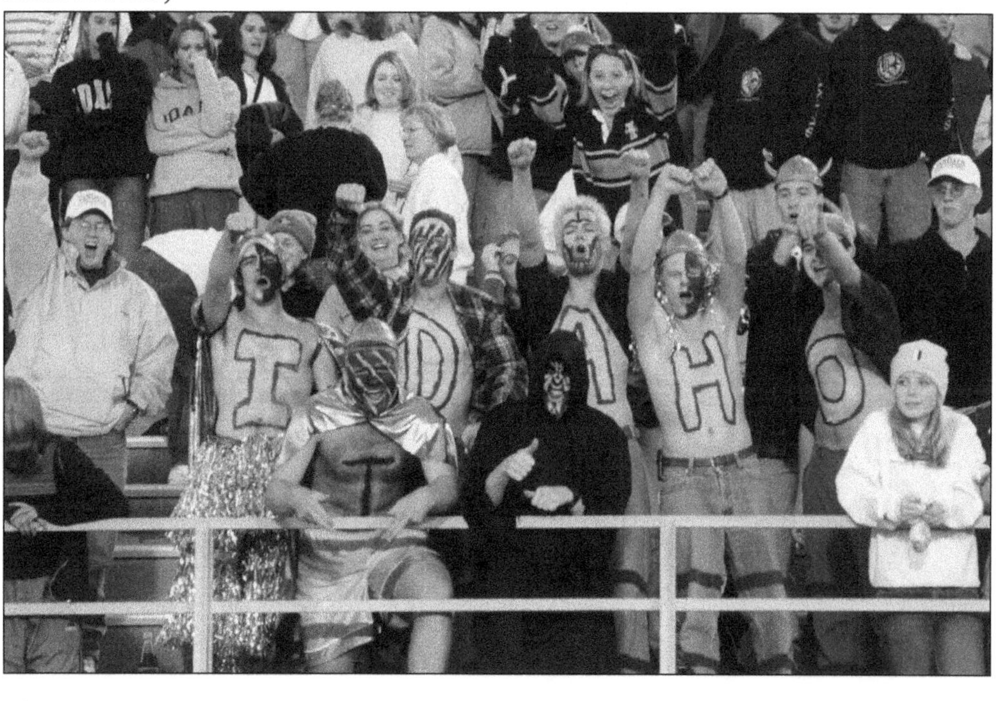

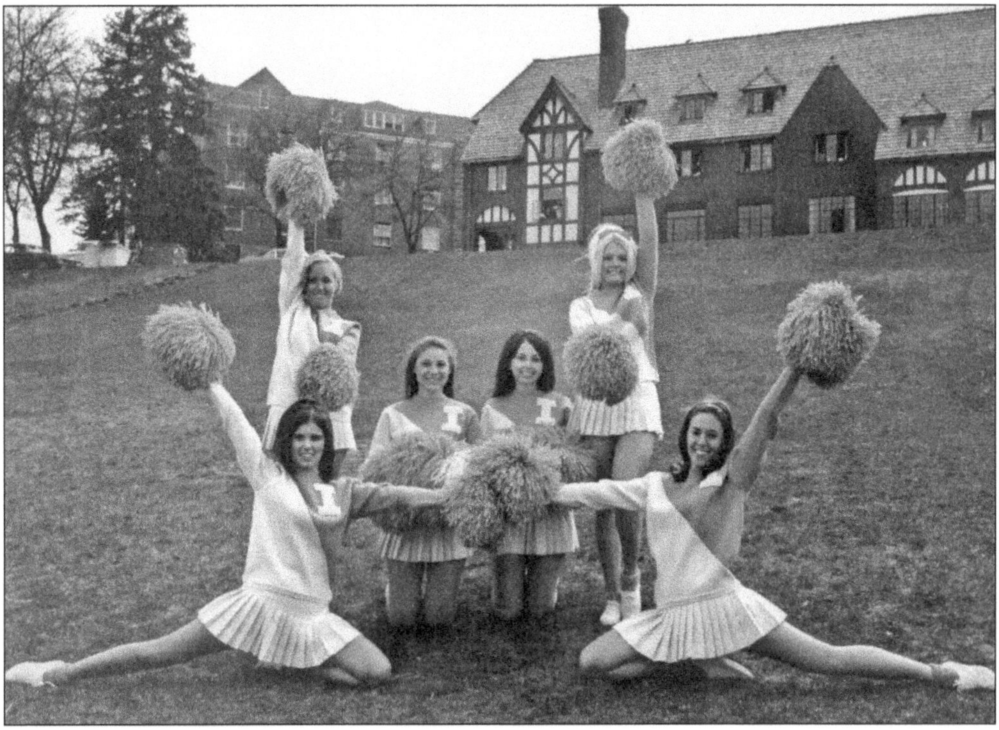

Early cheer squads were comprised only of men. Beginning in the 1950s, women entered the field and came to overshadow their male counterparts. Posing on the Delta Tau Delta lawn around 1970 are, from left to right, (first row) Barbara Benner, Jennifer Mattern, Valerie Plum, and Kleone Grotzinger; (second row) Debbie Maxwell and Connie Peterman. (SPEC, UA 1987-014.)

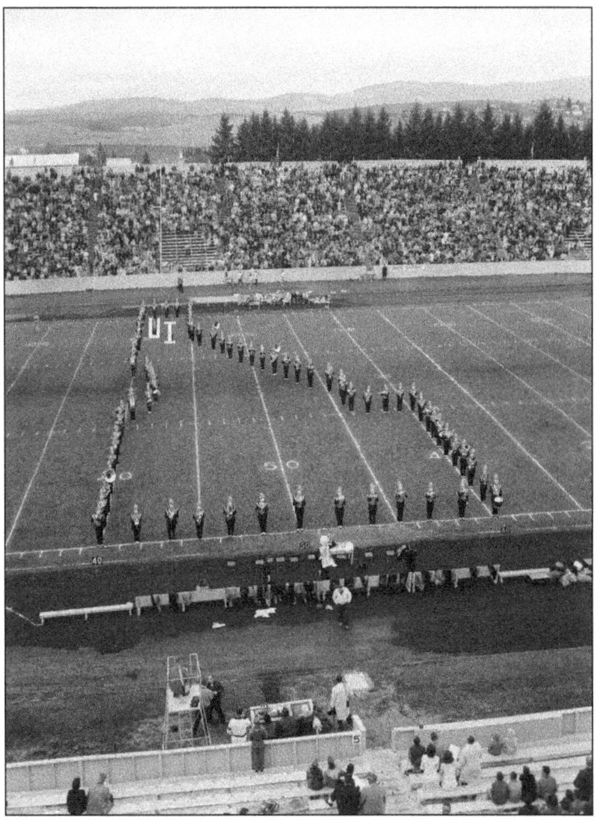

The marching band performs during halftime at the 1962 Homecoming game. The University of Idaho Sound of Idaho Marching Ban" is known for its vibrant performances at athletic events and continues to be an audience favorite. The Associated Students of the University of Idaho; the College of Letters, Arts, and Social Sciences; and the Lionel Hampton School of Music sponsor the band. (SPEC, PG 101-1507.)

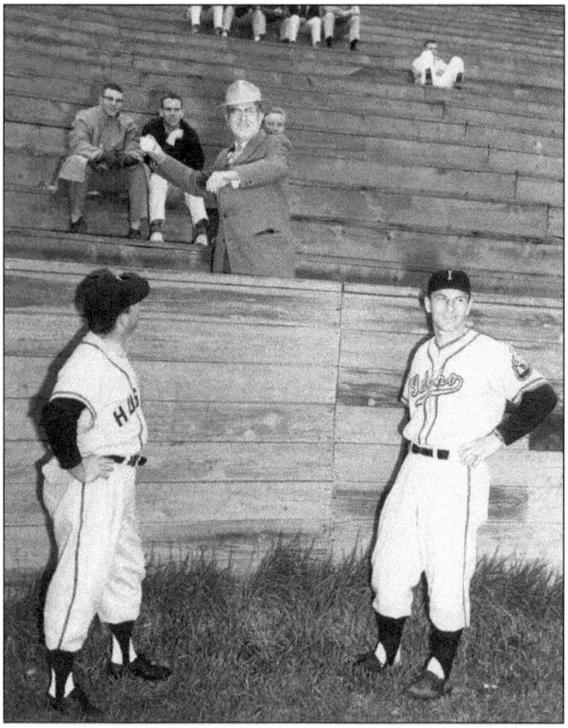

University of Idaho president Donald Theophilus throws out the first ball of the season at MacLean Field in 1961. The 1966 baseball team was UI's most successful, finishing the year 34-9 and ranked 18th in the nation. Bill Stoneman went on to play professional baseball and as Angels general manager won the 2002 World Series. The University of Idaho dropped baseball as an intercollegiate sport in 1979. (SPEC, PG 2-117-15a.)

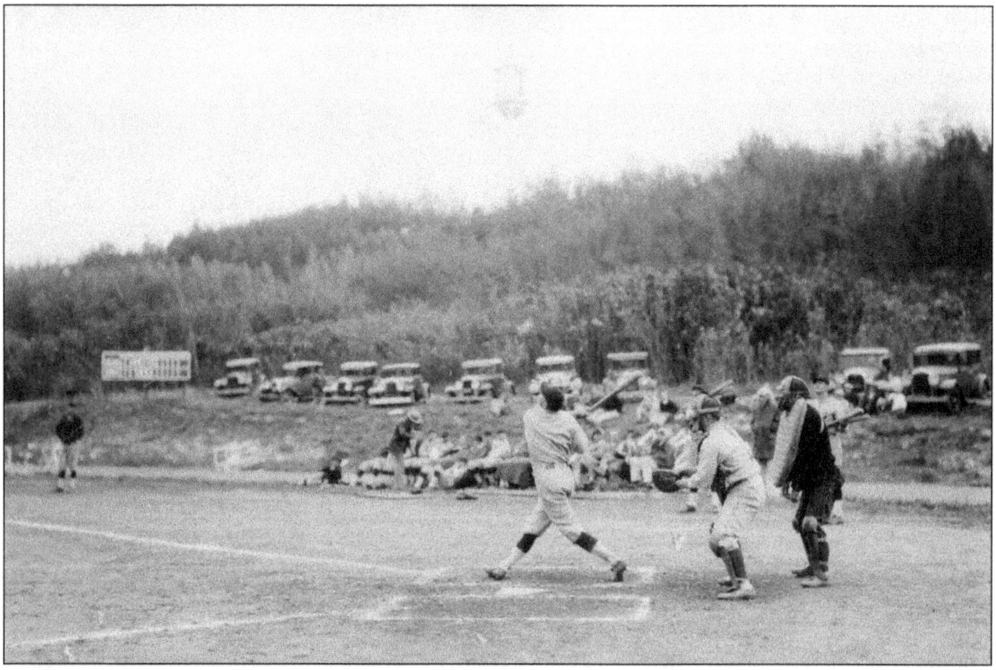

In 1967, the university's baseball venue moved from MacLean Field to Guy Wicks Field. Wicks was a three-year letter winner in baseball from 1921 to 1924. He returned to the University of Idaho in 1941 as basketball coach. Wicks Field is home to intramural sports and the Vandal soccer team. Wicks is a member of the University of Idaho Athletics Hall of Fame. Pictured is a UI vs. Washington State College baseball game. (SPEC, PG 2-117-070.)

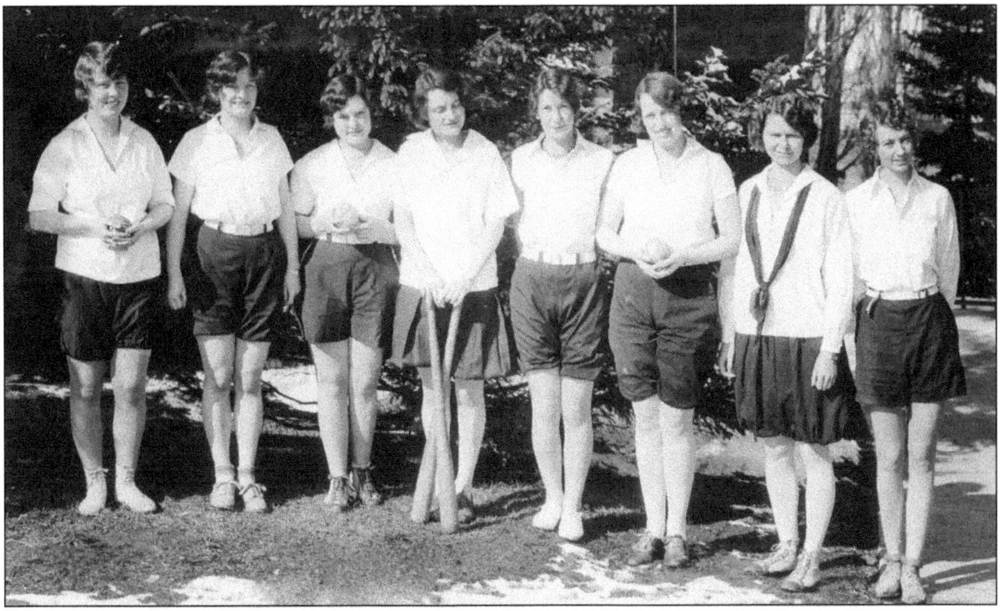

By 1925, baseball was the chief spring sport for women, having replaced field hockey. Idaho organized a local chapter and gained membership in the National Women's Athletic Association in 1923. To qualify for membership, women had to take part in at least two sports per semester. Pictured here is the 1930 women's baseball team. (SPEC, UA 2001-001.)

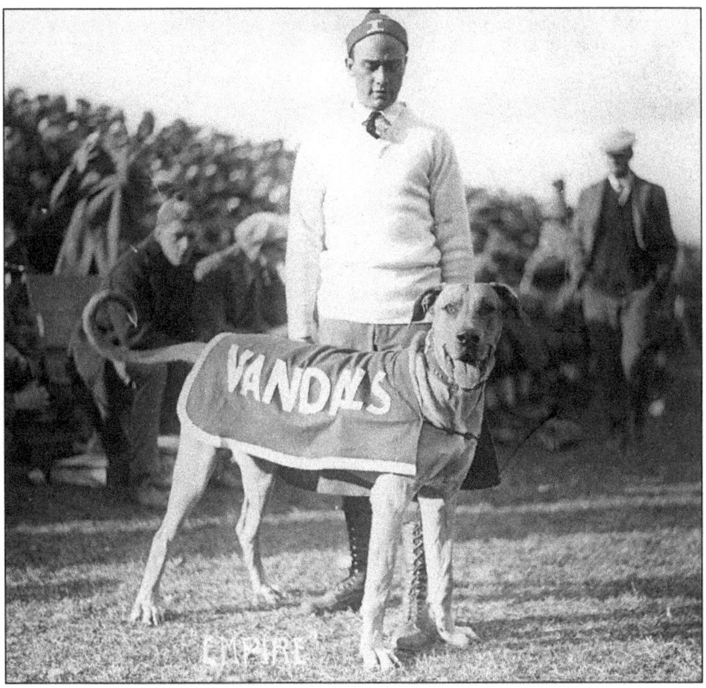

In 1911, the University of Idaho student body adopted a dress code for men that included green beanies for all first-year students. Male students were to wear the headgear at all times except when in bed. Here, an Idaho student sports the "I" beanie around 1923 with Empire the dog mascot. (SPEC, PG 92-1331.)

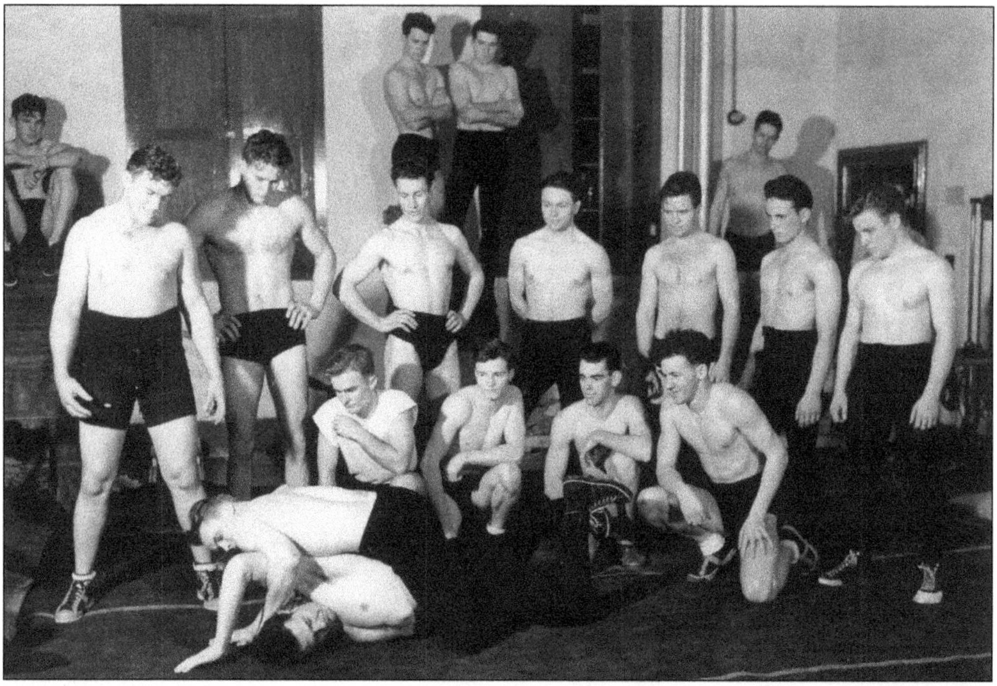

An Idaho wrestling team is pictured in the mid-1930s. The Vandals had intercollegiate wrestling teams until the post–World War II period, when the university discontinued the sport along with fencing and rifle marksmanship. Intramural wrestling continues at the University of Idaho. (SPEC, MG 5779.)

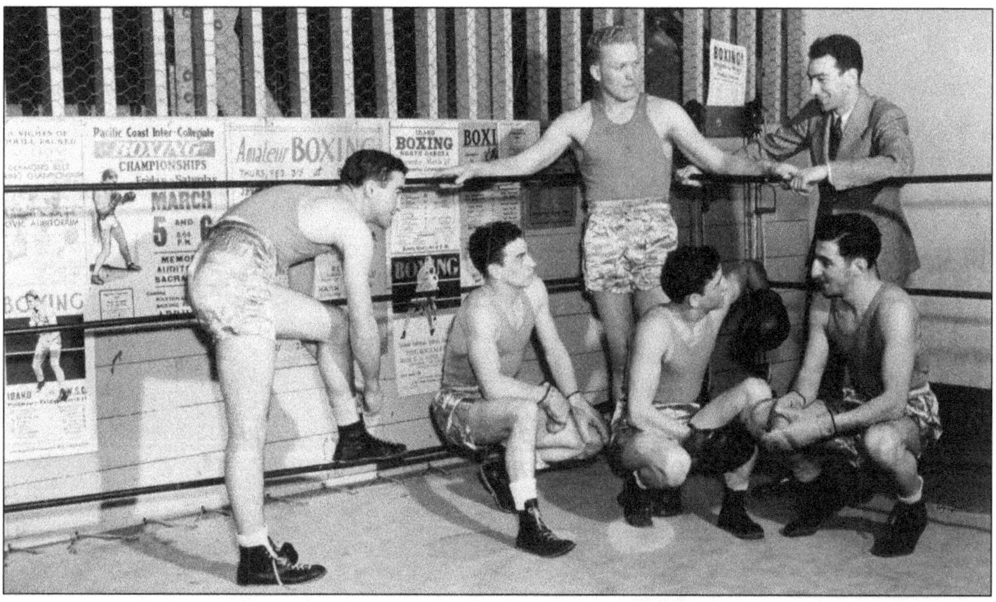

Student boxers talk with Coach Louie August in 1937. Following the lead of Rolly Shumway, the school's first NCAA champion, the boxing team embarked on 20 years of national prominence. Julian Benoit, Herb Carlson, Frank Kara, Ted Kara, Franky Echeverria, Luane Erickson, and John Webster were NCAA champions, the Karas being the first brothers to do so in the same year. UI was the national title holder in 1950. (SPEC, PG 2-125-24.)

Field hockey became an Olympic sport in 1980, the same year the university dropped it from the intercollegiate women's athletic program following a precipitous decline in interest across the Northwest. Here, the Idaho goalie stands her ground. (SPEC, PG2-116-08.)

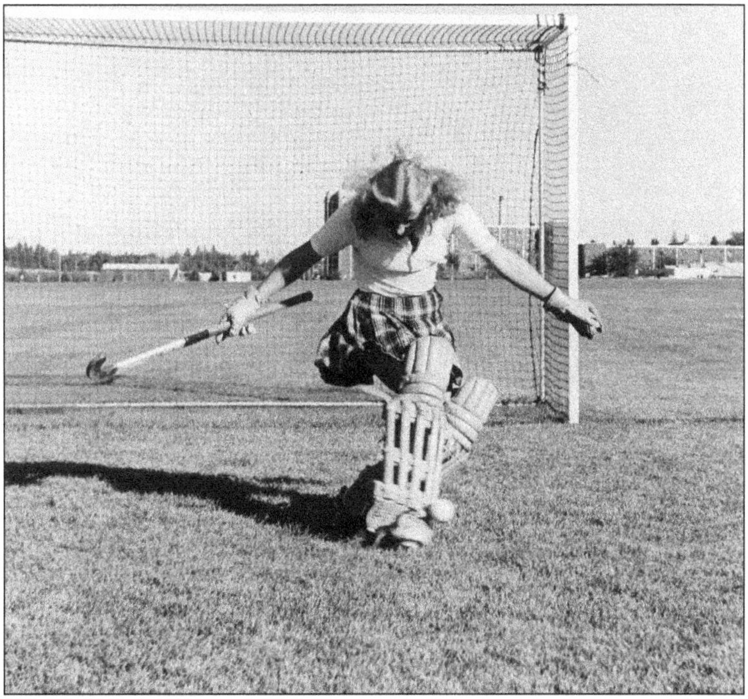

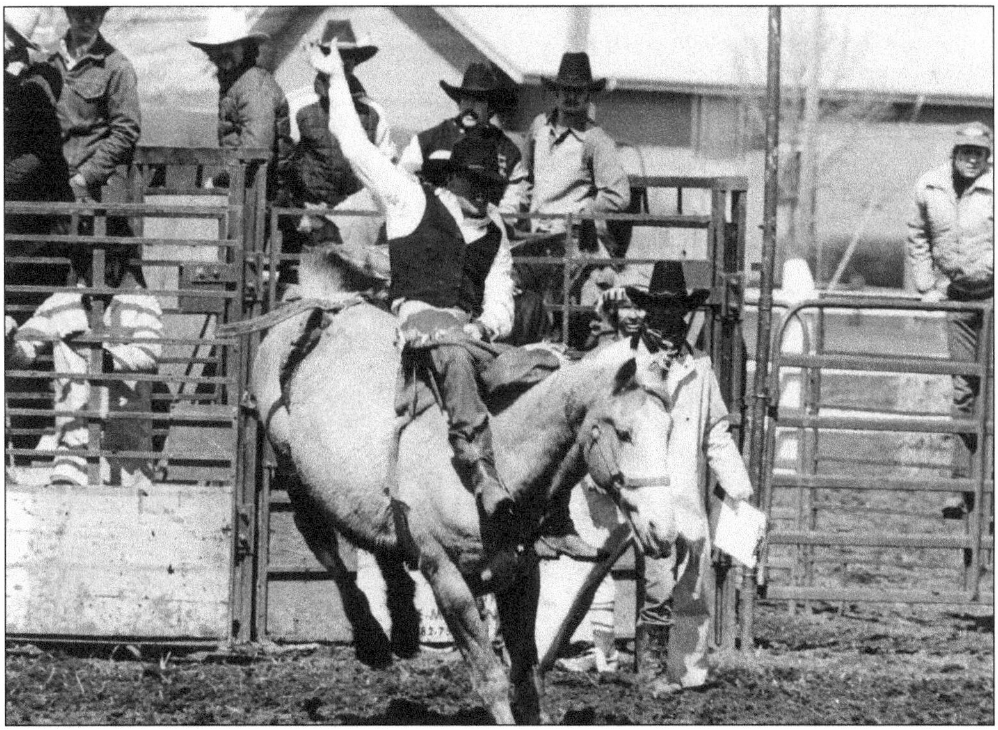

Club teams allow University of Idaho students to pursue athletic endeavors of their choice including climbing, cycling, fast-pitch softball, horse polo, ice hockey, lacrosse, rugby, skiing, snowboarding, soccer, table tennis, trap shooting, ultimate Frisbee, volleyball, water polo, and rodeo, shown here. (SPEC, UA 1991-040.)

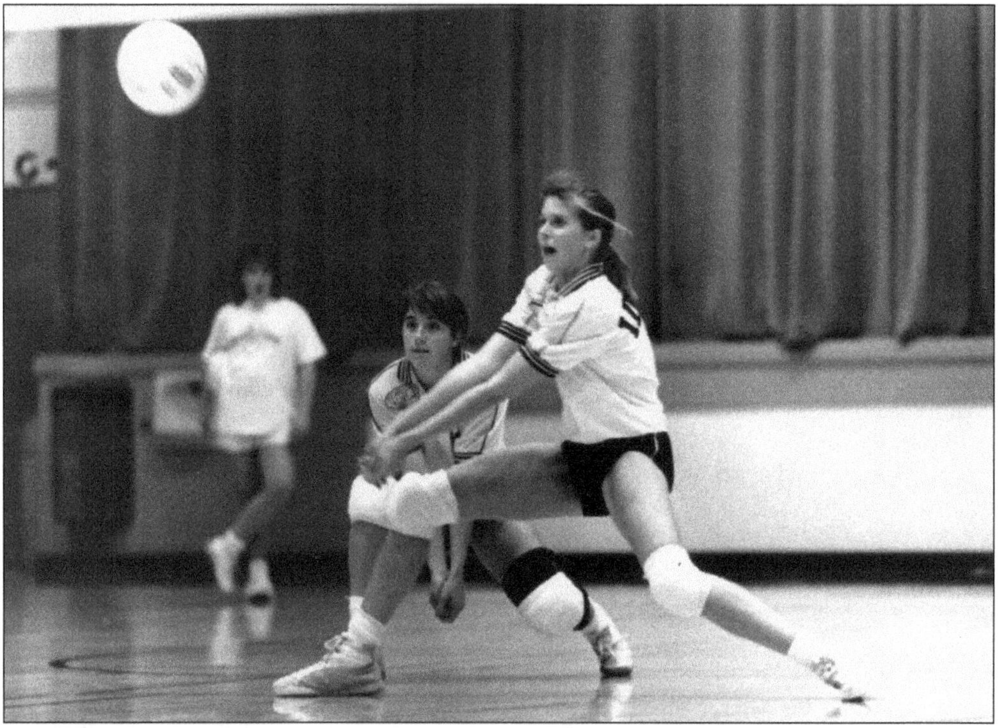

No Idaho women's volleyball team has garnered as many accolades as that of 1994. The team made it to the NCAA tournament round of 32 with a 31-3 record and was ranked 19th in the final national poll. Nancy Wicks was named the Big Sky Most Valuable Player and is a member of the University of Idaho Athletics Hall of Fame. (SPEC, UA 1989-027.)

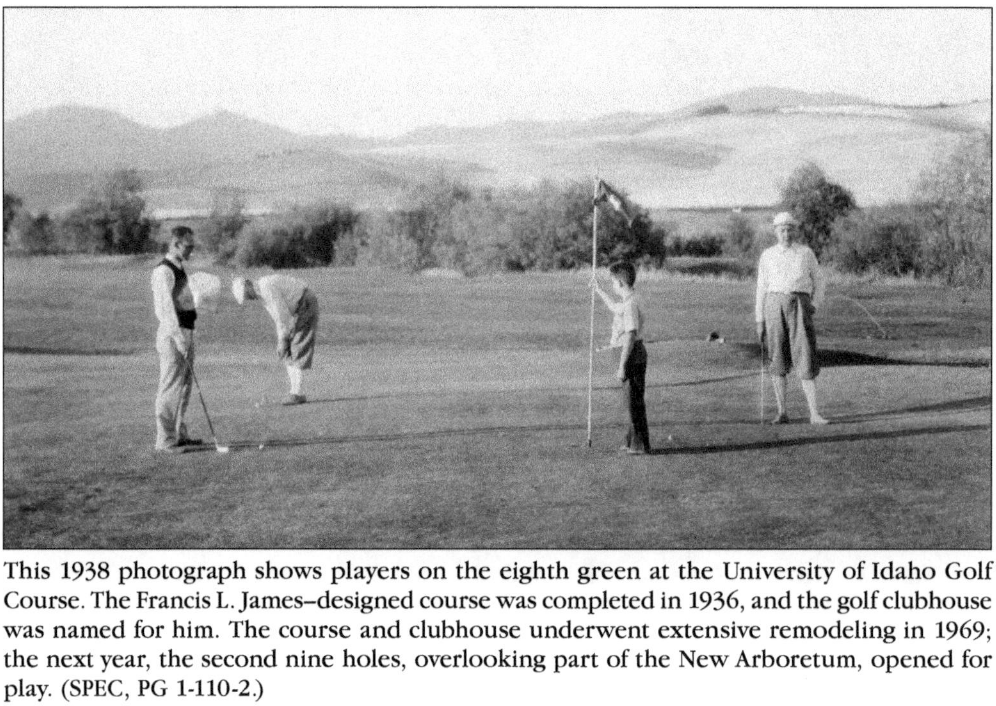

This 1938 photograph shows players on the eighth green at the University of Idaho Golf Course. The Francis L. James–designed course was completed in 1936, and the golf clubhouse was named for him. The course and clubhouse underwent extensive remodeling in 1969; the next year, the second nine holes, overlooking part of the New Arboretum, opened for play. (SPEC, PG 1-110-2.)

Kristen Armstrong, a 1995 sports physiology graduate, won two consecutive Olympic gold medals in cycling time trial. Armstrong retired following her 2008 Beijing victory. She began a comeback in 2010 following the birth of her son, Lucas, and was a gold medalist in London in 2012. (UI Photo Services.)

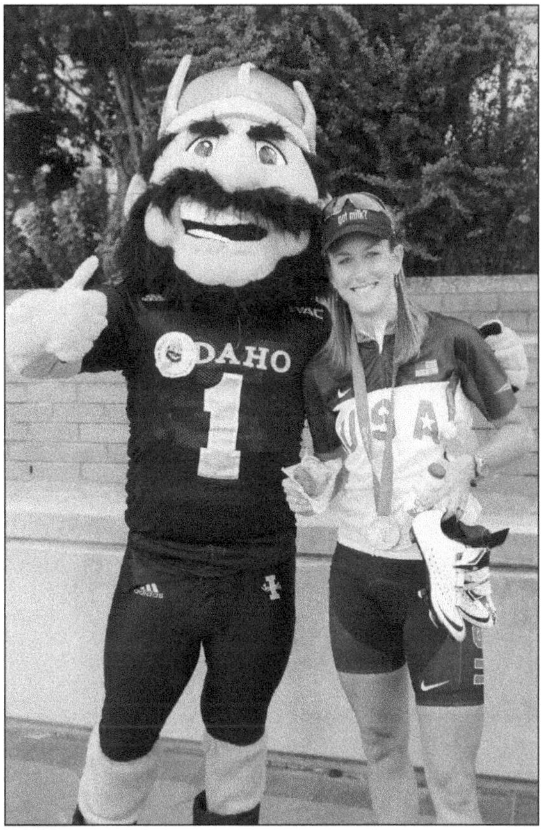

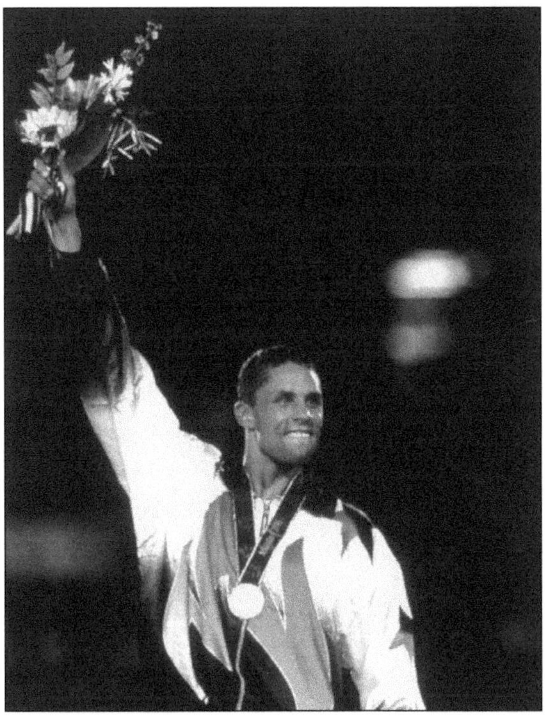

Dan O'Brien (1993) was a hurdler on the UI track team and was named a 1989 All-American. He won the 1996 Olympic gold medal in the decathlon. He is a member of the USA Track and Field Hall of Fame. The University of Idaho outdoor track and field facility is named for him. (UI Athletics.)

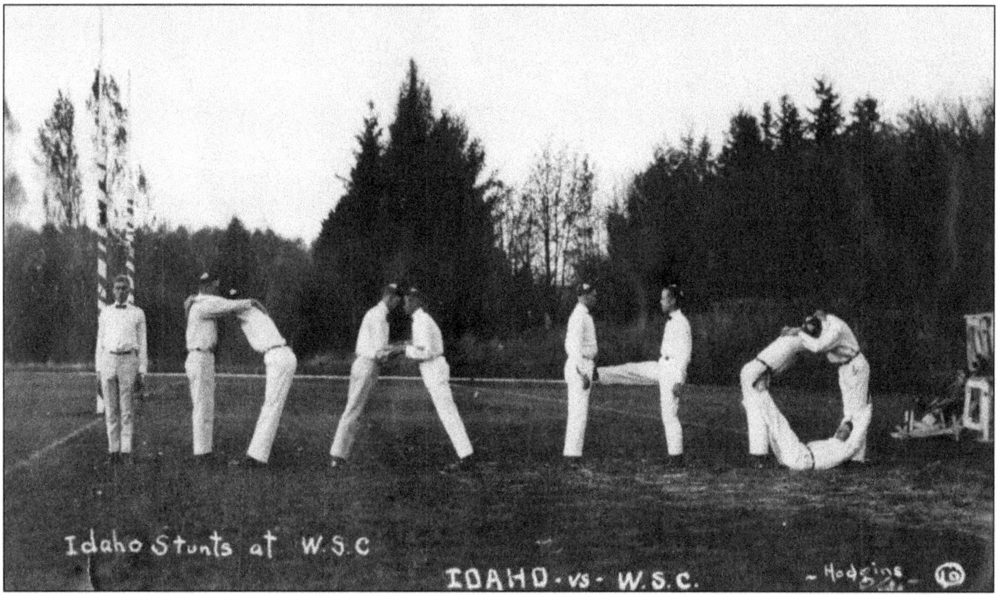

In one of the University of Idaho's best-known photographs, men spell "Idaho" as part of the 1921 Harvard Yell contest, a stunt competition during the annual Washington State College–University of Idaho football game. Idaho won the stunt competition again in 1922, when the audience waved yellow clothes while students sang "On Old Idaho." (Above, SPEC, PG 2-133-8; below, SPEC, PG 2-135-05.)

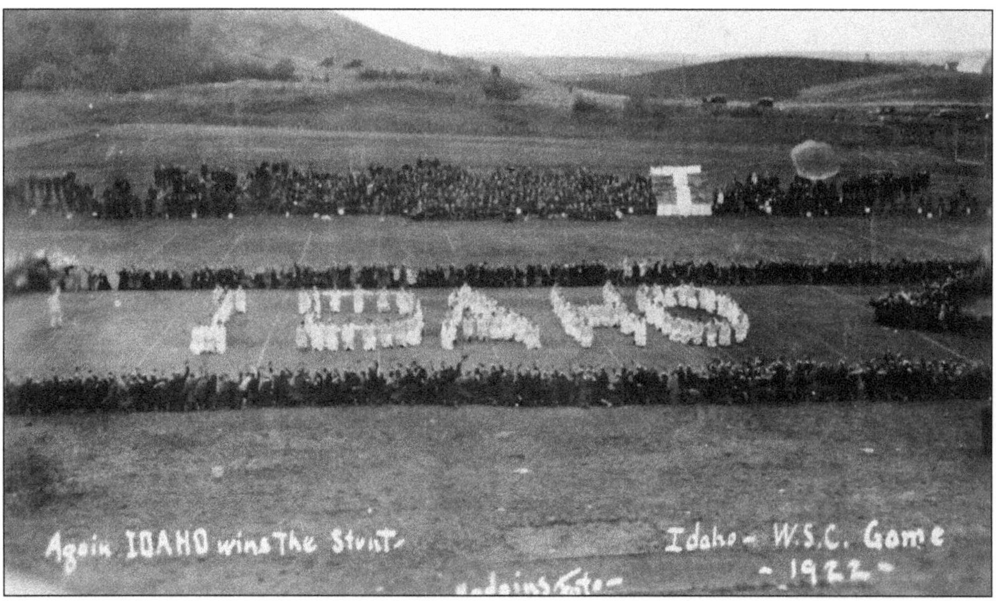

Four

Home Away from Home

The University of Idaho's Moscow campus is primarily residential and has been throughout its history. Idaho's geography, with its accompanying long travel distances, and Moscow's small-town atmosphere have both served to foster a campus environment where students build long-lasting personal relationships and often create their own entertainment. Homecoming Week is perhaps the best known of these and includes the traditional bonfire, a parade through the streets of downtown Moscow, a football game, and various reunions. The University of Idaho currently requires that all first-year students live on campus. This contributes to student success, aids in the building of community, and results in a dynamic campus environment.

Convinced that University of Idaho women needed suitable campus housing, the board of regents authorized the construction of Ridenbaugh Hall, dedicated in 1902. No appropriation was forthcoming for a men's dormitory, so Moscow residents provided the funding for Ernest K. Lindley Hall, named for the university president, in 1920. Currently, Residence Life offers students numerous choices ranging from themed halls to living and learning suites to more traditional dormitory accommodations to apartments. Students can explore a variety of social living arrangements and have access to academic support and exciting programming. Ethel Steel House provides a cooperative living experience for women.

For over a century, fraternities and sororities have occupied a prominent place in the University of Idaho landscape and provide living situations for almost one third of undergraduate students. Over the years, they have constructed graceful residences, beginning with Kappa Sigma, the first house built for a fraternity in Idaho, and including sorority Delta Zeta's impressive new house, occupied in 2015. Currently the Greek community includes 13 women's houses, 22 men's houses, and 6 nationally recognized multicultural Greek organizations.

An 18-hole golf course, a disc golf course, and the Student Recreation Center, featuring a 55-foot climbing wall, facilitate physical activity. Outstanding opportunities for skiing, hiking, and water sports are easily accessible. The University of Idaho is a perennial member of the President's Higher Education Community Service Honor Roll in recognition of the hours that University of Idaho students devote to service.

Moscow, Idaho, is the quintessential campus town; *Men's Journal* named Moscow one of the nation's five best places to live among college towns. Surrounded by the rolling Palouse hills, the community offers a safe and welcoming environment.

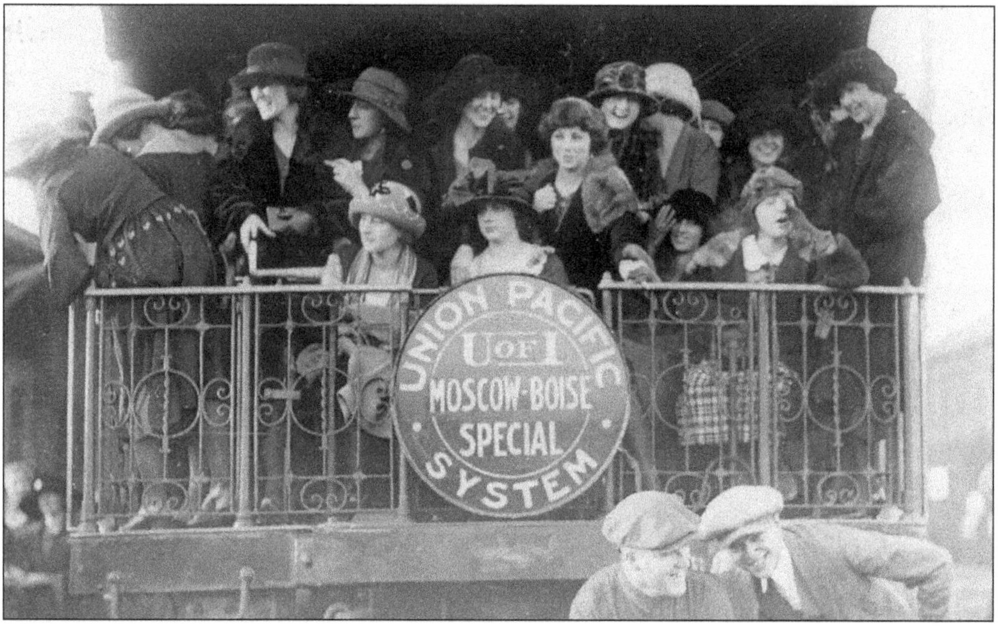

Students ride the Student Special train before 1915. Campus officials convinced the Union Pacific Railroad to provide low-fare trains to the university starting in the early 1900s. The Student Special started in southeastern Idaho with stops along the approximately 600-mile route. Its arrival in Moscow was an occasion for great fanfare and celebration. (SPEC, PG 92-1327.)

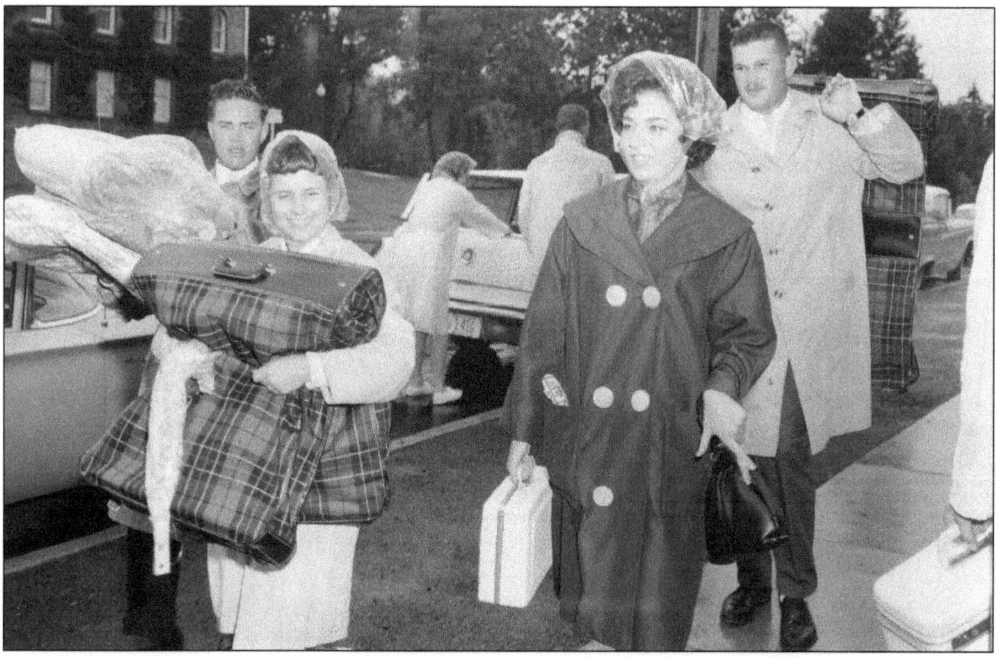

Student organizations the Spurs and Intercollegiate Knights help Gail Connell (right) move into her residence hall in 1962, when the student population was about 5,000. In recent years, campus administrators have provided move-in help to students as a first welcome to the University of Idaho. (SPEC, PG 101-1420.)

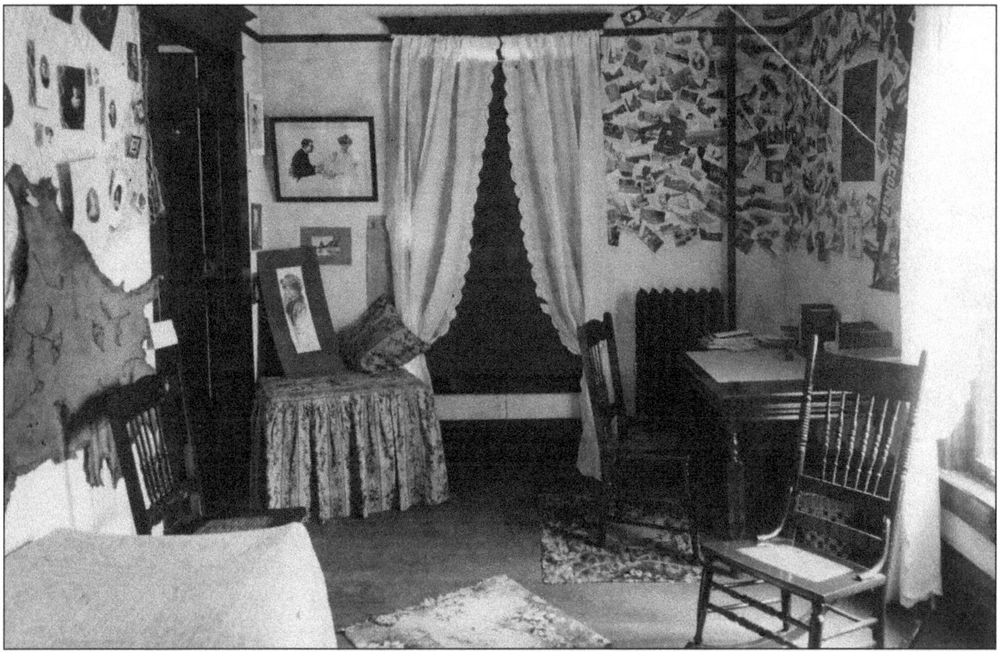

This student bedroom was in Ridenbaugh Hall in 1908. Women students brought all the comforts of home to adorn their rooms. The doctrine of *in loco parentis* allowed the university to regulate most aspects of student behavior. Until 1970, women students had to be in their residences at certain hours, while men did not have similar curfews. (SPEC, PG 1-58-14.)

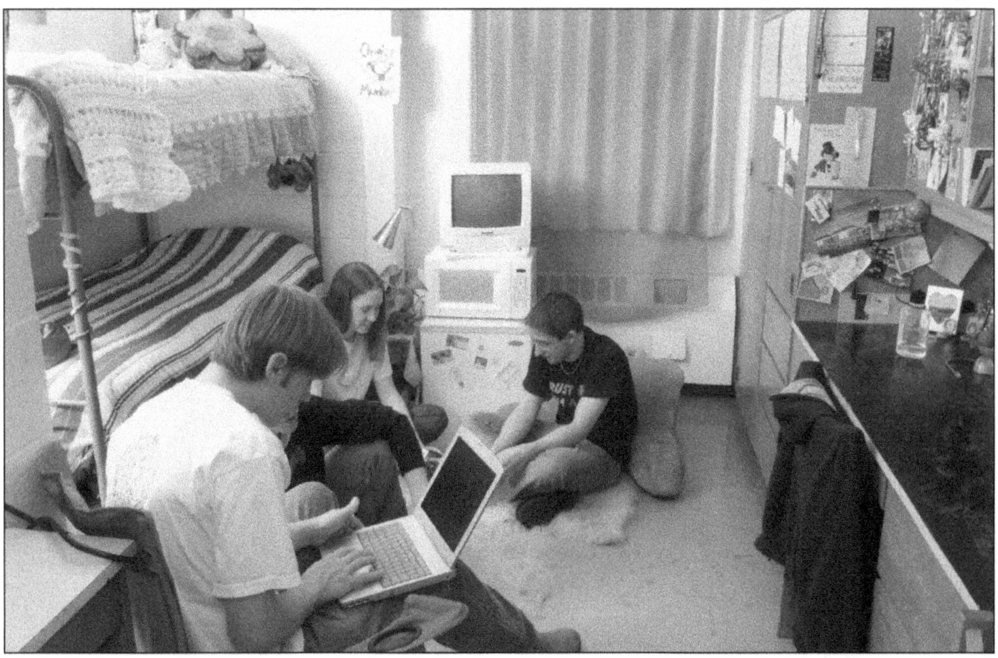

This is a dorm room almost a century later, in 2005. Visitors are no longer limited to a single gender, and computers and microwave ovens are de rigueur. The University of Idaho has 25 residence communities and one women's cooperative residence hall. Themed halls cater to a variety of specific interests. (UI Photo Services.)

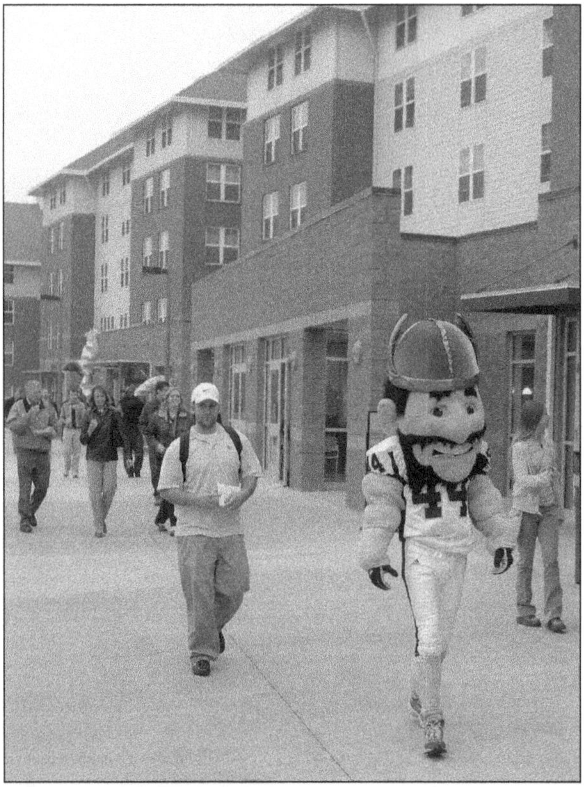

Mascot Joe Vandal walks near the Living and Learning Center around 2005. The LLC includes eight residence buildings for non–first year students. The University Honors Program, started in 1983, includes students from all undergraduate colleges and occupies one of the buildings. Yell leader Bill Currie made the first Joe Vandal entrance in the late 1950s. Although his appearance has changed, Joe continues to reign supreme among Idaho stalwarts. (UI Photo Services.)

Regina Bailey, accounting junior, occupies a telephone booth around 1989. Before the advent of cell phones, telephone booths in living groups were in constant use. Many residences set time limits for calls, and conducting a private conversation was sometimes difficult. (SPEC, UA 1989-027.)

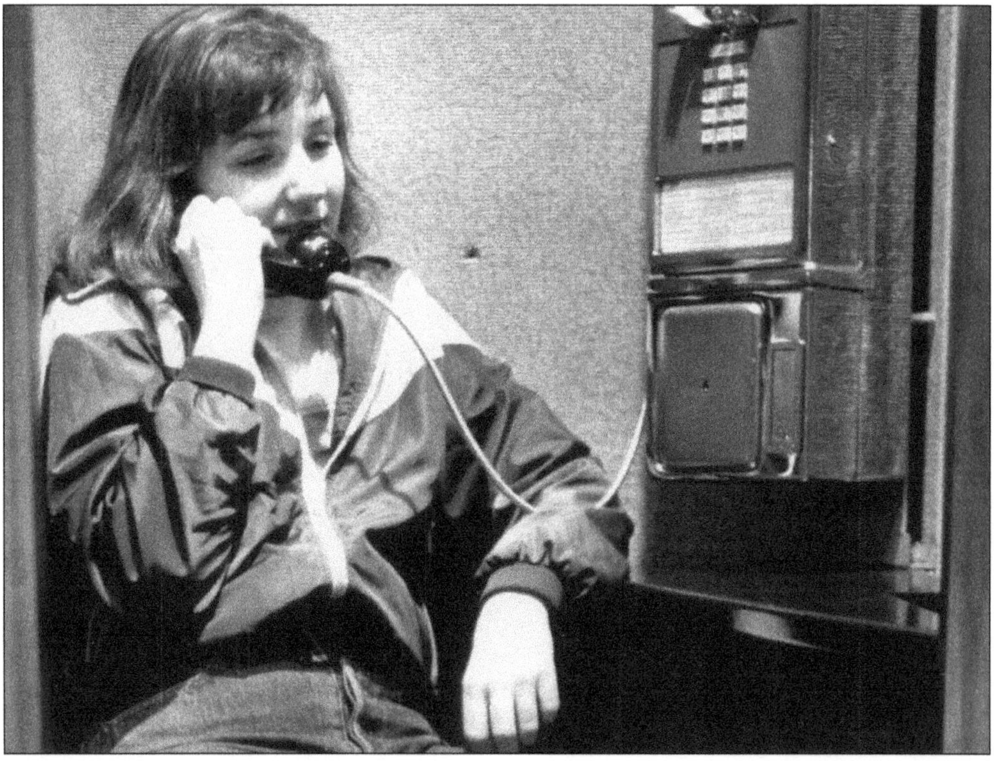

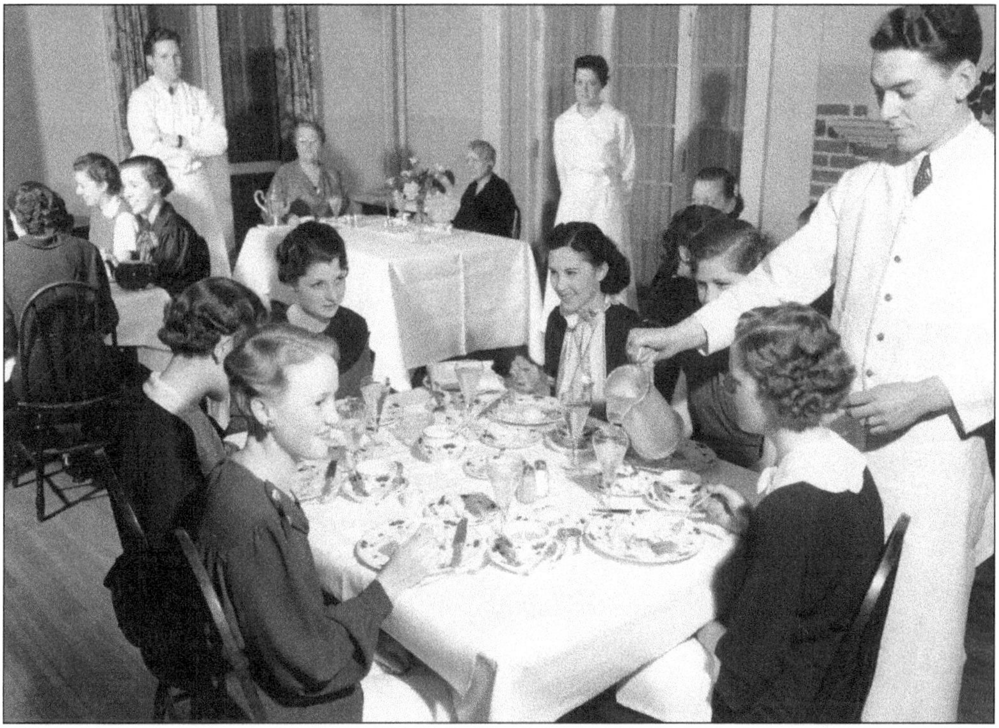

This 1936 image shows Hays Hall residents enjoying a meal. It was customary for students in residence halls and Greek houses to gather for sit-down meals served by uniformed "hashers." As the university grew and classes met throughout the day and into the evening, formal dining became less practical. (SPEC, PG 1-59-09.)

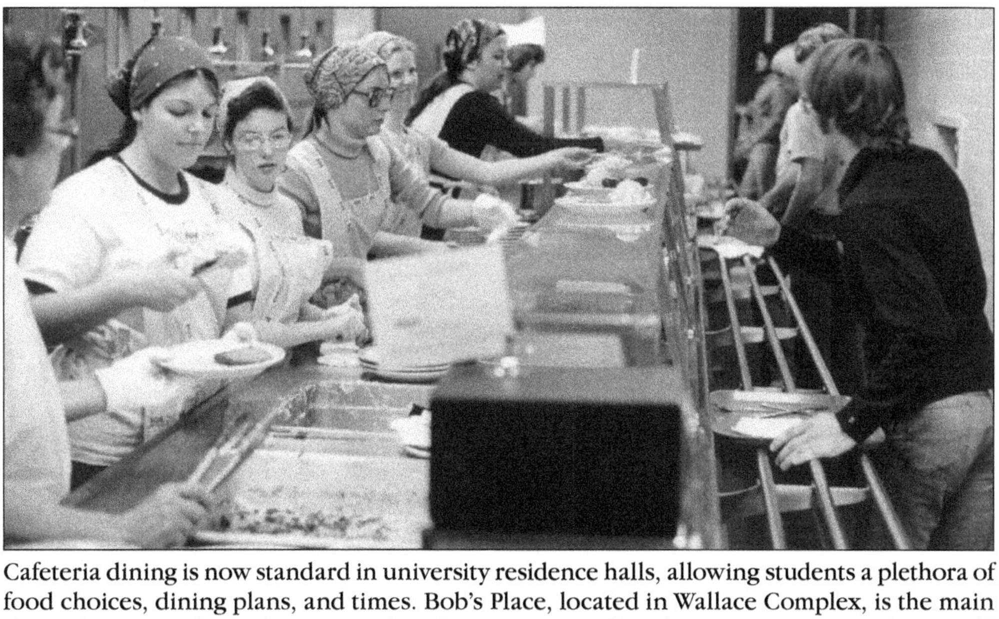

Cafeteria dining is now standard in university residence halls, allowing students a plethora of food choices, dining plans, and times. Bob's Place, located in Wallace Complex, is the main dining location. Shown here is Gault-Upham Dining Hall in the 1980s. Accommodating 344 men, Gault-Upham was torn down in 2003 to make way for the second phase of the Living and Learning Center. (SPEC, UA 1991-040.)

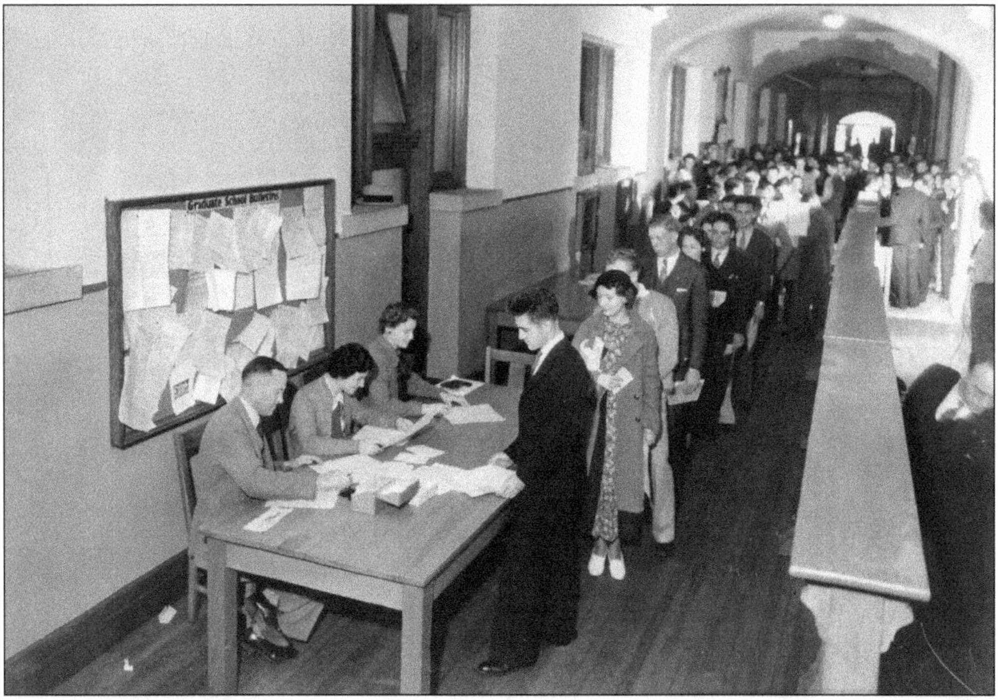

This registration line is in the main hall of the Administration Building in 1936. For two days, students stood in the "line that never ends" as more than 2,200 of them registered for classes that year. Temporary railings were in place to keep students moving in an orderly fashion. (SPEC, PG 2-78-4.)

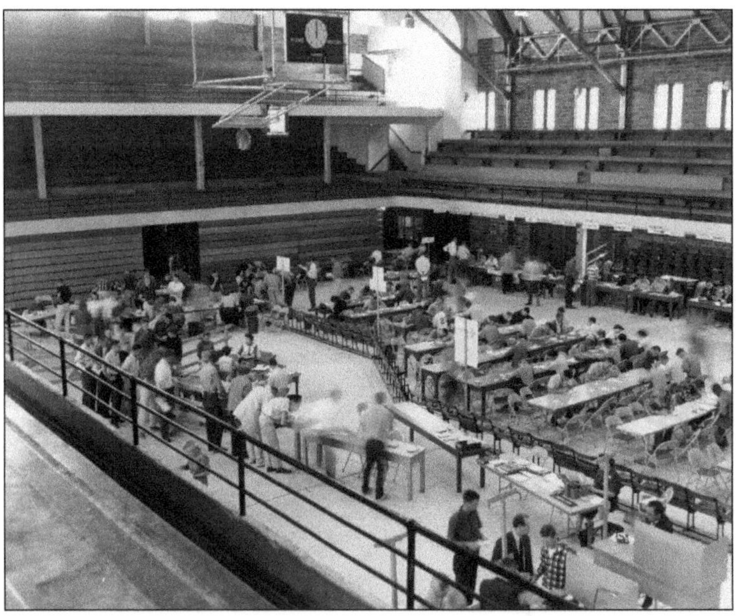

Registration takes place in Memorial Gym in 1960. Each department kept class lists for every class offering, and students signed them until the classes were filled. Planning a strategy for registration that would facilitate entrance to the most popular courses and times occupied students for hours. (SPEC, PG 2-78-025.)

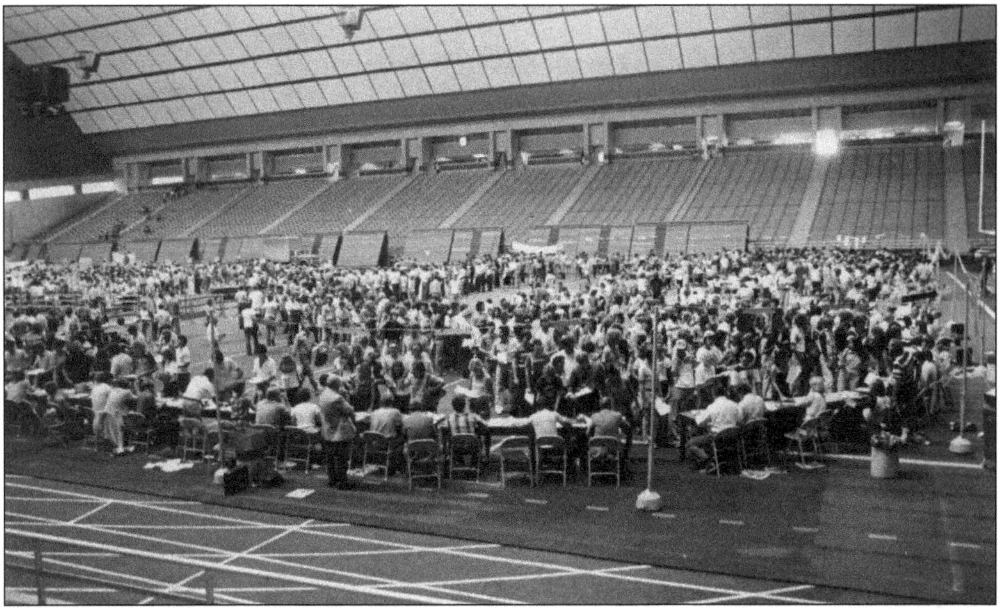

Registration is seen in the Kibbie Dome in September 1979, when enrollment was 8,698 students. The last Kibbie Dome registration took place in 1990. Students now register for classes online wherever they are, ending the need for mass registration sessions. (SPEC, UA 1991-040.)

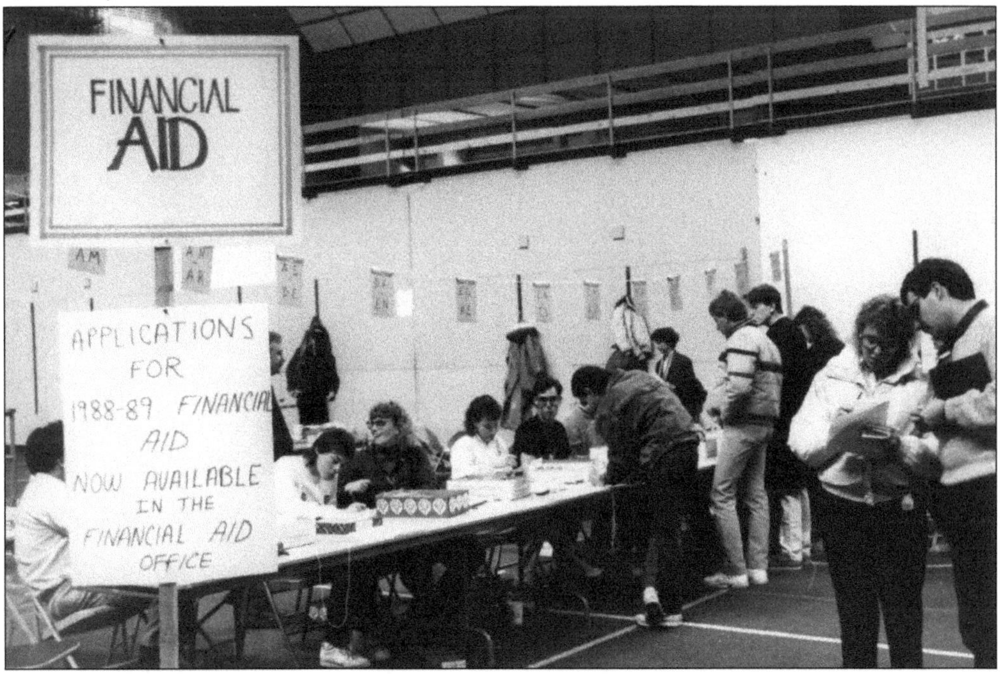

While the University of Idaho is ranked third for affordability among major public universities in the West, most students require financial aid. Although the federal government is the largest aid provider, the university offers more than $25 million in scholarships—more than any institution in Idaho. Students stand in line to fill out financial aid forms in the Kibbie Dome, an activity that is now completed online. (SPEC, UA 1989-027.)

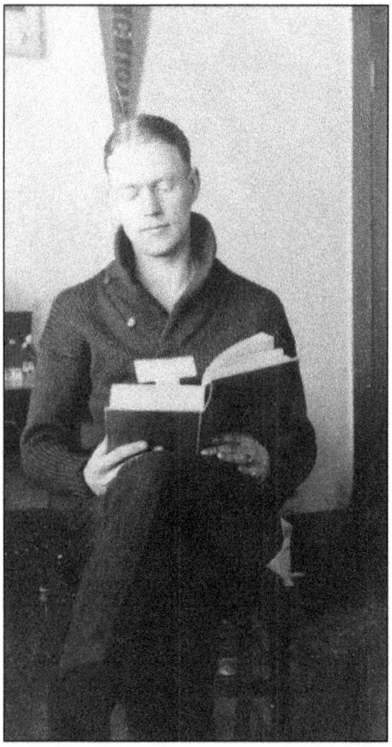

Students would often relax and study in their dorm rooms before the university included a large library. Here, a student reads a book in his dorm room in 1917 with a caption that reads "a student—of nothing!" Exploring a myriad of topics, including some not related to a major or degree program, is an important aspect of a university education. (SPEC, PG 2-268-1.)

The original infirmary was established in 1919 on University Street, site of the current Life Sciences South Building. The Student Health Building opened in 1936 and expanded in 1958. It included a 68-bed university hospital and provided a wide range of health services to University of Idaho students. Student health services are now contracted with a local physicians group. Pictured is the infirmary in 1937. (SPEC, PG 1-74-8.)

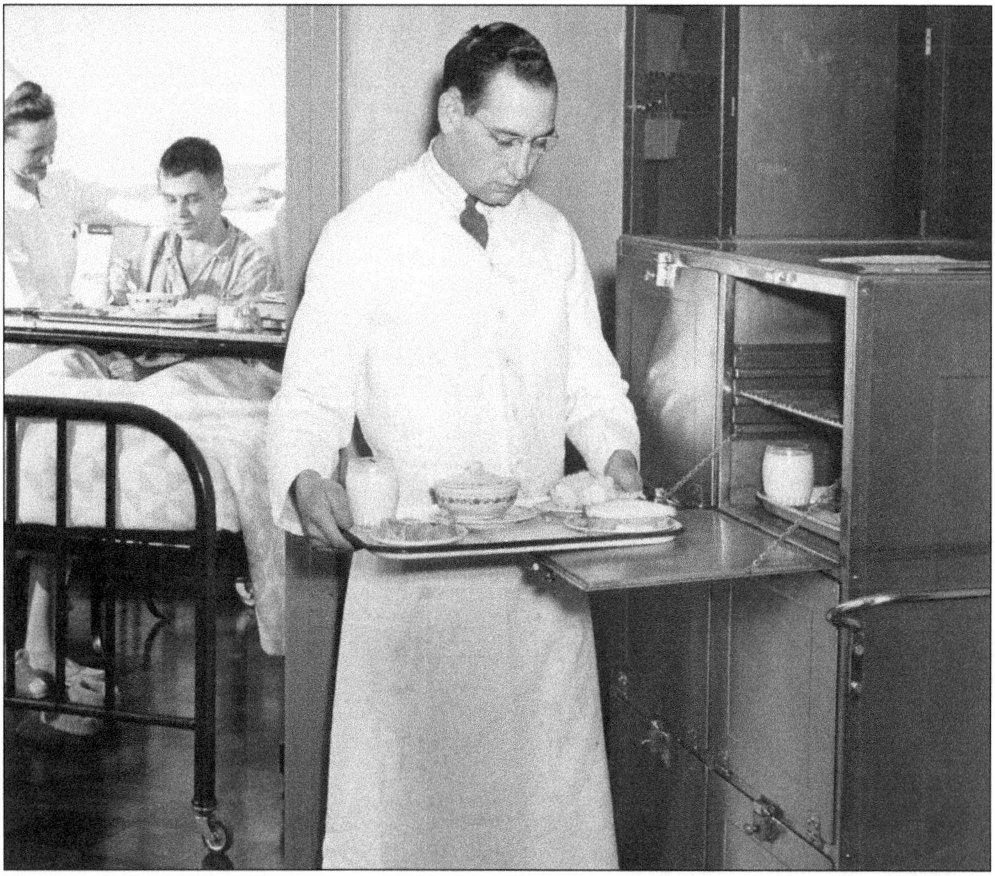

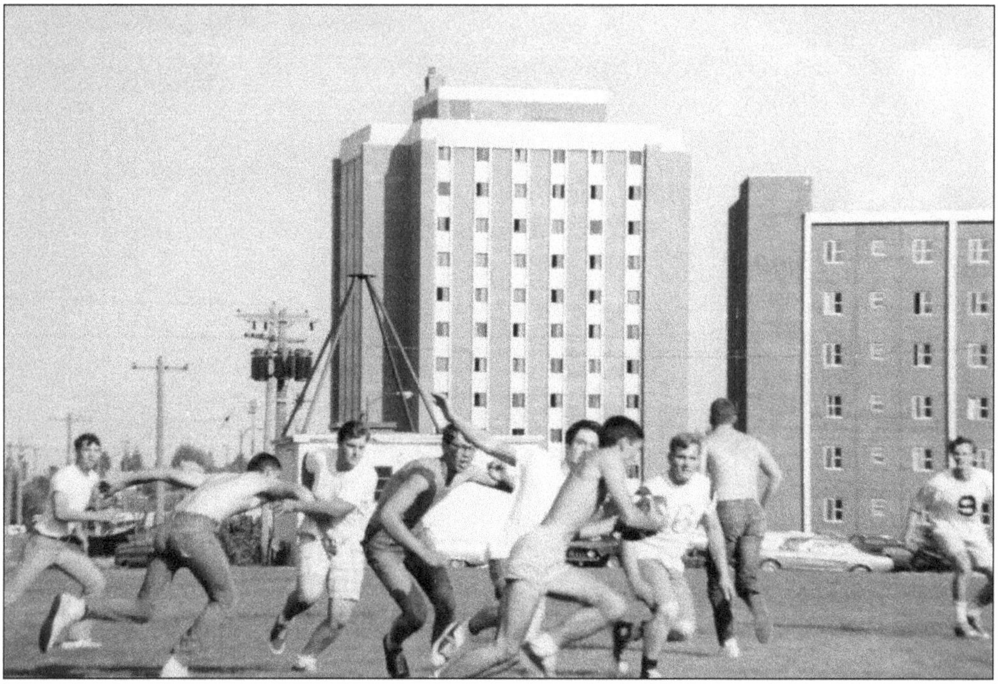

Men play touch football in the 1970s with Theophilus Tower in the background. Named for Pres. Donald R. Theophilus, "the Tower" opened in 1970 and was the first UI dormitory to house both men and women. At the time of its opening, the 11-story building was one of the Northwest's tallest. Tower Trick-or-Treat is a long-standing tradition where students provide a safe Halloween environment for area youngsters. (SPEC, UA 1987-017.)

Completed in 2002, the 85,000-square-foot Campus Recreation Center features a 55-foot climbing wall. Students have access to both wellness classes and workout machines as well as outdoor equipment for rent. In 2016, the facility was named one of the 20 most amazing campus recreation buildings in the country by Best College Reviews. Pictured here, new students test out the rock climbing wall at orientation. (UI Photo Services.)

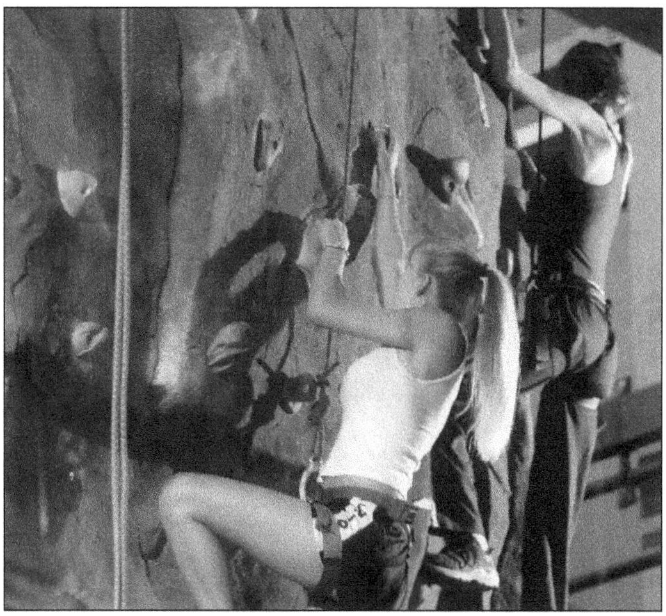

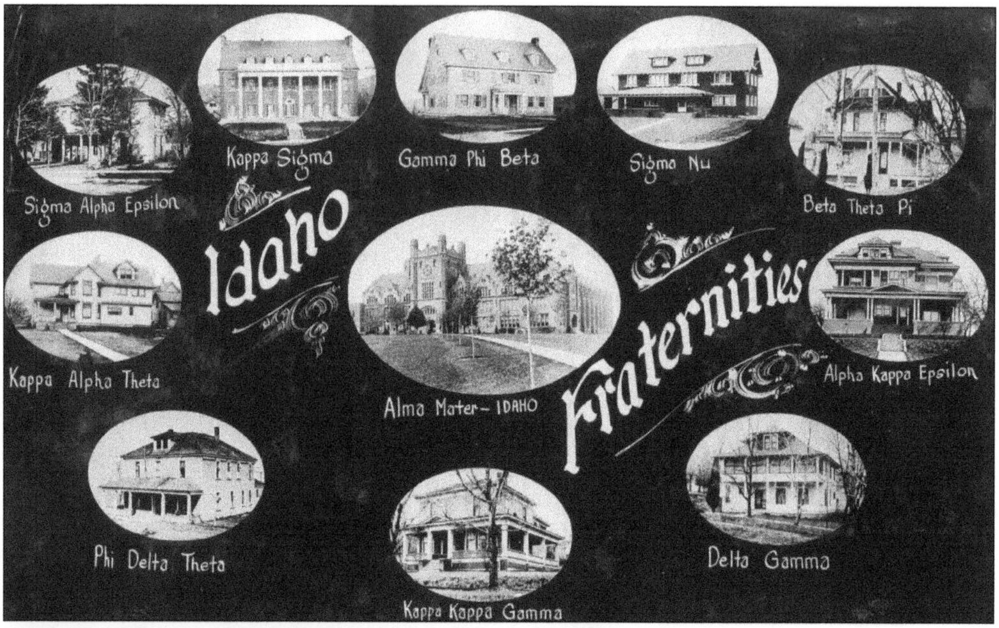

Greek living groups have been a fixture of the campus for over 100 years. This 1919 postcard features both men's and women's houses on campus. The label "fraternities" is appropriate, as that is the formal designation, except for sorority Gamma Phi Beta. The only house in this group still in use is Sigma Kappa, the first UI Greek house to construct a building specifically as its residence. (SPEC, MA 2015-42.)

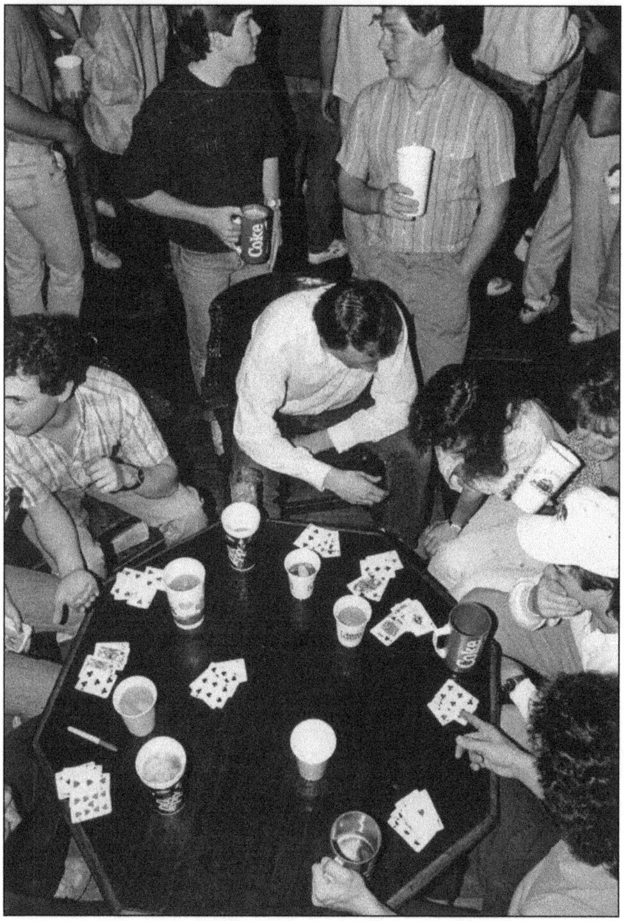

Exchanges between living groups were a frequent campus event. Members of residence halls and Greek houses would participate in social gatherings designed to foster acquaintance among students. It was not uncommon for men and women to line up according to height as a way to match couples. Here, the men of Sigma Nu and Beta Theta Pi entertain the women of Kappa Kappa Gamma and Delta Gamma. (SPEC, UA 1989-027.)

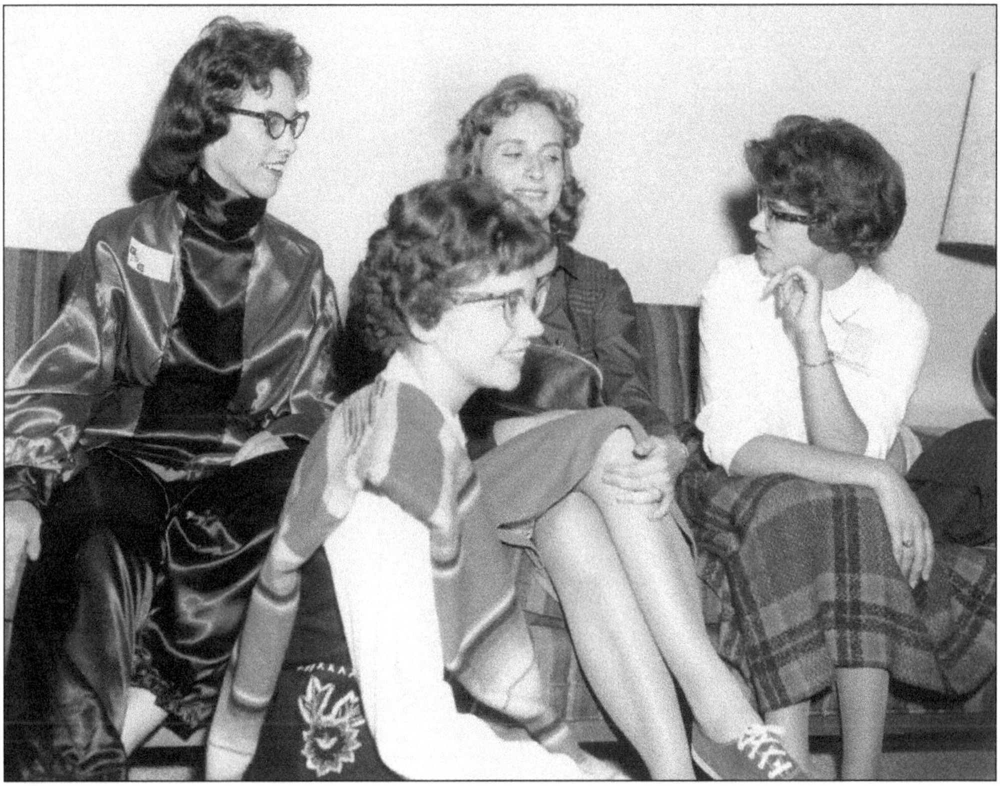

Sorority rush included formal parties where prospective members and current members sought to become better acquainted. The 1960 photograph above shows one such party. House members often presented skits and sang various songs during the rush parties. In recent years, the term "recruitment" has replaced "rush." Below is a formal rush tea hosted by Alpha Phi. (Above, SPEC, PG 2-49-8; below, SPEC, PG 2-50-3b.)

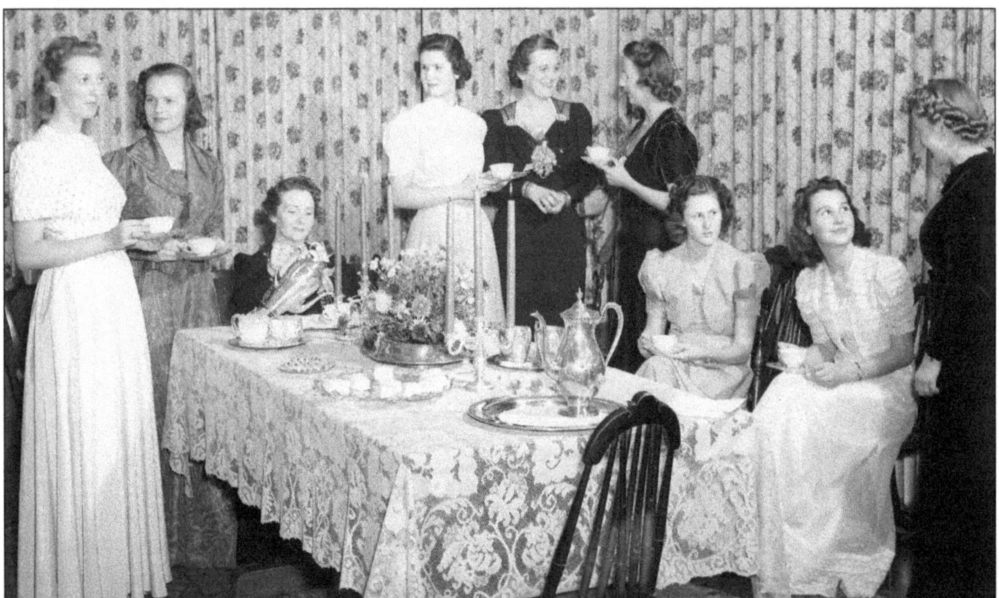

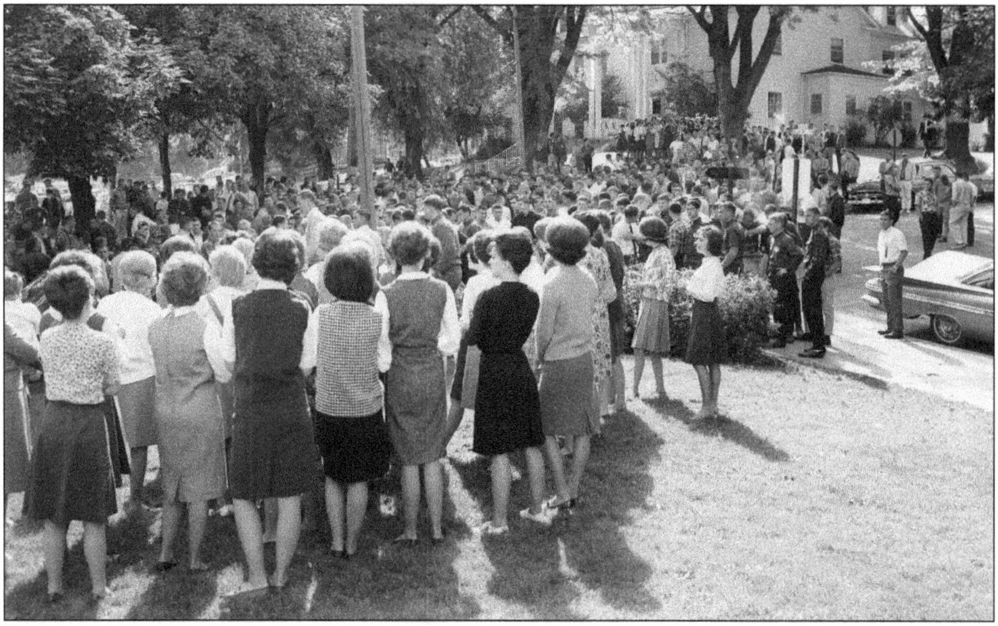

"Squeal Day" is pictured in 1964, named for the sound of several hundred women who have just received invitations to join Greek houses following rush/recruitment. Countless University of Idaho students retain a vivid memory of this occasion. Male students often line the streets to witness the ritual. (SPEC, PG 101-3429a.)

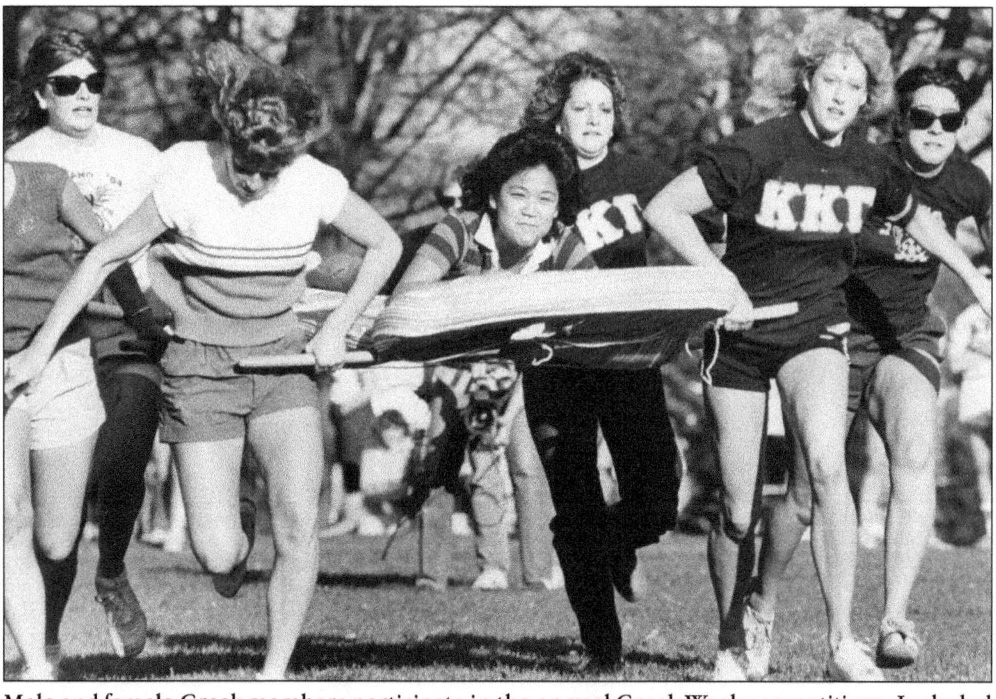

Male and female Greek members participate in the annual Greek Week competitions. Included are the Greek Olympics, house decorations, skits, songs, and an ice cream social. The week is designed to build Greek system unity and to highlight Greek philanthropic projects. Here, members of Kappa Kappa Gamma win the mattress race in 1985. (SPEC, PG 52-183.)

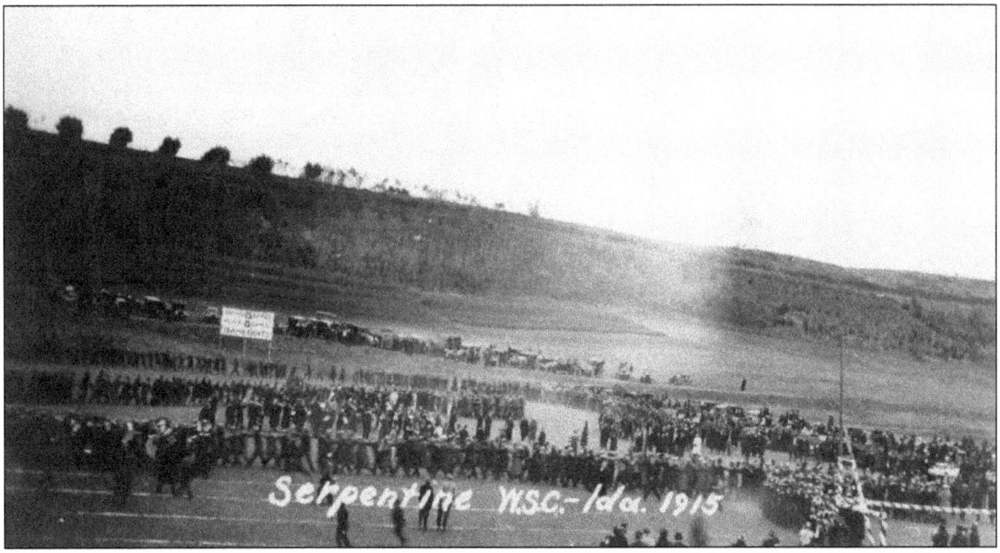

The first University of Idaho Homecoming took place in 1909. One of the main events was the Serpentine, which continues as a part of Homecoming Week and culminates in the bonfire. Pictured is the Serpentine during the Washington State College–University of Idaho football game in 1915. (SPEC, PG 2-115-1206.)

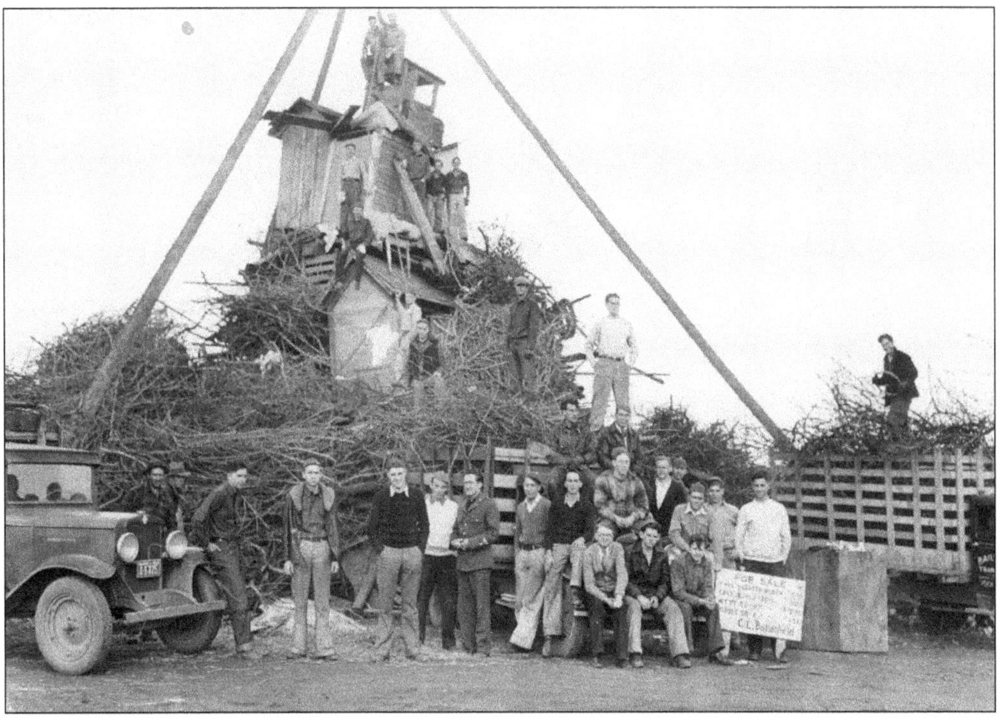

Freshmen students were assigned the task of building the bonfire pyramid during the early days, shown here before the Washington State College game in 1931. WSC was Idaho's perennial Homecoming opponent. In recent years, the Homecoming Committee has taken over responsibility for building smaller, but nonetheless exciting, bonfires. (SPEC, PG 2-102-7a.)

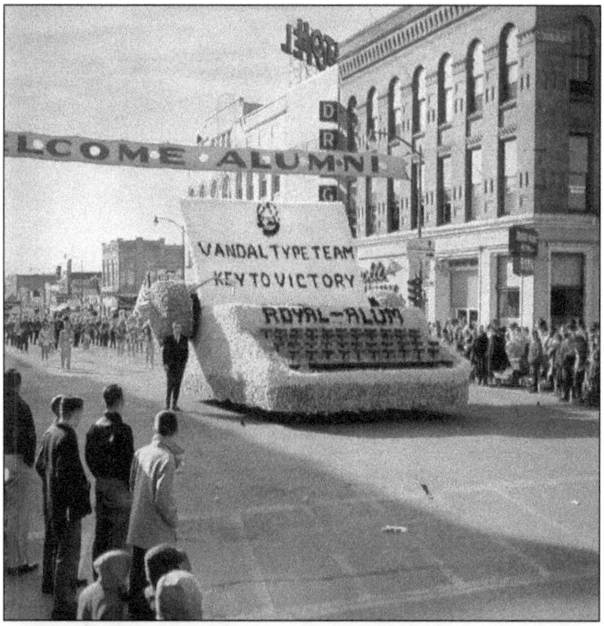

The annual Homecoming Parade continues to attract crowds to Moscow's Main Street. Pictured here in an image from the 1960 *Gem of the Mountains* yearbook, a 1959 float features the then ubiquitous, but now almost unknown, typewriter. Vandal alumna can be seen wearing the traditional "I" mum. (ASUI.)

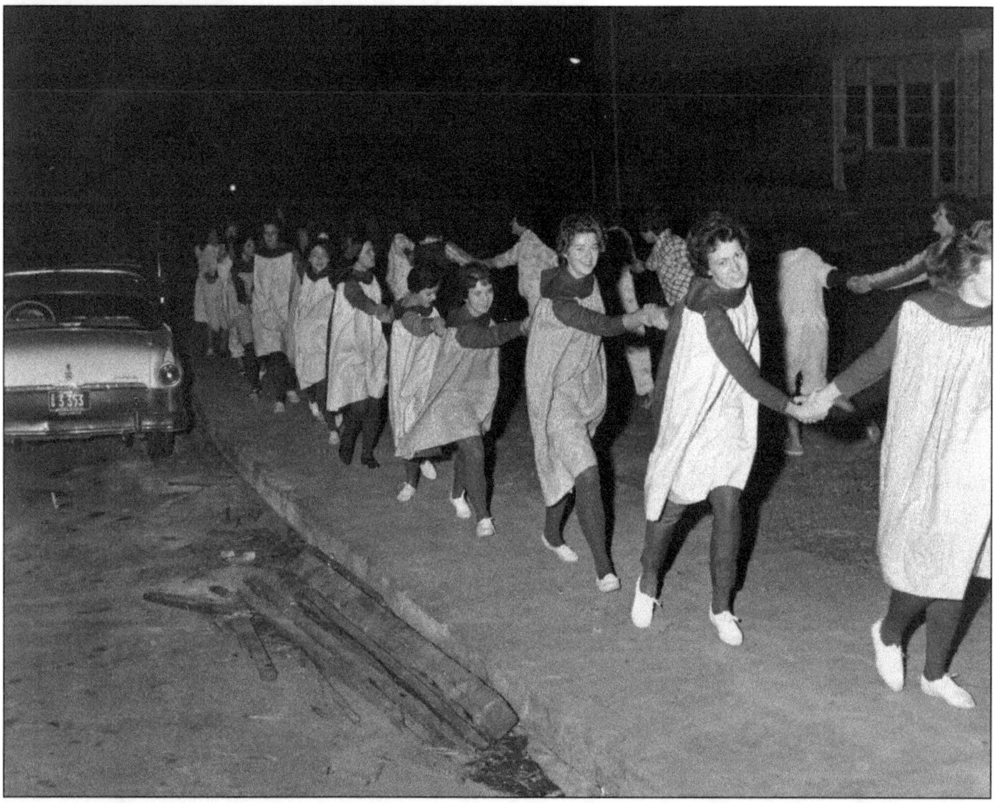

This pajama parade was held at the 1961 Homecoming. First-year female students from all university housing donned pajamas and paraded through men's living groups. In the early days, the parade ended downtown when pajama-clad men joined the women. (SPEC, PG 2-84-72d.)

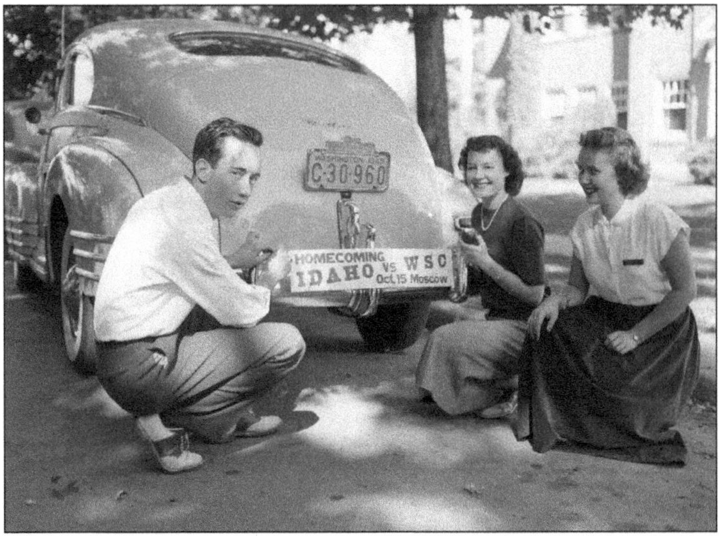

Students pose with a Homecoming bumper sticker in 1949. In the years following World War II, the University of Idaho experienced growth as students strived to return to more normal circumstances. Traditional college activities, such as Homecoming, enjoyed renewed popularity. (SPEC, PG 101-4544b.)

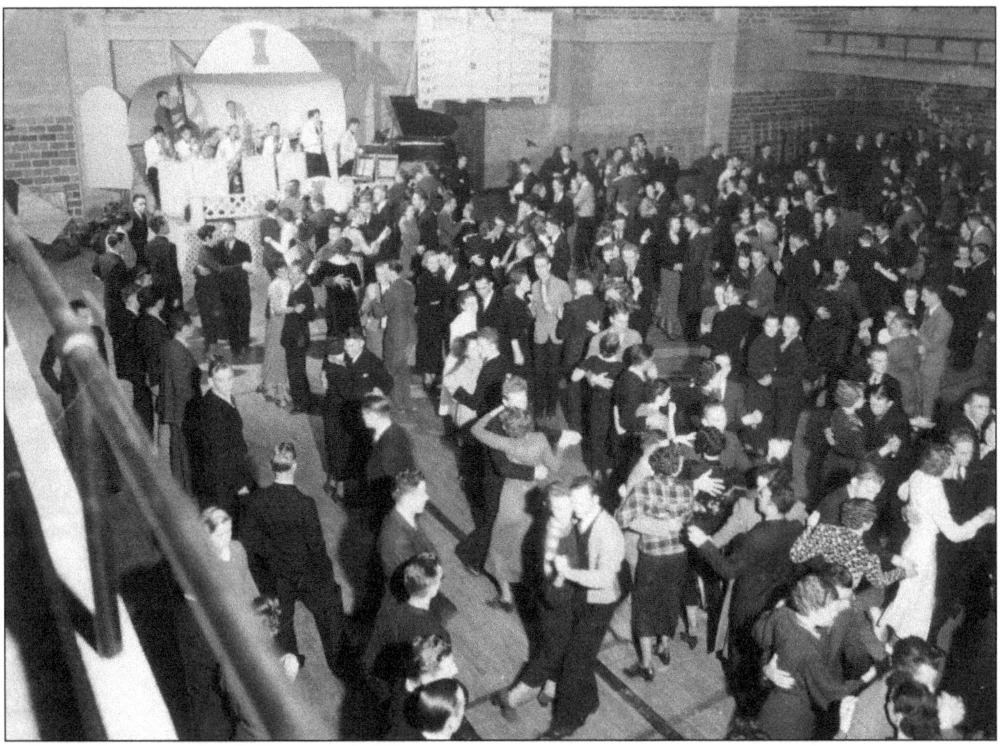

Dances have been a major source of entertainment at the University of Idaho since its beginning. Here, students enjoy the 1936 Homecoming Dance in the Memorial Gymnasium. In 1910, the Senior Ball, Junior Promenade, Sophomore Frolic, and Freshman Glee entertained students. The Military Ball, Foresters Ball, Engineers Ball, and various living group dances were important social occasions. Students collected dance cards where they recorded their dance partners. (SPEC, PG 2-84-15.)

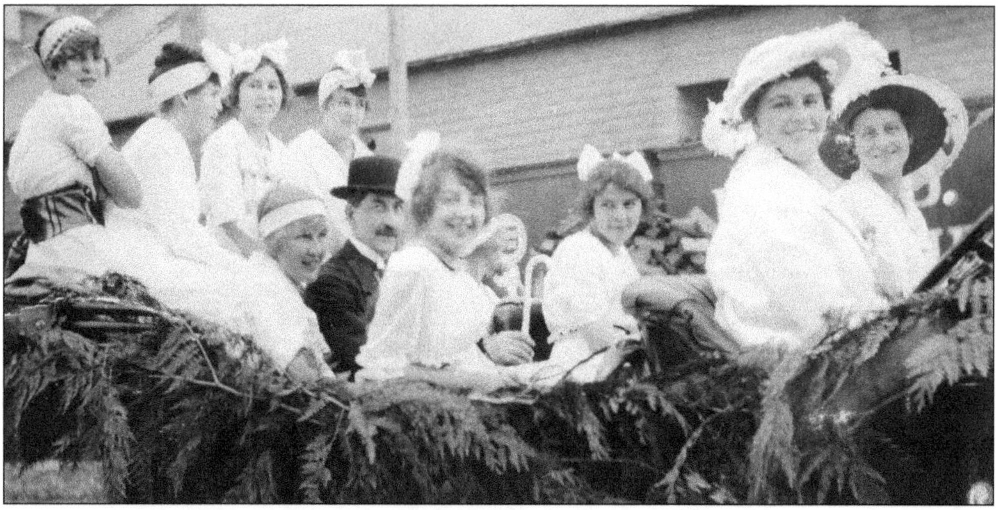

Students are "off to the fair" during the World War I era. For more than 100 years, the Latah County Fair has showcased area agriculture and livestock production. The early September event still attracts students for food and fun. Other popular local events include Mardi Gras, the annual Renaissance fair, and the weekly downtown farmers' market, which draws people from the region from May through October. (SPEC, MG 170.)

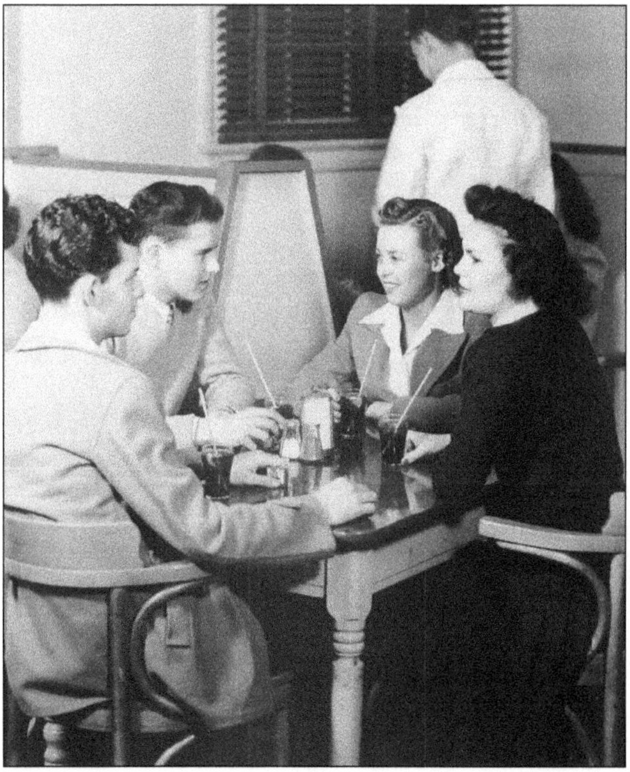

A typical campus scene shows students enjoying a soda in 1942. Students dressed more formally in comparison to later years. Campus life continued while Idaho students worried about the draft and soldiers fighting overseas during World War II. From left to right in this image from the 1942 *Gem of the Mountains* yearbook are Jim Freeman, Jim McCluskey, Kay Ash, and Ramona Larkin. (ASUI.)

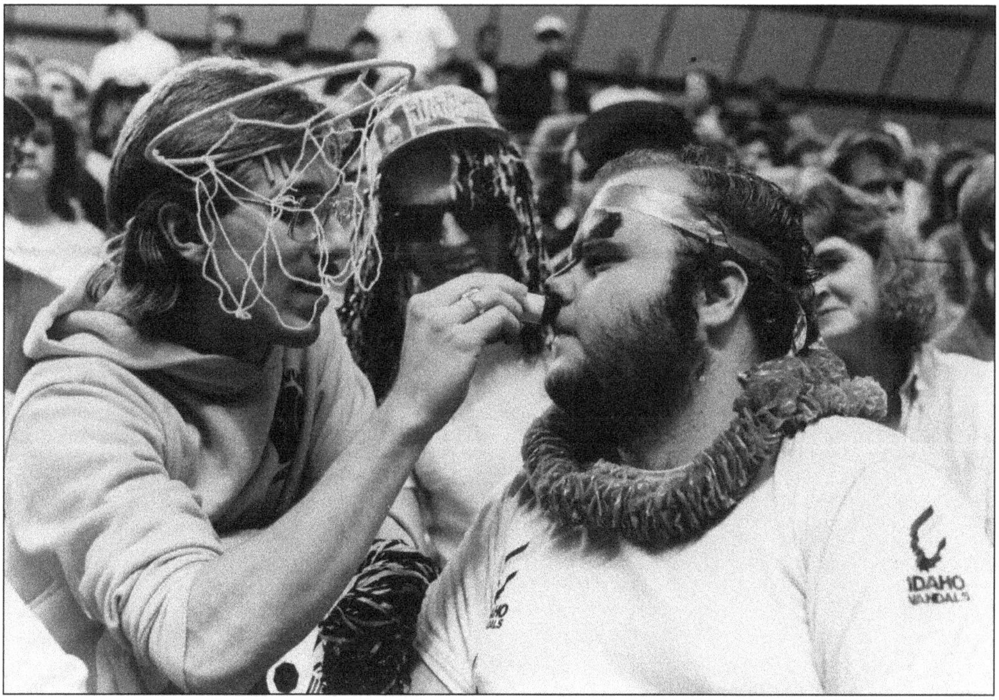

Fans and students Andy Knutson (left) and Jeff Pullinin (right, with lei) prepare for the 1986 University of Idaho–Boise State University basketball game with face painting. The rivalry game was guaranteed to pack the ASUI-Kibbie Dome. (SPEC, UA 2003-015.)

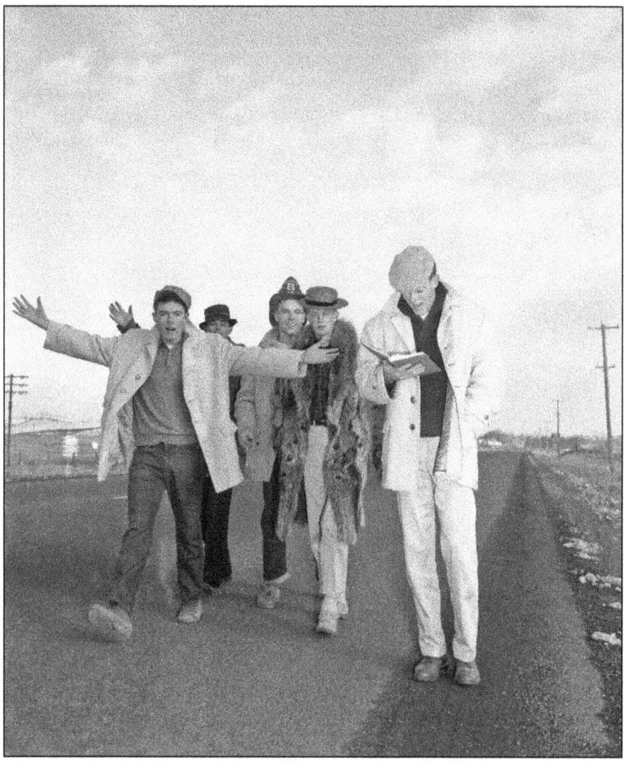

The Loser's Walk originated in 1938 and was discontinued in 1969. The student body of the institution whose football team was defeated in the annual University of Idaho–Washington State University football game made the walk between Pullman and Moscow. In 1957, Hale Henson occupied himself during the nine-mile walk with a book. (SPEC, PG 101-1002.)

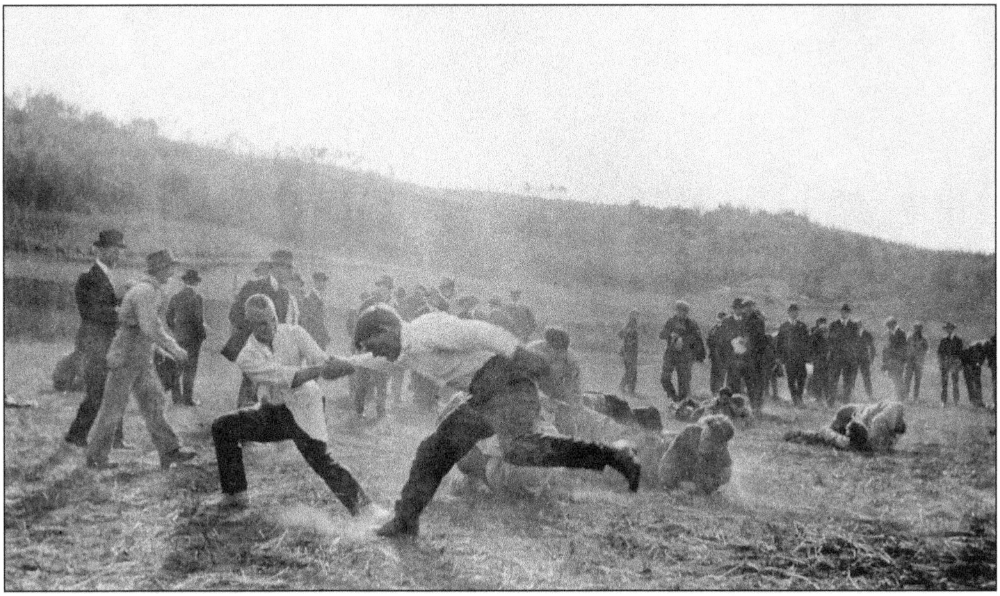

Each fall, annual contests occurred between the sophomore and freshman classes. Events included the Hulme fight (pictured in 1916), tug-of-war, and flagpole rush. In the evening, the Bury-the-Hatchet Dance reunited the two classes. Frosh men were required to wear a green beanie until Campus Day in May, which included a gala and bonfire where caps were discarded by freshmen moving into the sophomore class. (SPEC, MG 170.)

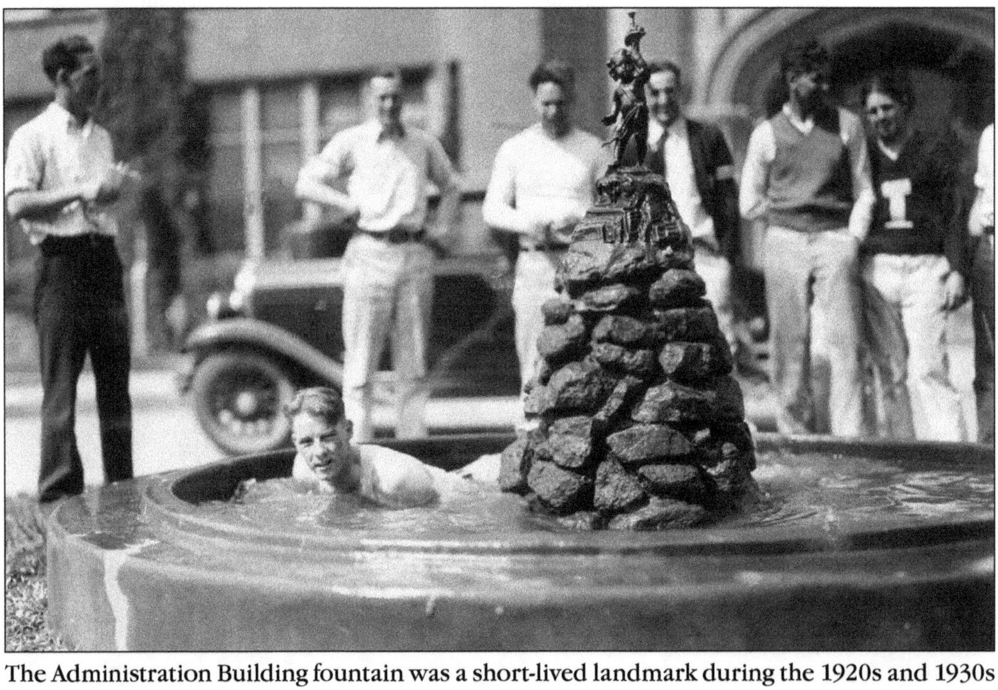

The Administration Building fountain was a short-lived landmark during the 1920s and 1930s that was removed due to a tradition called "Dunking the Frosh." The fountain was the site of nearly nude dunking for non-senior students caught occupying the "I" Bench, regardless of the weather. The fountain was first topped with a cupid statue, later replaced by a sea horse that was allegedly stolen by students. (SPEC, PG 1-112-01.)

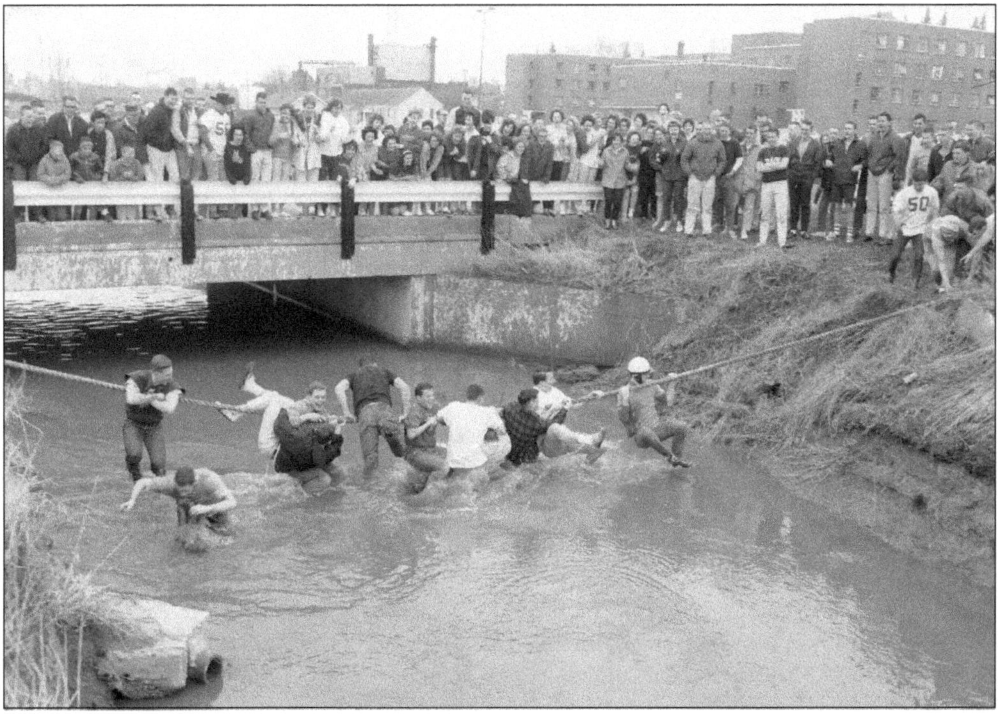

The Annual Frosh Tug-of-War contest at Paradise Creek and pie-eating contests were both part of new student orientation and continued to attract large crowds of students cheering on their teams. In recent years, first-year students have engaged in a day of service as part of new student orientation. Shown above is the 1963 Annual Frosh Tug-of-War at Paradise Creek; below is the pie-eating contest during Frosh Week in 1966. (Above, SPEC, PG 101-2875; below, SPEC, PG 101-3497.)

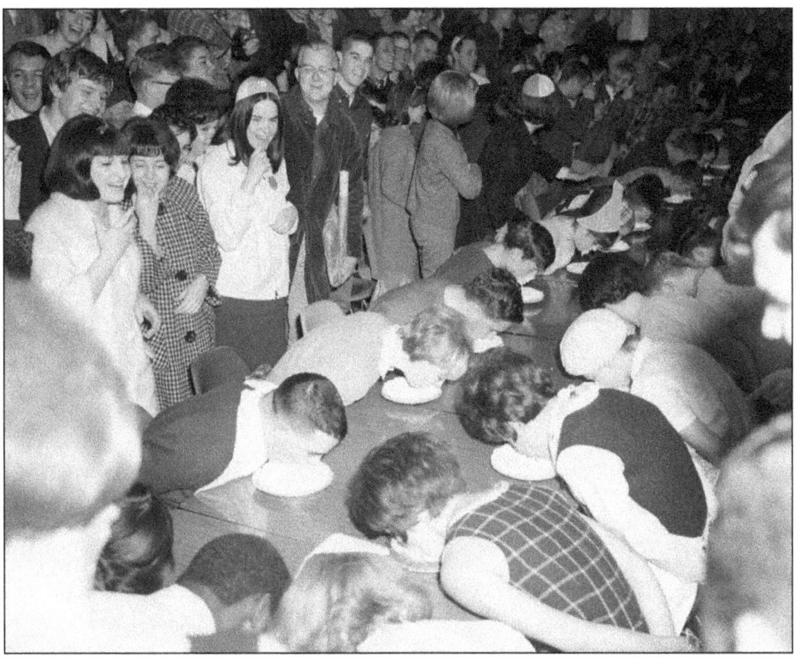

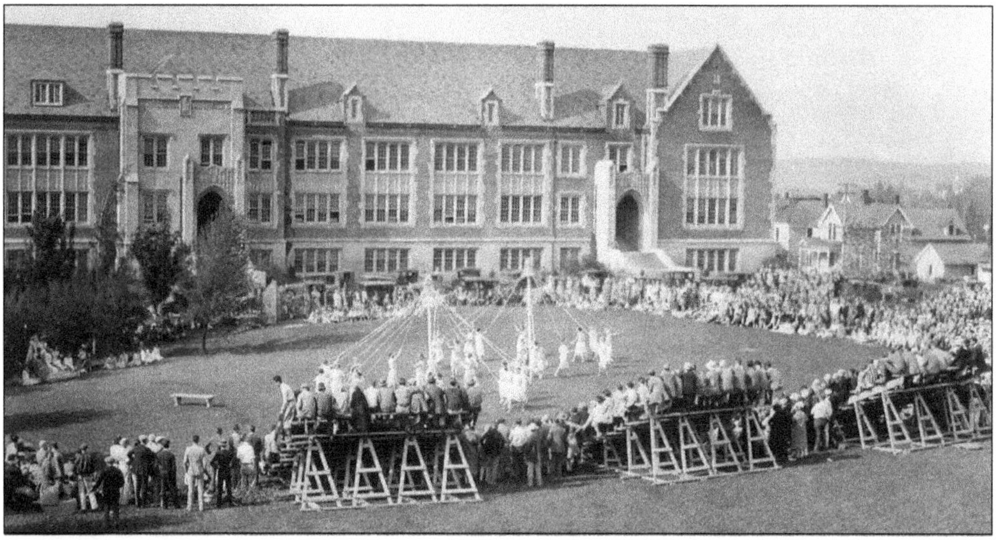

Pictured is the May Day celebration in 1928. Following a national trend, campus May Day celebrations started in 1910 on the Administration Lawn. The day began with senior women, attired in Grecian robes and carrying a syringa chain, processing from the University Gardens to the Administration Lawn. The May Queen coronation and induction for the Mortar Board and Silver Lance honor societies were highlights, as was the maypole dance. (SPEC, UA 1987-005.)

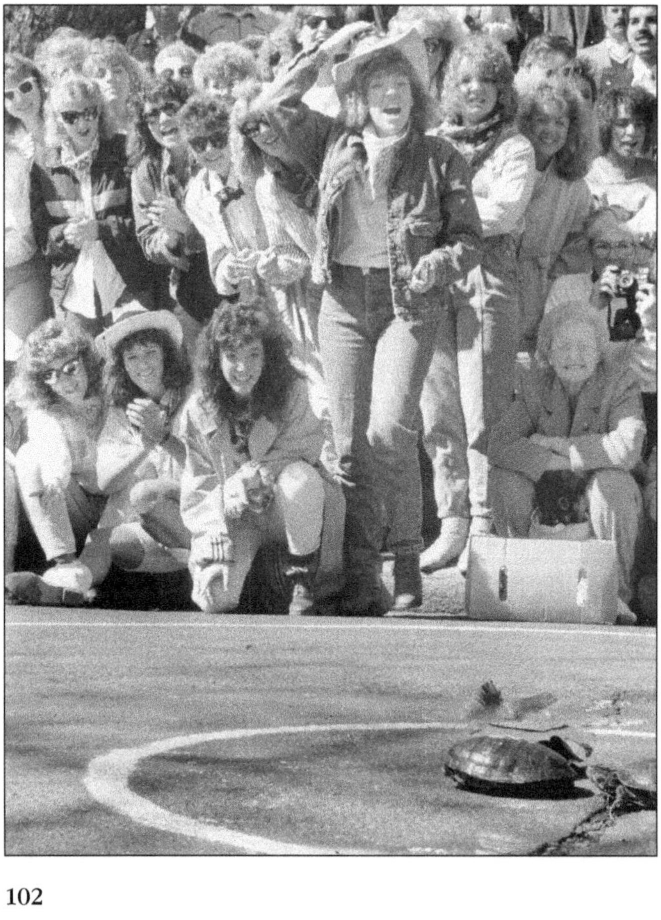

The Turtle Derby was started in 1958 by John Chapman (1958; honorary doctorate, 2009) and Phi Delta Theta. Held on Mother's Weekend, the Turtle Derby raises funds for local charities. Women from each residence hall and sorority adopt a turtle, perform skits, and cheer on their turtles. The venue is comprised of two concentric circles—the Ooh Pah Pah Dow! (SPEC, PG 52-573.)

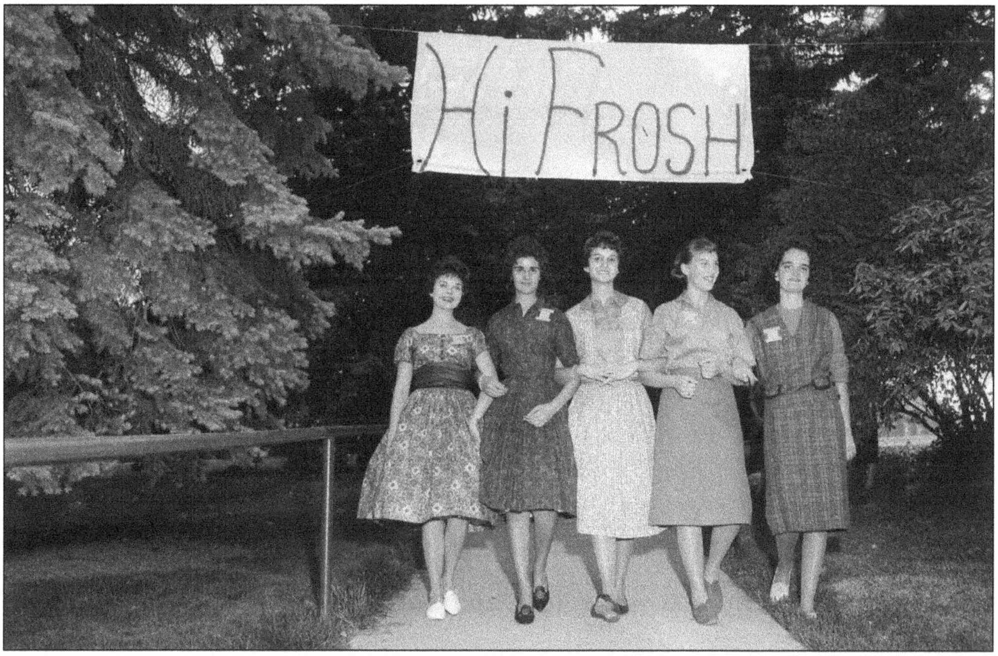

Women walk arm in arm up "Hello Walk" in 1960 during freshman orientation. Campus dress code required that women be attired in skirts or dresses. For years, if the weather was well below freezing, the dean of women's office would inform living groups that this dress requirement was temporarily suspended and pants for women were allowed. (SPEC, PG 101-2293.)

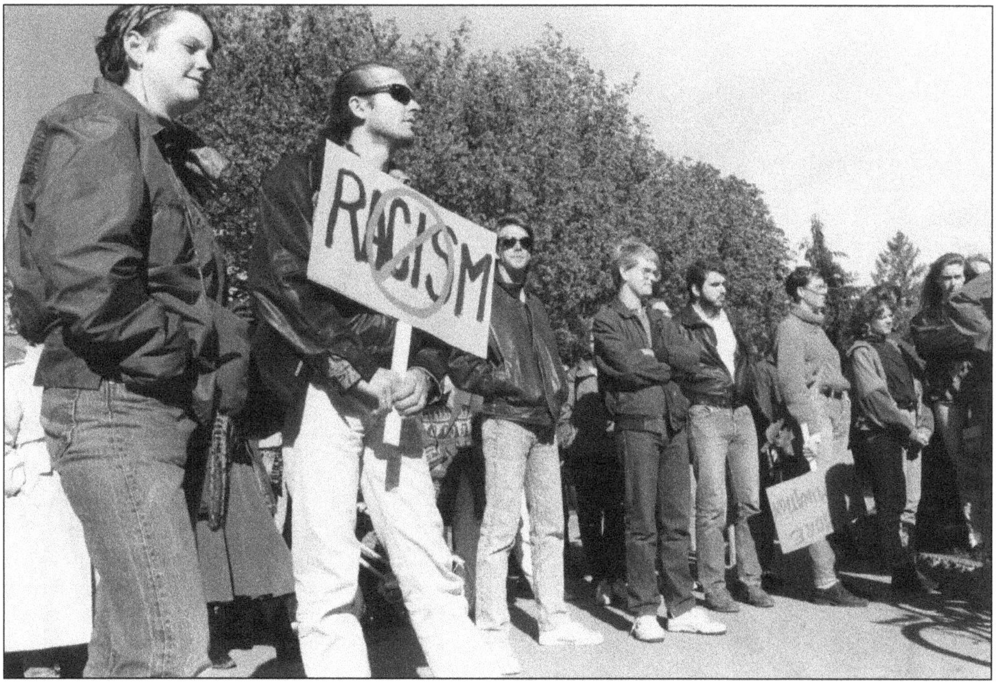

Through the years, University of Idaho students have demonstrated on behalf of many causes. Here, they engage in an anti-racism protest in 1991. The students are listening to ASUI president David Pena before beginning a march across campus. (SPEC, UA 2003-015.)

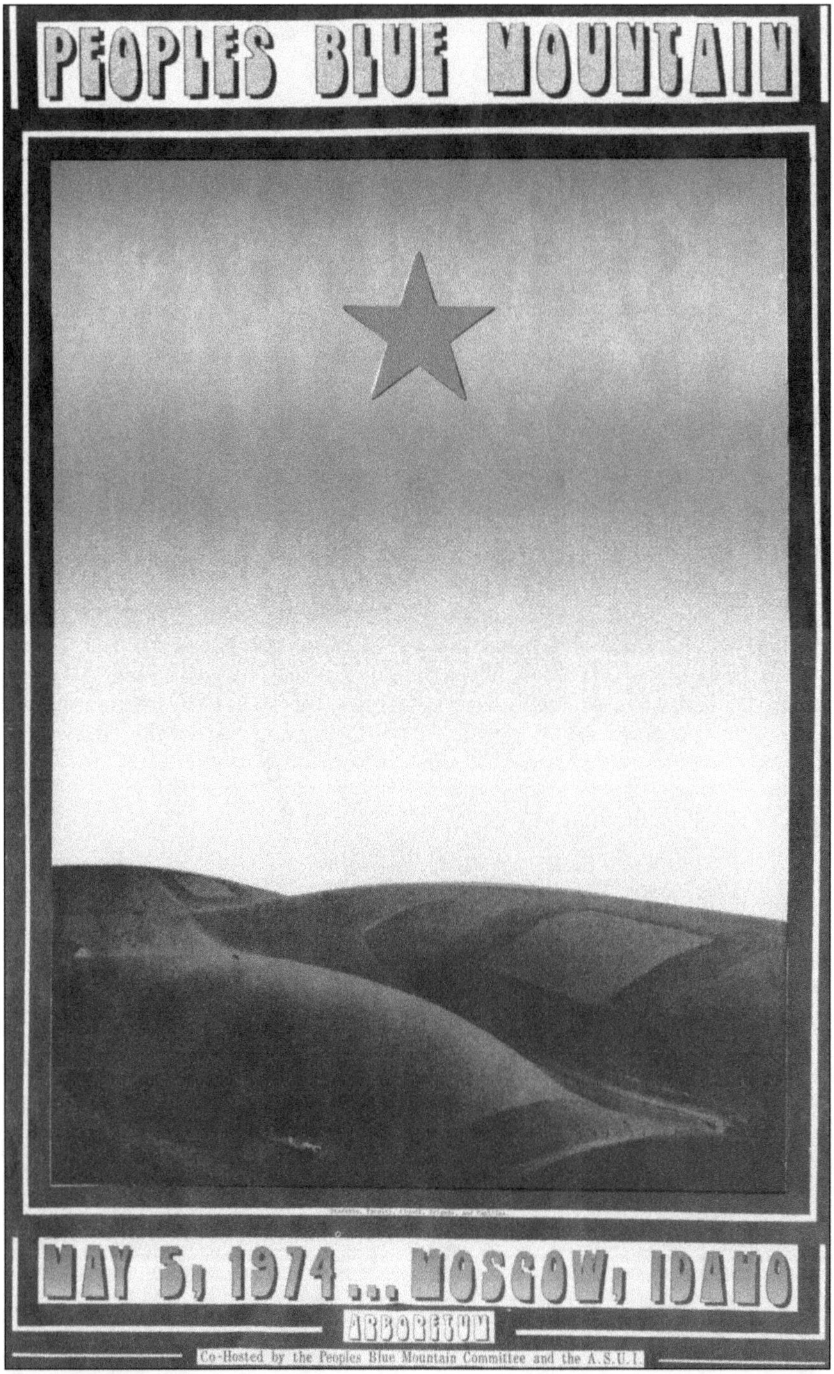

In 1970, UI students organized the first Blue Mountain Rock Festival as a fundraiser for the American Civil Liberties Union. The second festival was dedicated to students slain at Kent State University. The *Argonaut* printed its entire May 3, 1974, edition in blue ink to promote the festival advertised on this poster. An estimated 10,000 students attended in 1974, but in 1975, Pres. Ernest Hartung banned the event from campus. Rumors of illegal substance abuse and illicit student behavior prompted Hartung's action. (SPEC, VF Campus Life and Culture.)

Five

Organizations

The University of Idaho features 200 student organizations, many of which have a long history on campus, beginning with the Associated Students of the University of Idaho, founded in 1904. ASUI represents students' voices in campus affairs. The University of Idaho Alumni Association, founded in 1899, represents over 100,000 living alumni. Mom's Weekend in the spring and Dad's Weekend in the fall continue to be among the most popular events; for a few years, these were celebrated together as Parent's Weekend.

Providing military training was part of the Morrill Act mandate, and the University of Idaho has a long tradition of embracing its military roots. An armory building, completed in 1906, facilitated training in the military arts. In 1945, Navy and Air Force ROTC joined the long-established Army program. Annually, Military Appreciation Day is a well-attended football weekend. The Spanish-American War Statue and Memorial Gymnasium both recognize University students who died in military service.

The arts occupy a central place at the University of Idaho. The Lionel Hampton School of Music presents more than 300 concerts each year. As part of the university's 125th celebration, a new Steinway grand piano, a gift from private donors, graces the Administration Building Auditorium, home to the popular Auditorium Chamber Music series. Students, faculty, staff, and community members enjoy productions at the Hartung Theater and a new black-box theater, the Forge, located in the CLASS Annex (formerly the Industrial Technology Building). The dance program is one of few in the region, and in association with Festival Dance, sponsors a number of performances. The university operates the downtown Moscow Prichard Art Gallery, which mounts several exhibitions a year.

Recreational and faith-based opportunities for students abound. Intramural and club sports allow students to pursue any athletic endeavor that interests them. Outdoor Recreation offers rental equipment and excursions to students, faculty, and staff. Students have access to faith-based programming through the Campus Christian Center, the LDS Institute, and the St. Augustine Center.

The Tutxinmepu Powwow, India Night, Confucius Institute celebrations, Cruise Around the World, Cinco de Mayo, Day of the Dead, and many other events celebrate the many cultural traditions of University of Idaho students and faculty. The university has distinct offices in Multicultural Affairs, the Office of Human Rights, Access and Inclusion, and the Office of Tribal Relations to foster practices that make all feel welcome on campus. The campus boasts 20 recognized minority student groups.

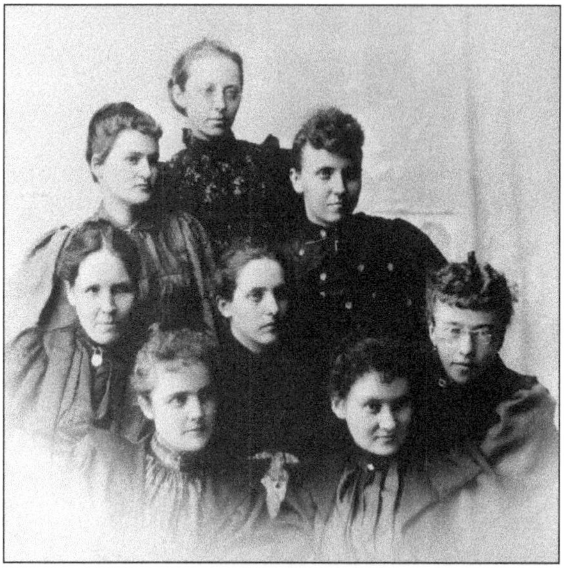

The Faculty Wives Club poses for a group photograph in 1897. Clockwise from top center are Jennie Gault, Martha Fox, C.W. McCurdy, Millicent Bonebright, Ellen Aldrich, Kate Henderson, Florence Chrisman, and Sarah Ostrander (center). Once the university faculty included more women, the Faculty Wives Club disbanded. Athena, established in 1987, is open to all staff, faculty, and administrators interested in promoting inclusion and an equitable climate for women.(SPEC, PG 4-2-1.)

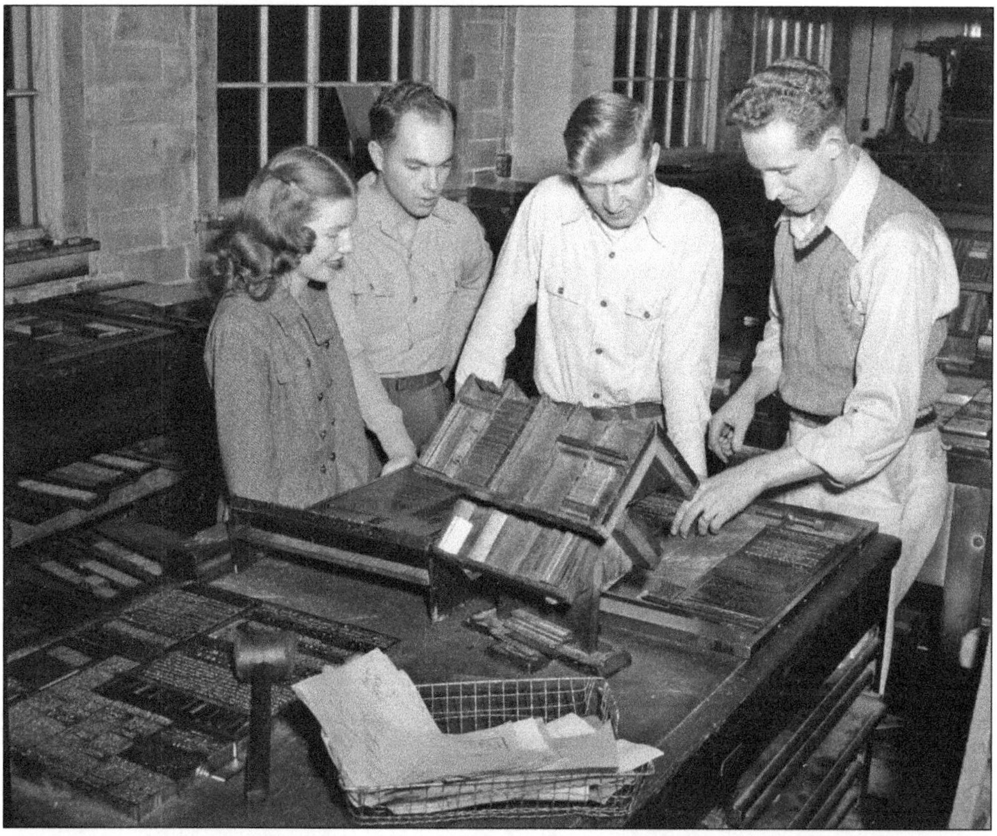

The University of Idaho student newspaper, the *Argonaut*, has been in circulation since 1898. Pictured are students working on the newspaper printing press in 1949. The *Gem of the Mountains* yearbook first appeared in 1902 and was published until 2004. The *Blue Bucket* magazine was the official humor publication of ASUI, published from 1923 until 1940, when it was ruled out by a majority on the student executive board. (SPEC, PG 92-1680.)

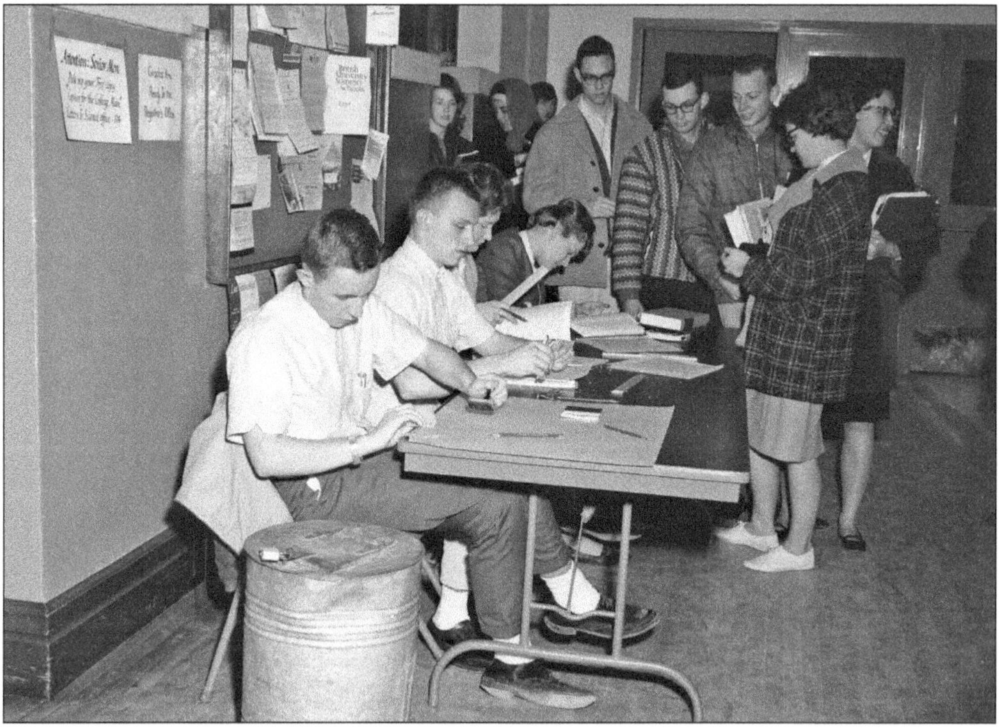

The Associated Students of the University of Idaho, founded in 1904, is a vital part of the university community. Shown above are students tallying votes at the 1964 election; below, students Hans Weger (left) and Seton Foster hang campaign signs outside the University Classroom Center. The ASUI student government now employs its own government relations representative during the Idaho legislative session to present student opinions in Boise. ASUI officers play an important role in the annual fee-setting process for students as well as deciding how the fees are allocated. ASUI sponsors a number of highly regarded student service programs, including Alternative Spring Break trips to both United States and international locations. (Above, SPEC, PG 101-2851; below, PG 52-658.)

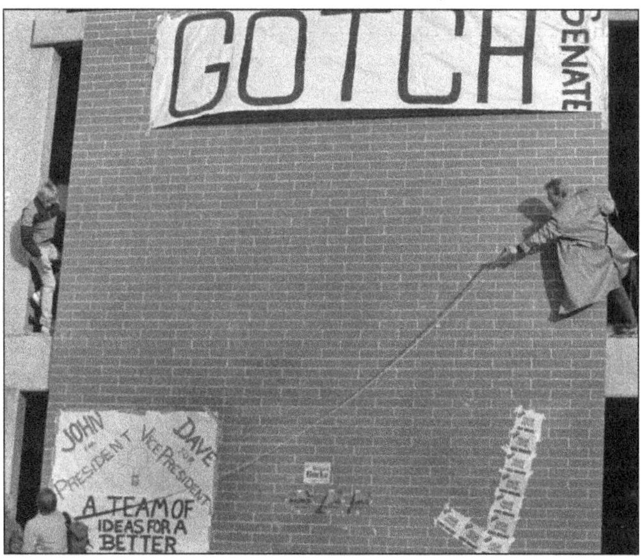

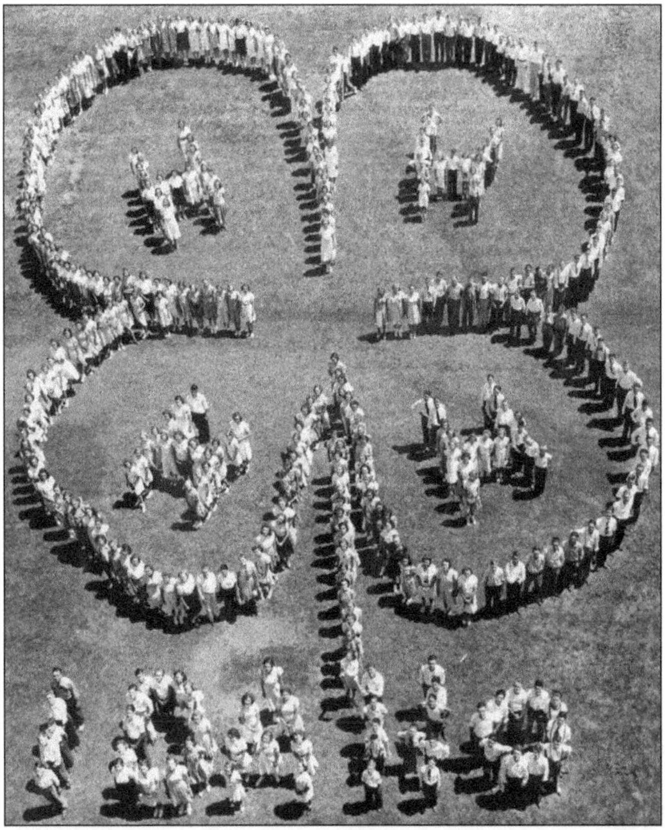

Idaho 4-H is a key part of UI Extension. The first 4-H "Short Course," precursor to the annual 4-H Congress, took place in 1923. At left, on June 19, 1940, participants created the 4-H symbol; the clover's four leaves stand for Head, Heart, Hands, and Health. Below, in 1977, attendees posed with Idaho US senator James McClure (juris doctorate, 1950; honorary doctorate, 1981), a longtime UI advocate. McClure Hall was named for him in 1992. The UI 4-H Youth Development program reached 56,786 youth in 2015 with the help of 3,198 volunteers across the state. Senator McClure's congressional papers are part of the Library's Special Collections and Archives. (Left, SPEC, PG 1-164; below, SPEC, PG 4-1-100b.)

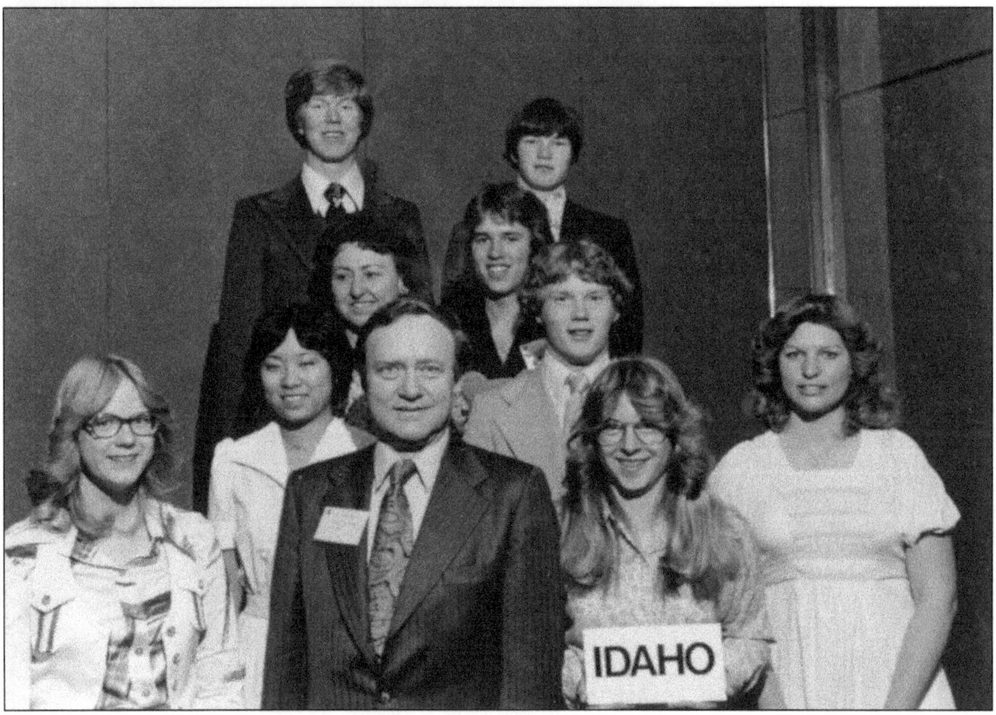

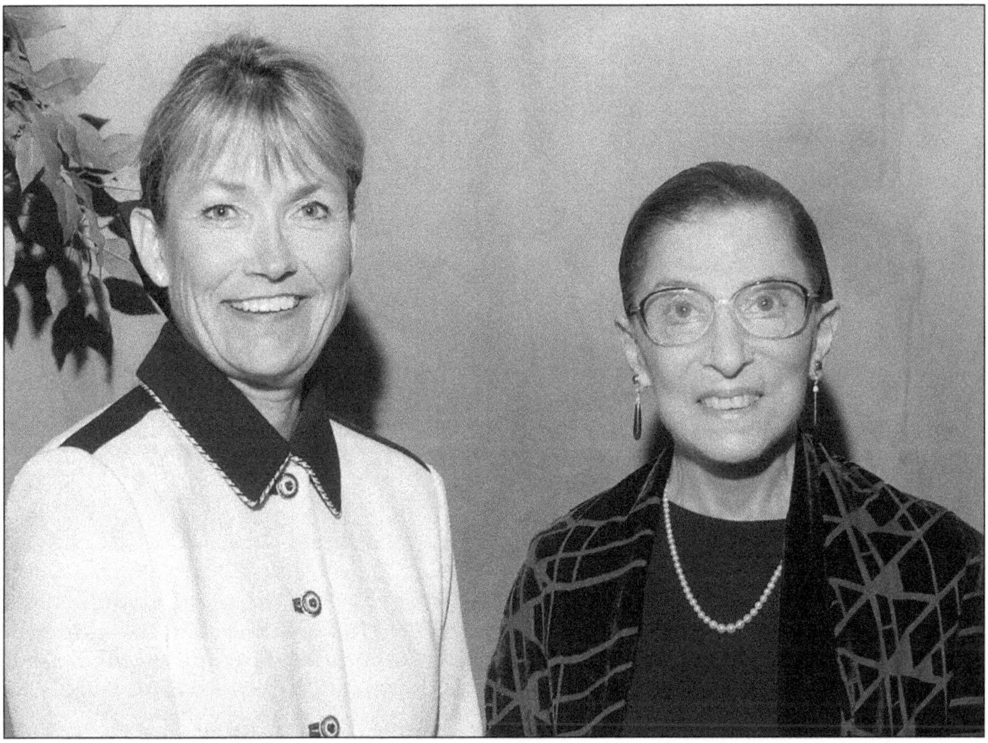

Idaho native and district court judge Sherman J. Bellwood (1939) funded the largest endowed lectureship at the University of Idaho, which brings prominent people to campus to discuss issues of justice and law. Speakers have included Chief Justice John Roberts and Supreme Court justices Sandra Day O'Connor, Antonin Scalia, and Ruth Bader Ginsburg (right), pictured here with Linda Copple Trout (1973, 1977), the first woman member of the Idaho Supreme Court. (UI Photo Services.)

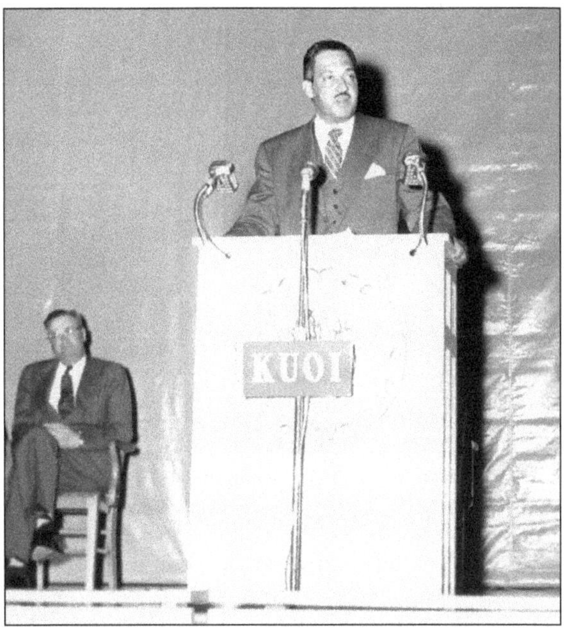

Since 1948, the Borah Foundation has sponsored a symposium devoted to the understanding of the causes of war and the conditions for peace, planned by students, faculty, and staff. NAACP counsel Thurgood Marshall delivered the 1954 opening address. Other notable speakers include Benjamin Spock, Eugene McCarthy, Betty Williams, Arun Gandhi, and Nobel laureates Frederik de Klerk and Oscar Arias. (SPEC, PG 4-5-4.)

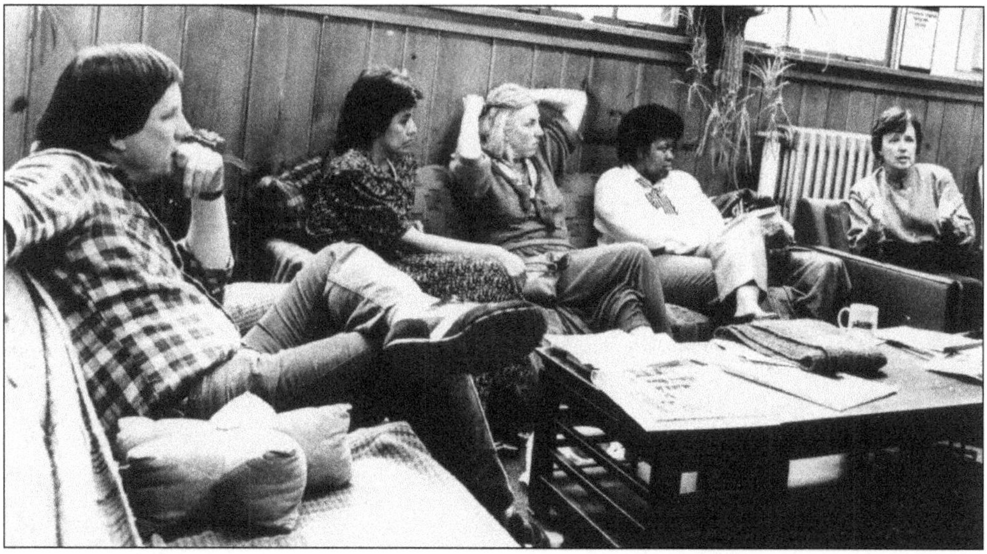

The University of Idaho Women's Center is one of the country's oldest. The Women's Caucus filed a complaint against the university with the Idaho Human Rights Commission and the Equal Employment Opportunity Commission in 1973. To avoid litigation, the university signed a 1974 conciliation agreement. The agreement mandated permanent funding for the Women's Center, which celebrated its 40th anniversary in 2014 with Gloria Steinem as keynote speaker. (SPEC, PG 52-657.)

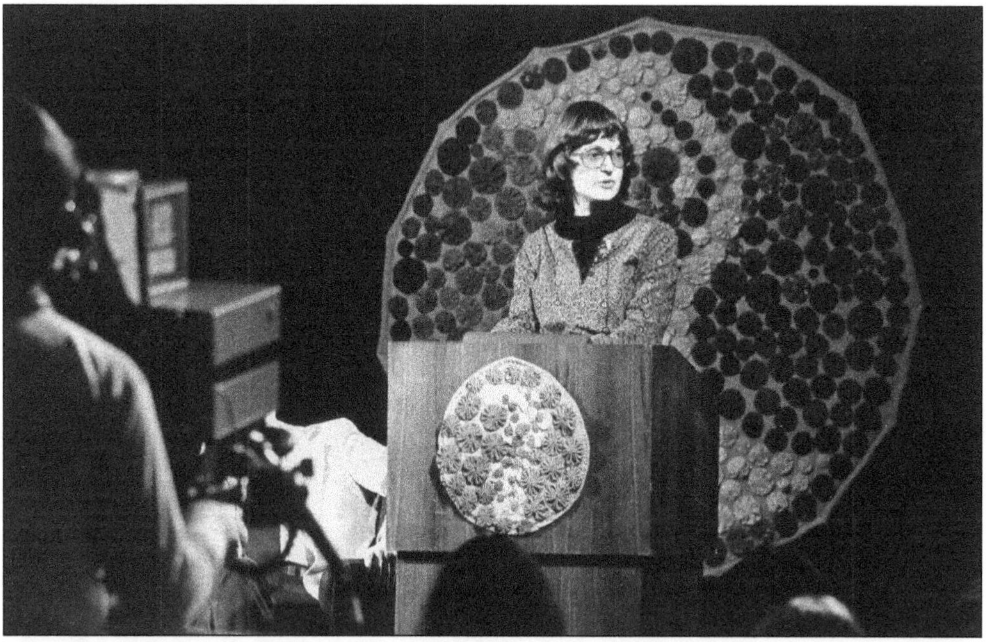

The University of Idaho prides itself on its inclusivity. Shown here is the Androgyny Symposium, held during the 1990s in the Student Union Building. Beginning in the fall of 2005, the LGBTQA coordinator has conducted comprehensive programming, including Safe Zone training for faculty and staff to provide support and resources to students needing assistance. The university community honors LGBTQA students earning degrees at Lavender Graduation. (SPEC, UA 1991-040.)

The Native American Student Center empowers Native American students through student support services and tribal networking. The Native American Student Association, which meets in the center, is open to all students interested in Native American culture and issues. The University of Idaho established the Office of Tribal Relations to help foster relationships with tribes in the region. Pictured is a student at Winter 2007 Commencement. (UI Photo Services.)

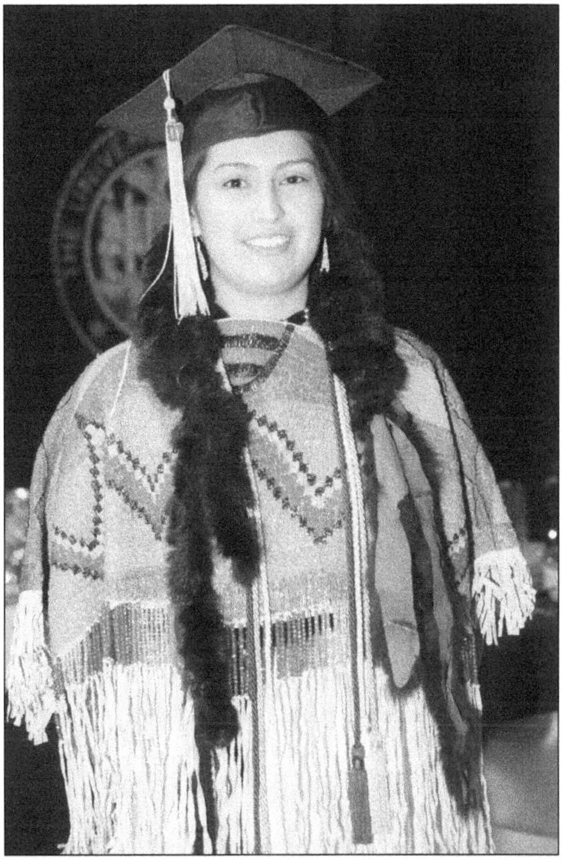

The first Indian Awareness Week took place in 1979 and included a Native American Student Association–sponsored powwow. The Tutxinmepu Powwow has become one of the university's signature events (pictured here in 2009). Tutxinmepu means "the place where the deer loses its spots" in Nez Perce. People from across the Northwest and Canada come to participate in the annual powwow. (UI Photo Services.)

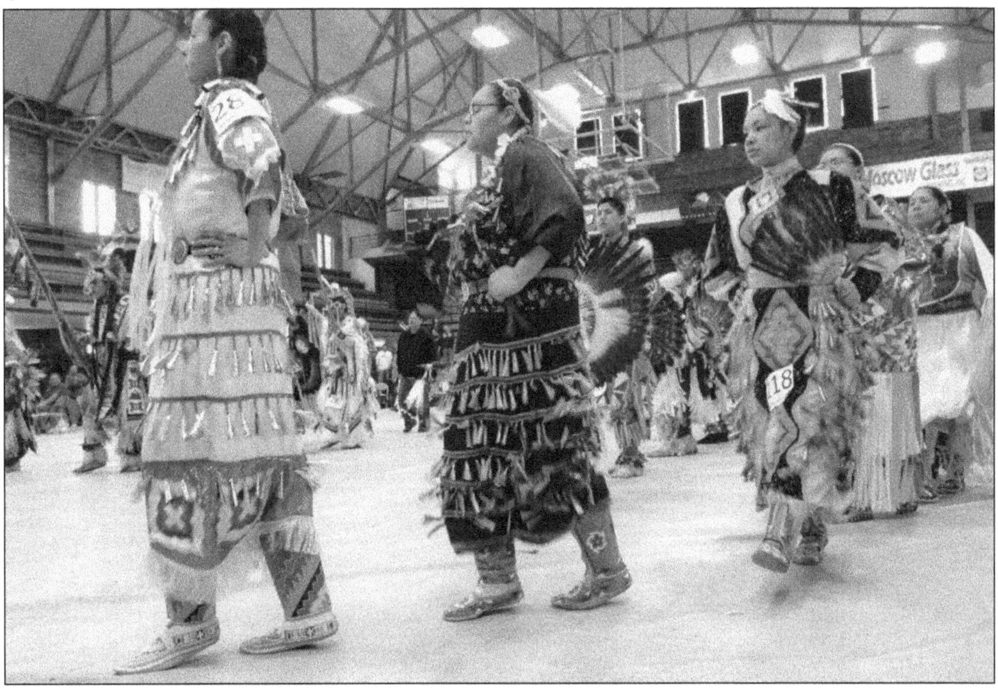

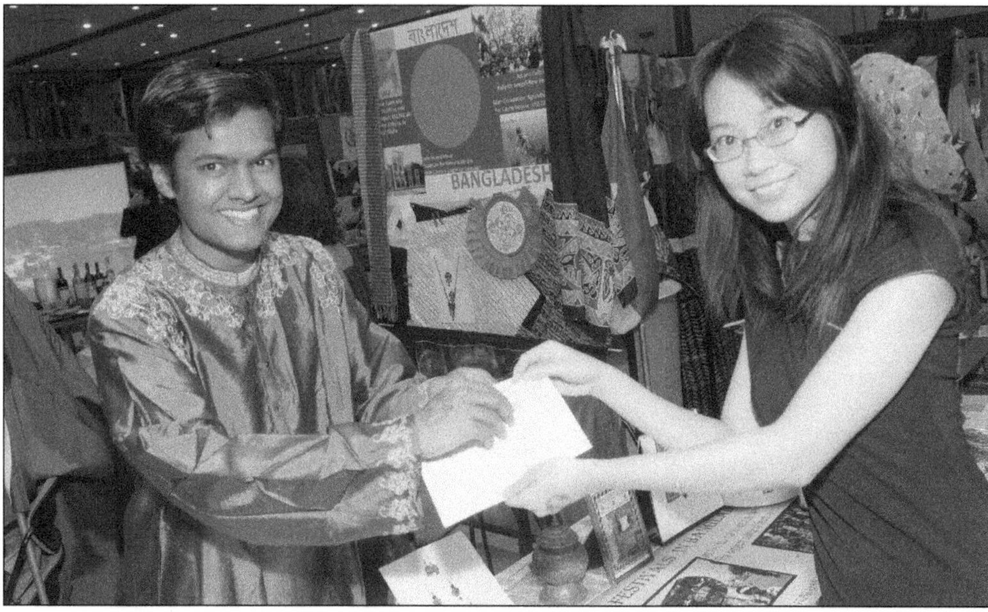

Cruise Around the World, shown here in 2008, is the largest international student event on the Palouse. It features live performances and food from more than 30 countries around the world. Through the International Programs Office, student organizations facilitate other popular cultural events, including Taste of Nepal, Japanese Festival, Africa Night, and Lunar New Year. (UI Photo Services.)

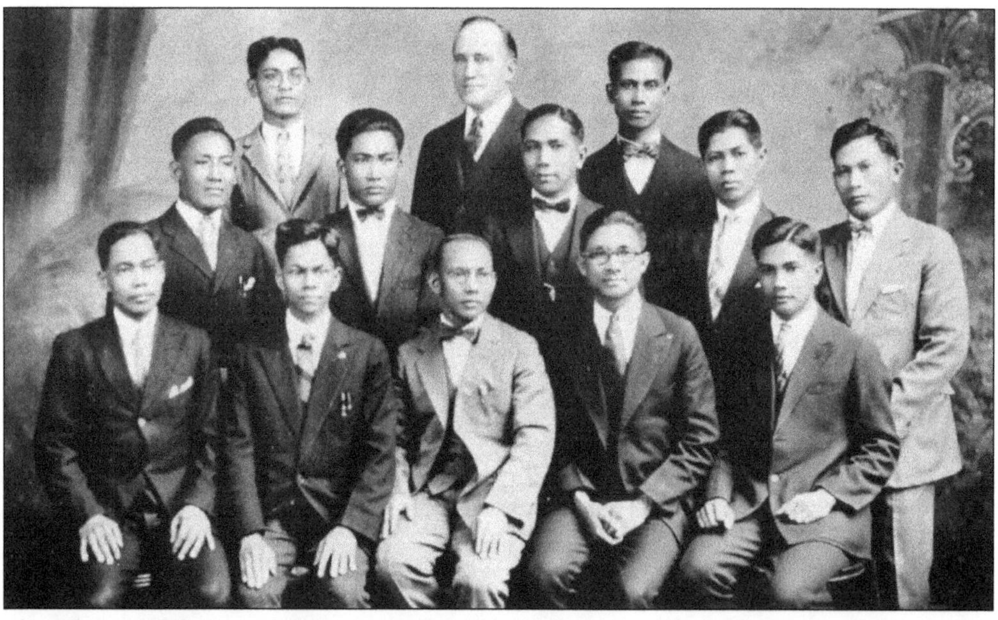

The Filipino Idahoans Club is pictured in the 1925 *Gem of the Mounatins* yearbook. The club strived to keep the American public informed about the Philippines, to study American institutions and how the people of the Philippines could benefit from them, and to foster social interactions. Similar student organizations exist today, including the Indian Students Association, Nepali Student Association, the Black Student Union, and Chinese Students and Scholars Association. (ASUI.)

KUOI (pronounced que-ee) first broadcast on November 15, 1945. At that time, it was the only student-operated radio station in the Pacific Northwest. Now part of the National Public Broadcasting system, it is still student-owned. The station features all musical genres. Pictured is Megan Harris working the 89.3 FM booth in 1986. (SPEC, UA 2003-015.)

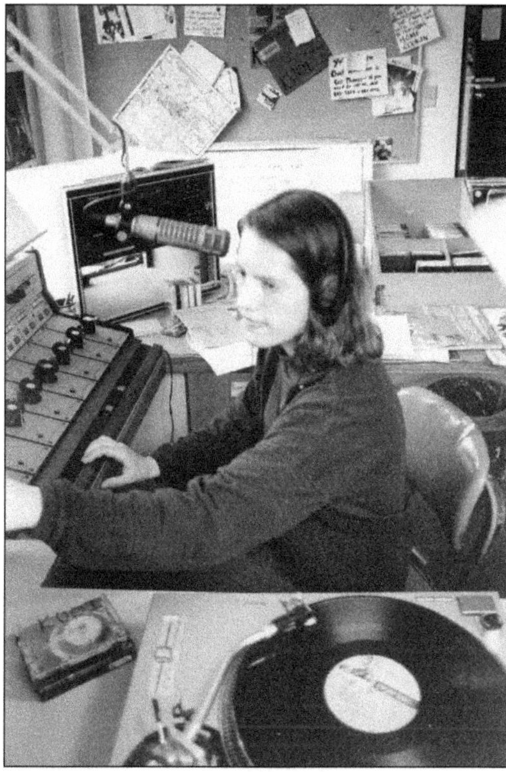

Sponsored by the Associated Foresters of Idaho, the log-rolling competition was one of many events related to logging culture on campus. Throughout Idaho's history, timber has been a major industry. Loggers engaged in competitions based on the industry's requisite skills. (SPEC, PG 52-442.)

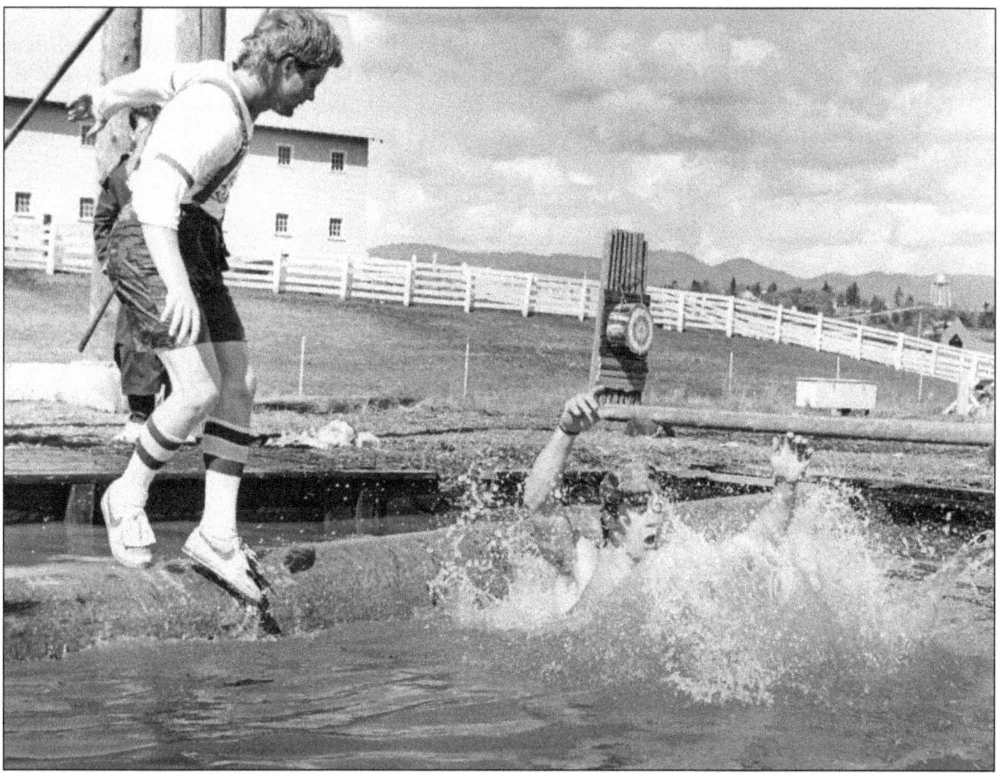

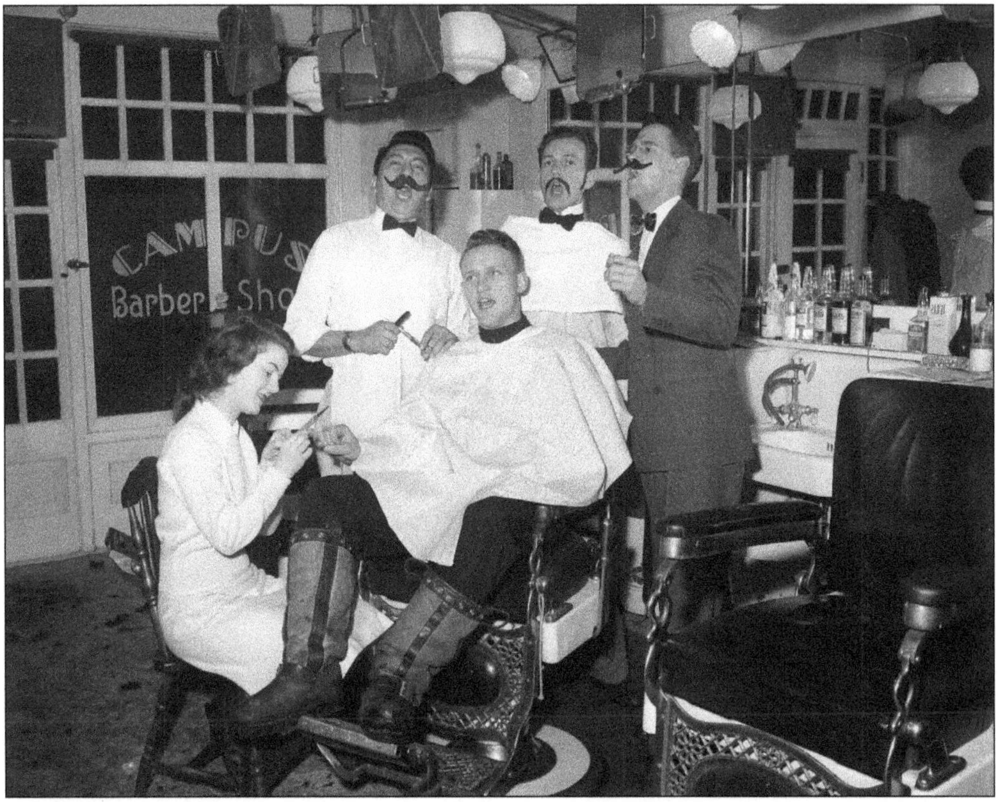

As a residential campus, the University of Idaho offers students the opportunity to explore a variety of interests and find outlets for their various talents. The only real limits and boundaries are those of imagination. Above, a 1947 barbershop quartet performs in the Campus Barber Shop. Below, members of the Society of Creative Anachronism compete in medieval traditions wearing historical costumes. (Above, PG 92-1773; below, SPEC, UA 2003-015.)

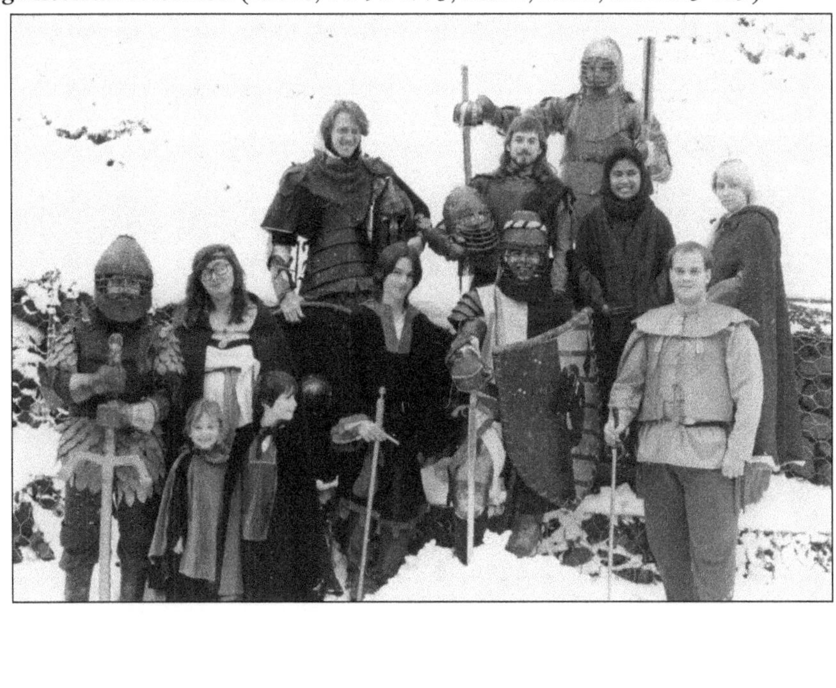

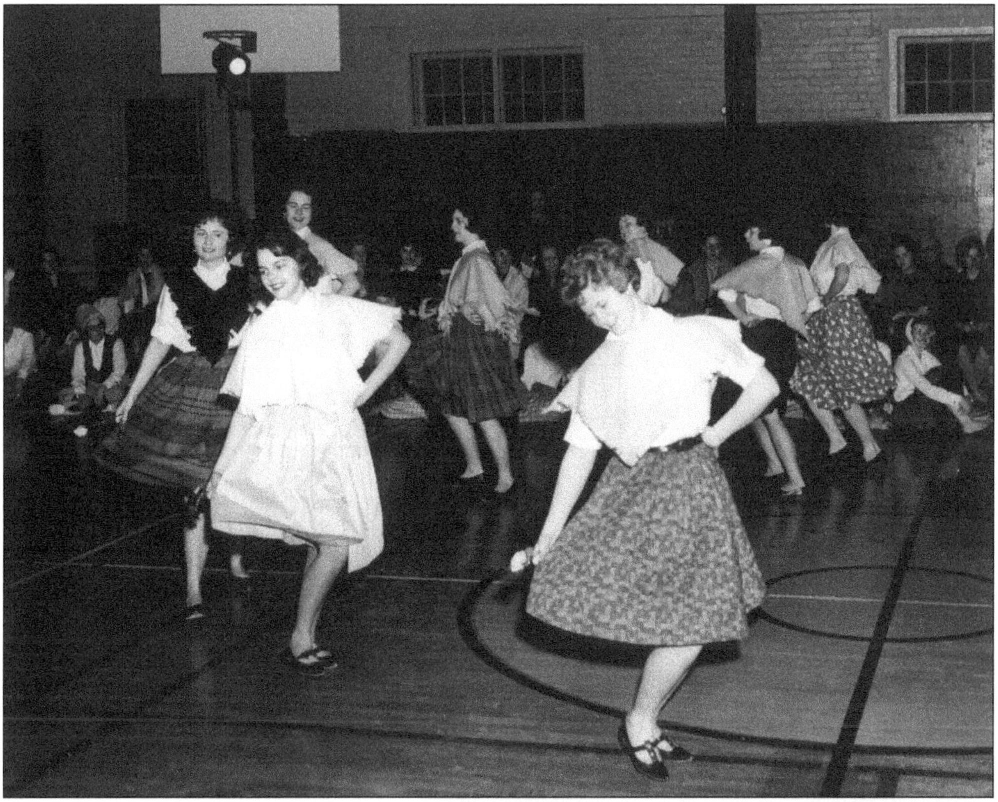

Dancing was one of many programs offered through the Women's Recreation Association and was considered a physical activity for women. Pictured are women dancers in Memorial Gym. In the 1960s, Orchesis, a modern dance group, presented annual Christmas and May Fete programs. (SPEC, UA 1987-005.)

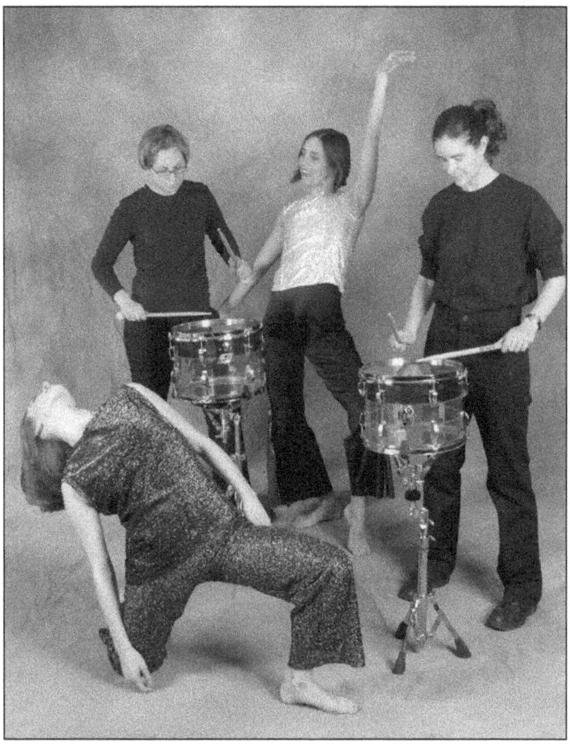

DancersDrummersDreamers (shown here in 2008) came from the imagination of music professor Daniel Bukvich and longtime dance professor Diane Walker. For 25 years, sold-out performances have featured students involved in the UI dance program, the music program, and across campus. The production has traveled to various schools in the region to showcase their art. (UI Photo Services.)

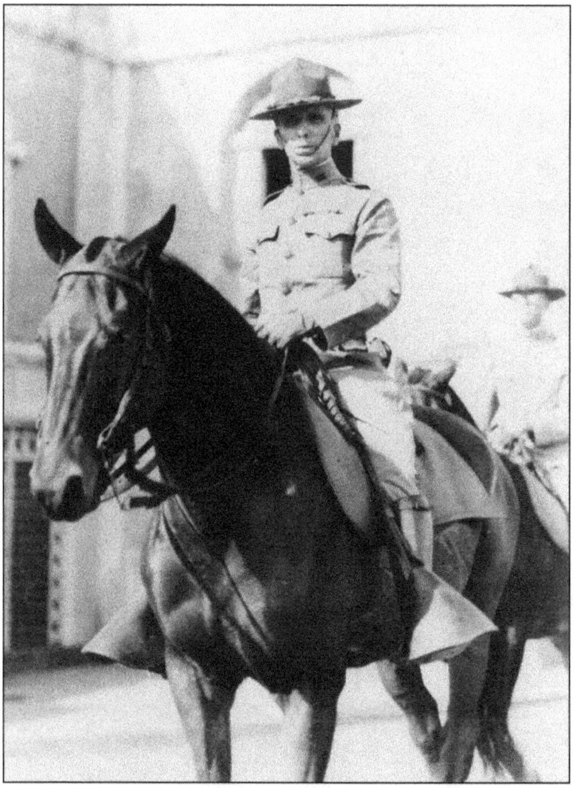

Edward Chrisman arrived on campus as a lieutenant in 1894, led troops in Cuba during the Spanish-American War, and was promoted to brigadier general in World War I. He returned to Moscow and retired from active duty in 1932. The UI Army ROTC unit is named for him, and Chrisman purportedly often proclaimed that for him it was "duty, honor, country, and the University of Idaho." (SPEC, PG 3-47n.)

In 1926, rifle was the only women's athletics team to engage in intercollegiate competition. The coed Vandal team battled opponents from across the country, including the universities of Washington, Maine, Nevada, South Dakota, California, Kansas, and Michigan State. "Company C" (Calico) began in 1897 as a fun unit to appear in public performances but soon drilled with the same precision as military men on campus. (SPEC, PG 1-208-08.)

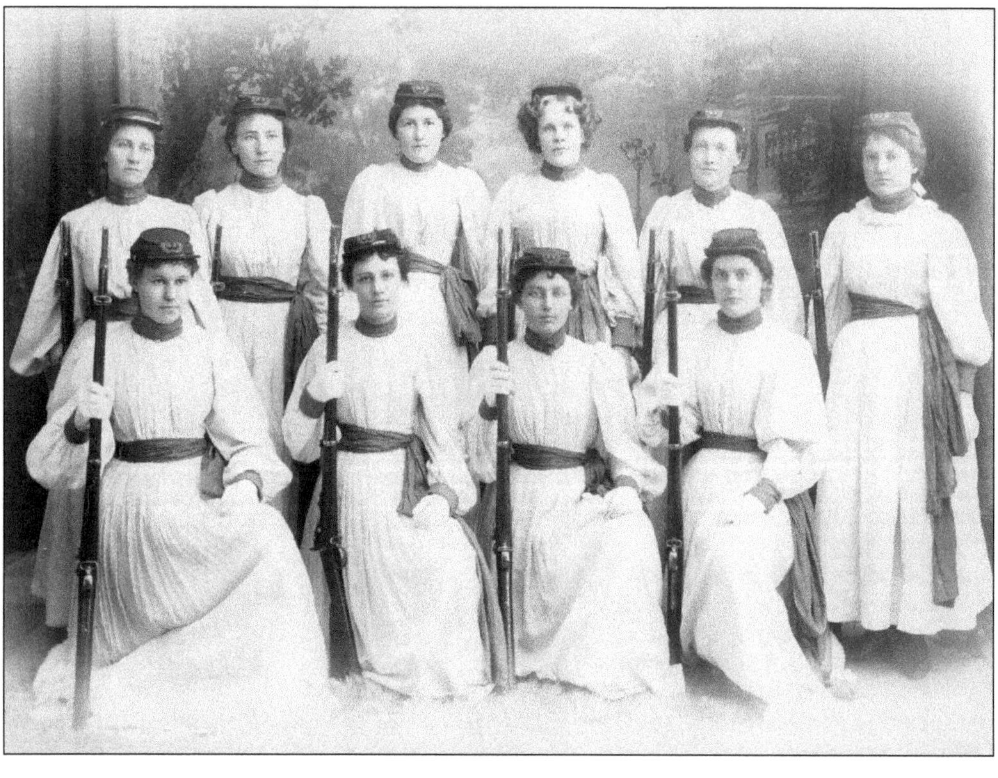

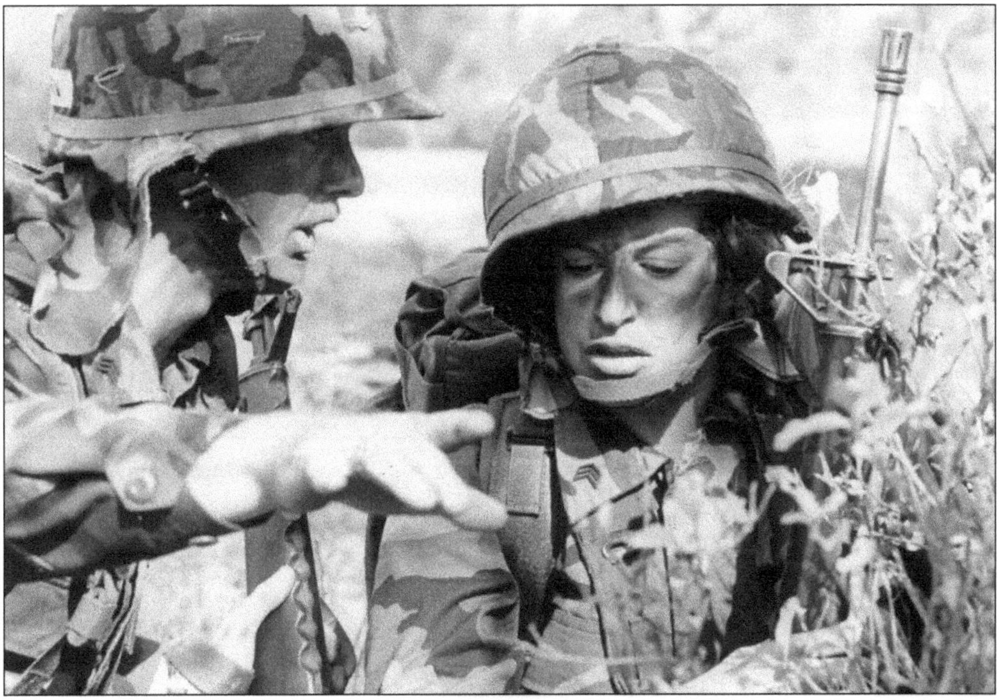

Greg Wooten and Renee Sink participate in a maneuver during ROTC exercises near Harvard, Idaho, in 1987. US Marine colonel Janice Scott assumed command of the Navy–Marine Corps Officer Education program at UI in 1985. She was the first woman commander in the country to hold such a post. (SPEC, UA 1989-027.)

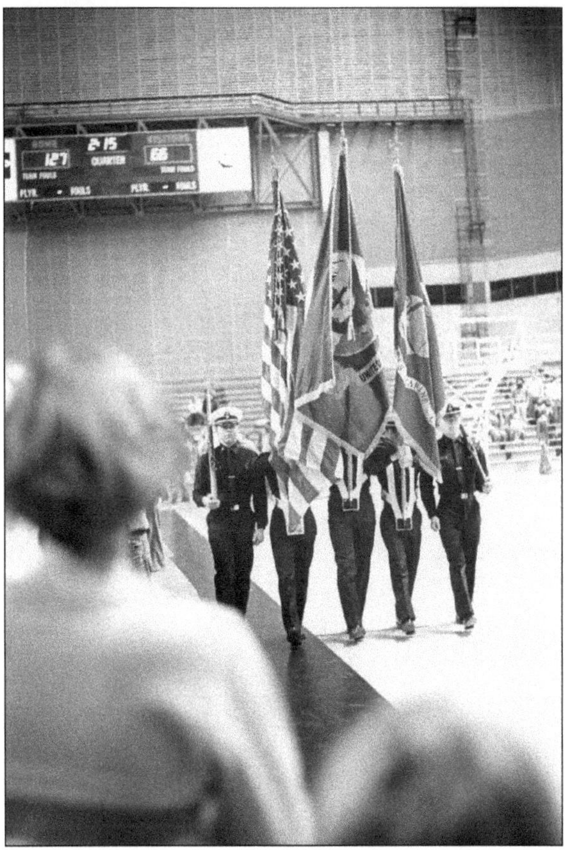

The color guard enters the Kibbie Dome. UI graduate Ross E. Rowel was the first Marine to receive the Distinguished Flying Cross and the first Marine aviator to become a general. Reginald T. Myers received the Congressional Medal of Honor during the Korean War. Operation Education, launched in 2006, is a leading scholarship and assistance program for veterans and their spouses serving the nation since September 11, 2001. (SPEC, UA 2001-001.)

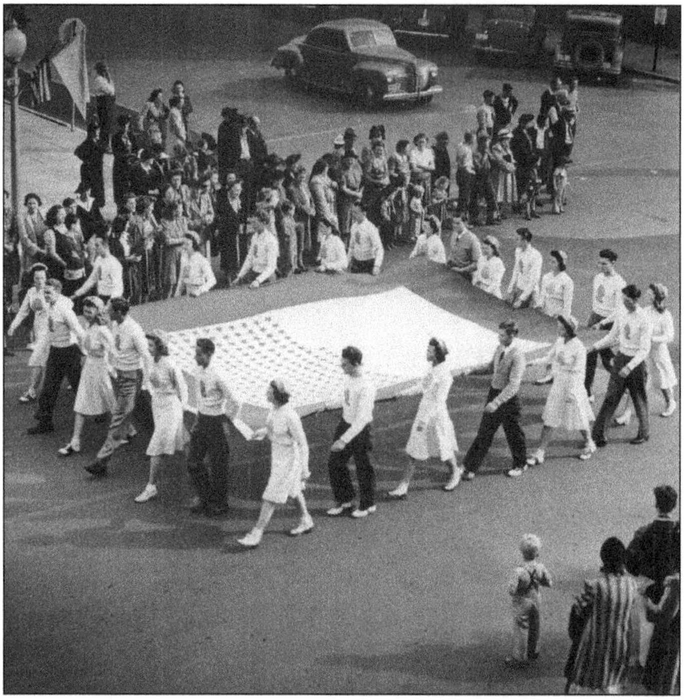

Ghormley Day Parade, pictured in the 1943 *Gem of the Mountains* yearbook, honors University of Idaho students serving on active duty with the armed forces. Spurs and Intercollegiate Knights, the women's and men's sophomore honor societies, carry the university's service flag, featuring a star for each student in the military. (ASUI.)

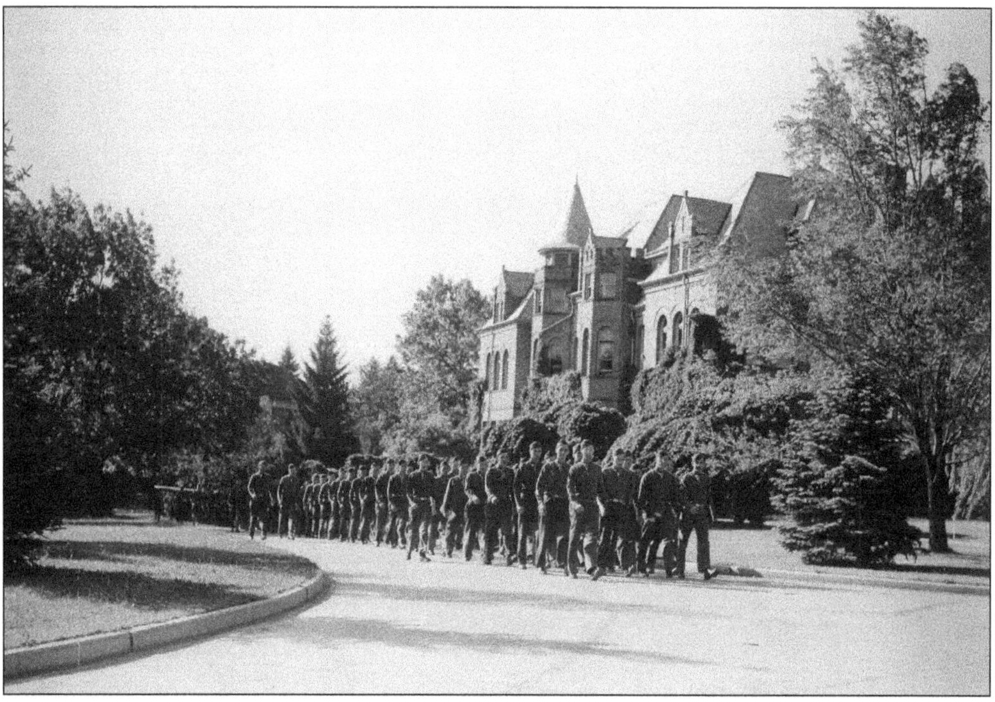

Military training was part of the Morrill Act obligation and has been present at the university from the beginning. Pictured are uniformed cadets in 1943. The 35th Marine Corps commandant general, James F. Amos, was a member of the class of 1970 and commencement speaker in 2012. The campus veterans' center is named in his honor. (SPEC, PG 6-4-11.)

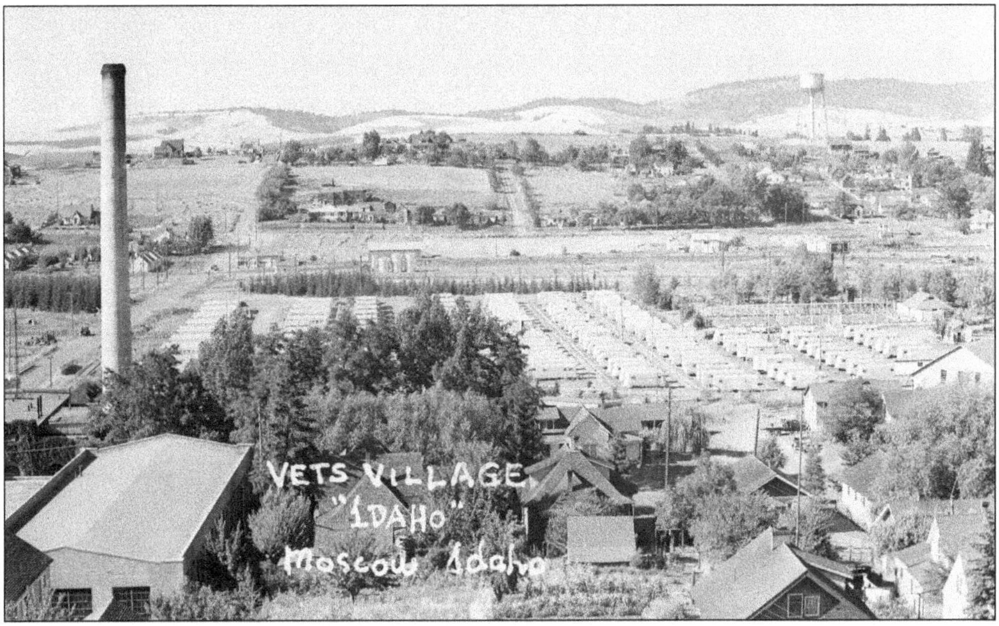

Following World War II, returning veterans took advantage of the GI Bill, and they and their families created a housing shortage. The university addressed this through the Reconversion Housing Project for Veterans by adding trailers and prefabricated housing both on campus and north of downtown Moscow. This 1948 aerial view of West Sixth Street shows the "Vets' Village." (SPEC, PG 1-120-4.)

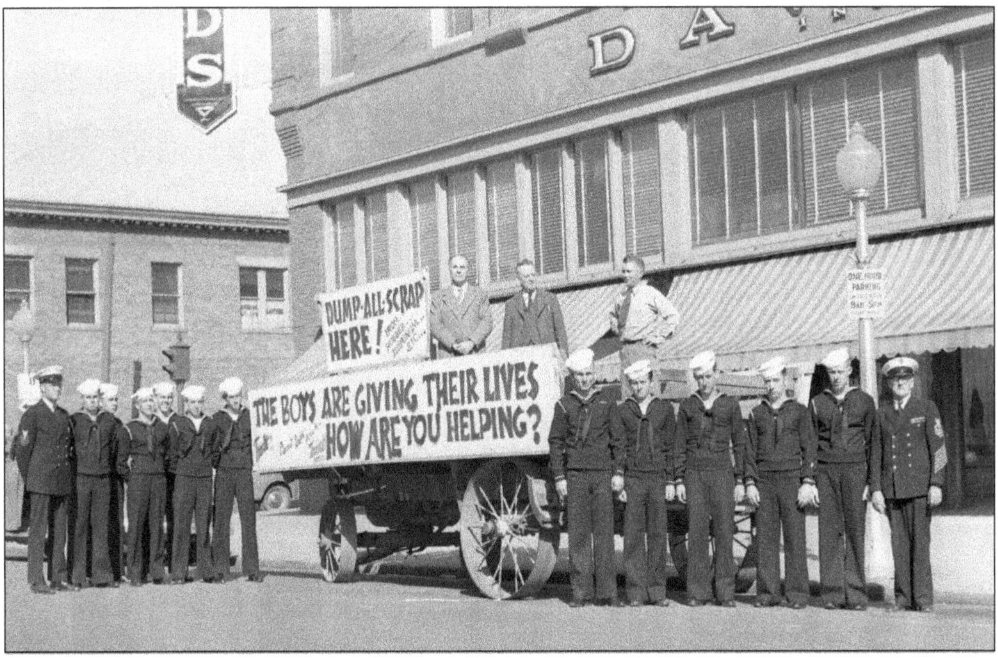

This Navy scrap metal drive took place in 1945. This wagon with the slogan "The Boys Are Giving Their Lives How Are You Helping?" is in downtown Moscow outside David's Department Store. UI hosted a Navy radio training school during World War II, and Navy ROTC came to campus in 1945. (SPEC, PG 92-829.)

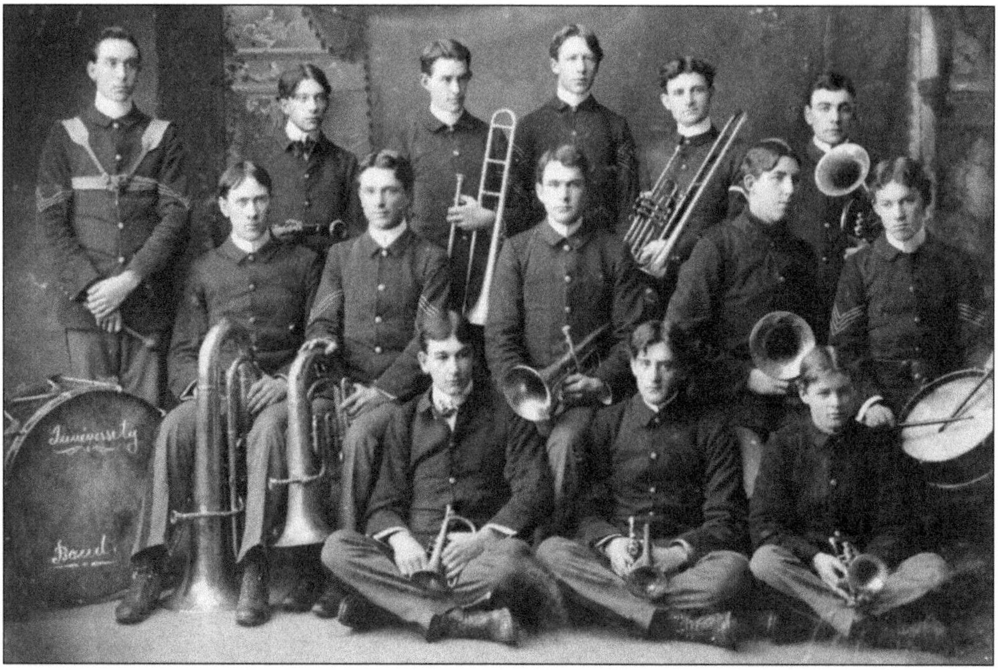

Instrumental music has a long history at the University of Idaho. Shown here is the 1903 university band. Current Lionel Hampton School of Music ensembles are concert band, symphony orchestra, wind ensemble, and four jazz bands. Choral groups are Jazz Choir I and II, the Vandaleers, the Men's Chorus, and the Women's Chorus. Other musical societies on the Idaho campus date to 1900. (SPEC, PG 2-82-20.)

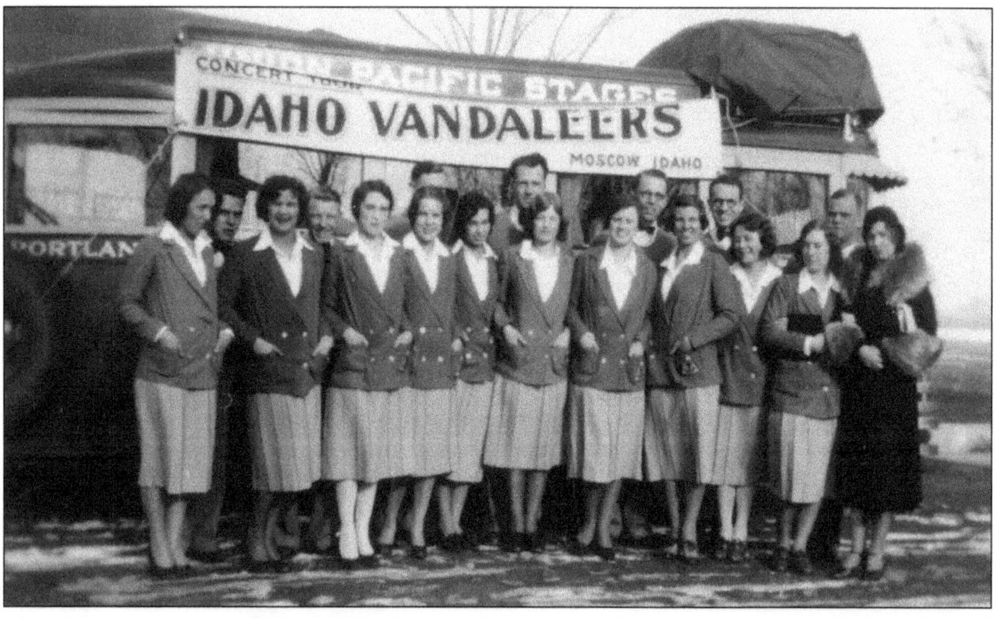

The university concert choir, the Vandaleers, first appeared in 1930. The group has performed throughout the region and embarked upon European tours in 1971 and 2010. The Vandaleers visited Latin America in 1975. Here, the Vandaleers stand beside the Union Pacific Stage as they prepare to tour Idaho. (SPEC, PG 2-112-40.)

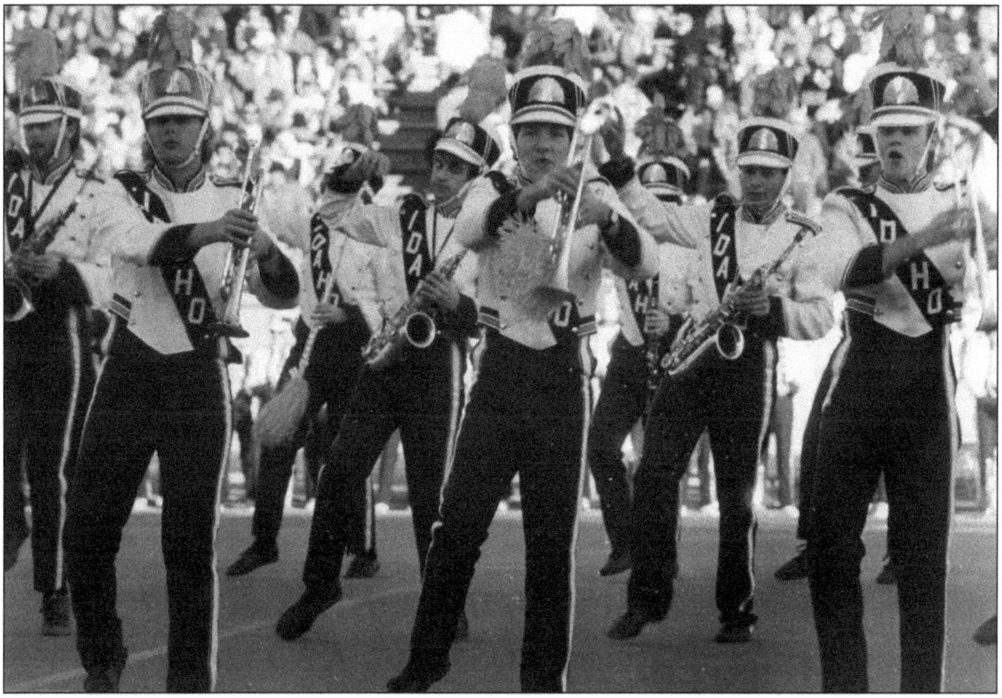

The ASUI and the Lionel Hampton School of Music present the Sound of Idaho Marching Band for halftime performances, shown here in the 1980s. Anyone affiliated with the University of Idaho may join without audition. Many former members return to march with the alumni band during Homecoming. (SPEC, UA 1989-027.)

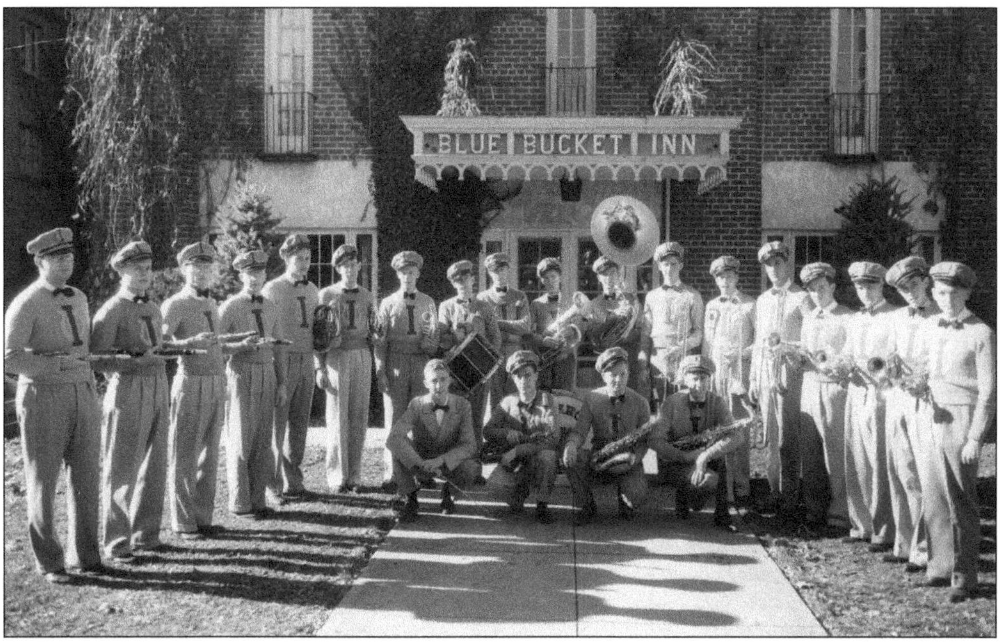

The pep band first performed in 1919 and appeared at various locations around the state and region. It is shown here in front of the Blue Bucket Inn in 1938 with director W.E. Chase. The current iteration of the pep band performs at basketball games. (SPEC, PG 2-108-26.)

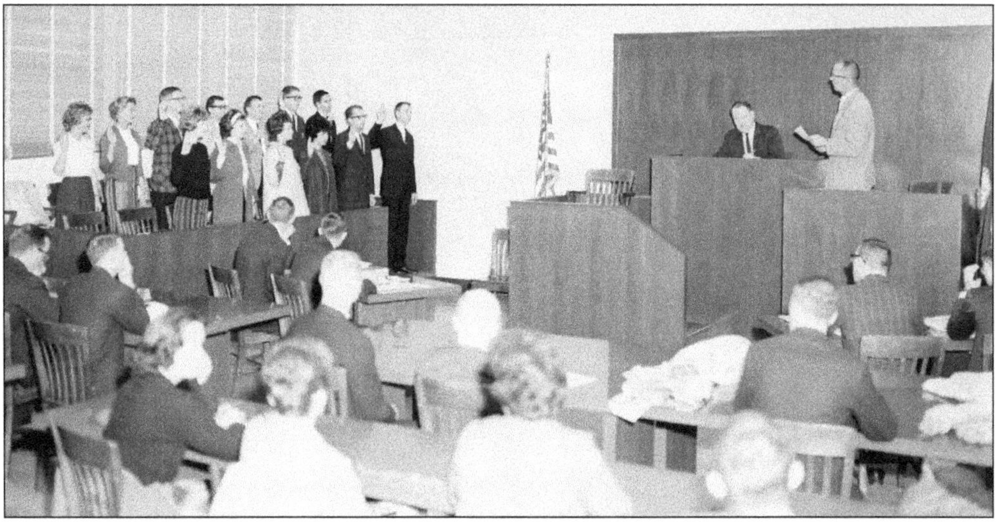

The Student Bar Association oversees student organizations and provides law students access to shared governance. The College of Law offers a number of practical experience opportunities, including moot court, mock trial, appellate advocacy (McNichols), and the trial advocacy program for third-year students. The college is known for its pro bono requirement, clinics, and externship opportunities. Law students are pictured participating in a mock trial in 1963. (SPEC, PG 101-1734.)

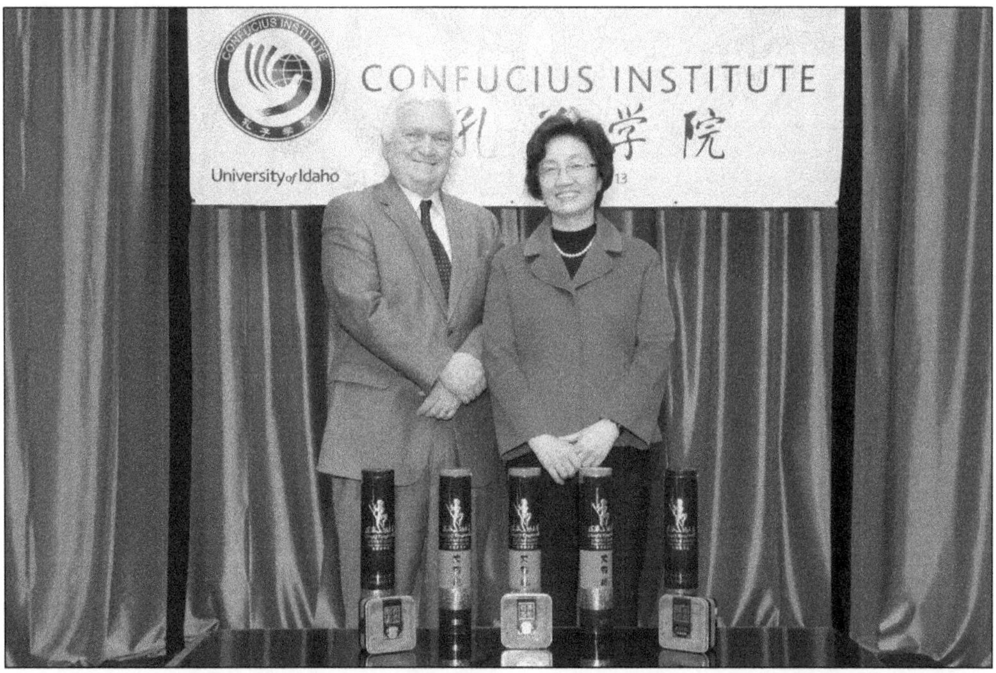

The University of Idaho Confucius Institute is Idaho's first. A partnership with South China University of Technology, the Confucius Institute was formally opened in 2013. The institute offers Chinese language courses, sponsors cultural events, and arranges the celebration of Chinese holidays. The Confucius Institute plans to offer Chinese language and culture classes in Boise. Pictured are interim president Don Burnett and president of the South China University of Technology Wang Yingjun at a gala opening. (UI Photo Services.)

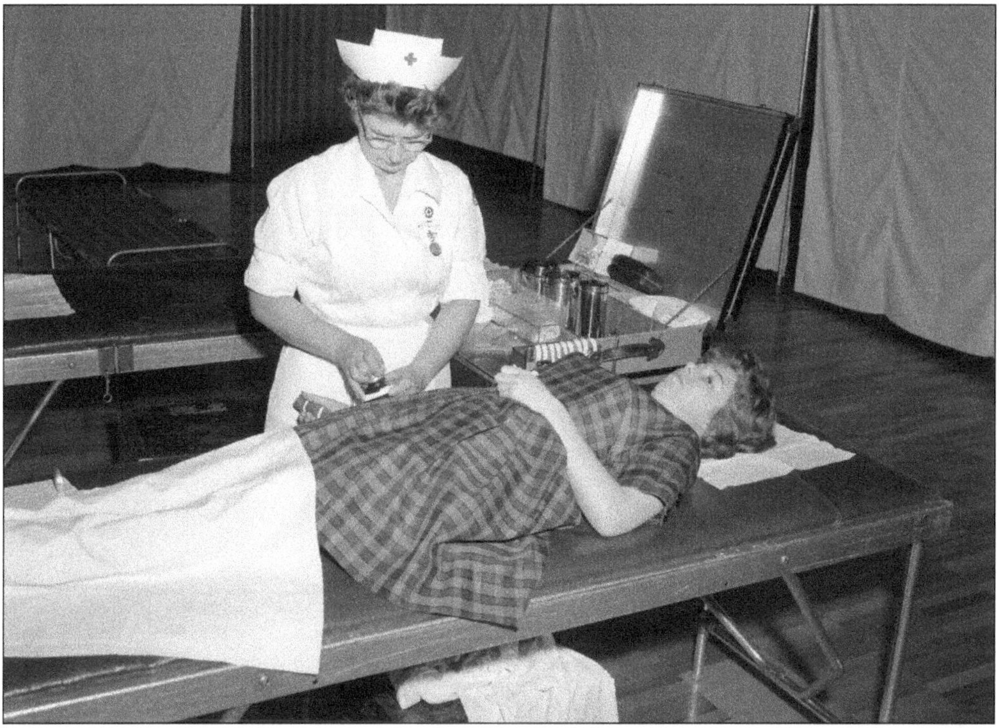

The campus blood drive was an annual event for years. Living groups across campus competed to donate the most blood, and the University of Idaho claimed to be "the bloodiest campus in the United States." Giving blood continues to be just one aspect of Vandal service. Here, a student gives blood during the annual blood drive in 1963. (SPEC, PG-01-1775.)

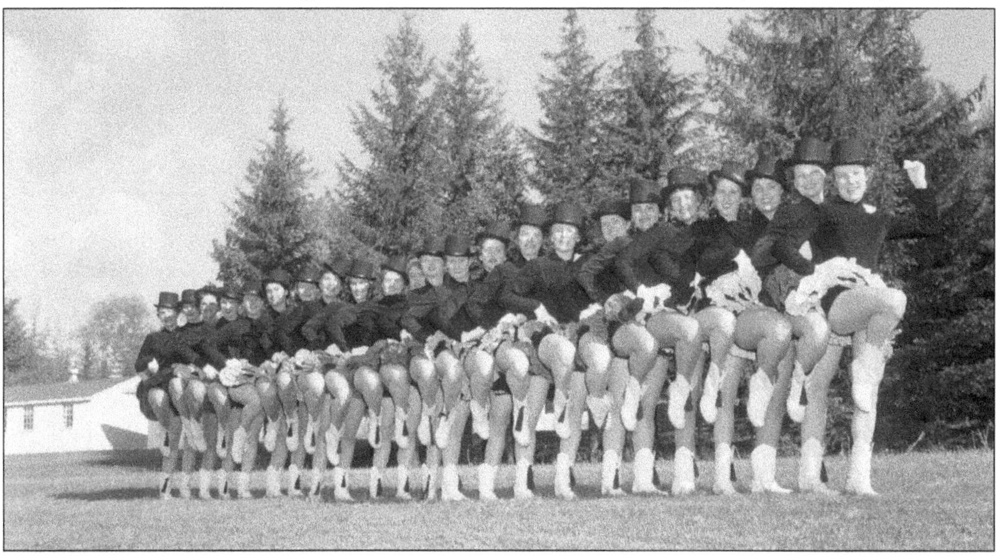

The Vandalettes Drill Team performed during halftime at football games, along with the marching band. The group traveled to many away games, and at basketball games, they often provided entertainment during intermission. By the 1970s, rehearsal had become so time-consuming that group members earned one credit for "Musical Pageantry." Here, the Vandalettes pose in formation in 1957. (SPEC, PG 101-411.)

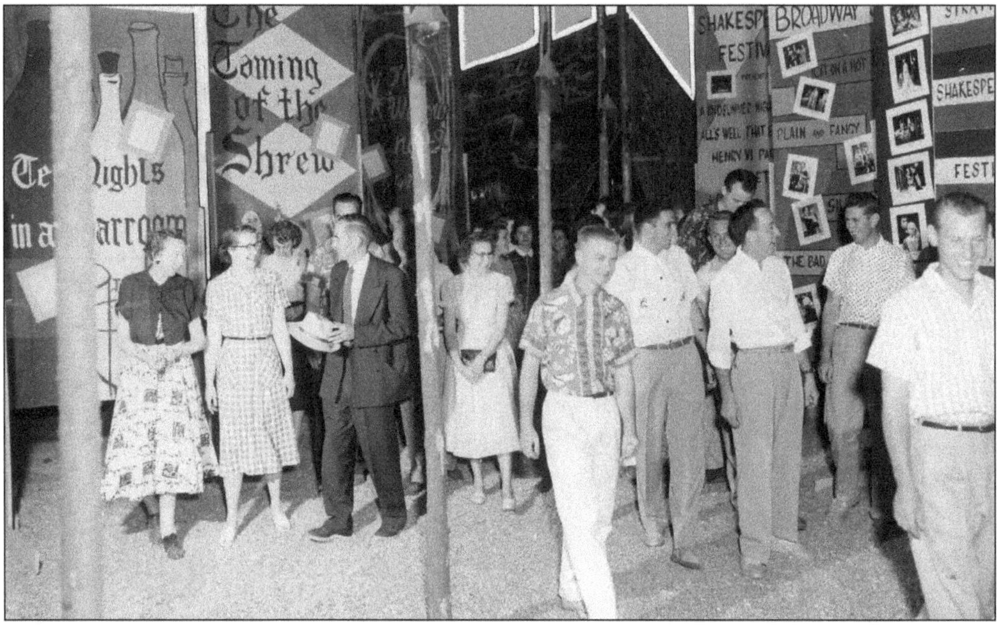

Seldom a week goes by at the university without an opportunity to attend dramatic productions, concerts, recitals, or art exhibitions. Here, an audience leaves a 1955 summer production, part of entertainments patterned after New England's famous barn theaters and held at the fieldhouse. For 60 years, Idaho Repertory Theatre brought professional summer theater to the Palouse. (SPEC, PG 2-184-2.)

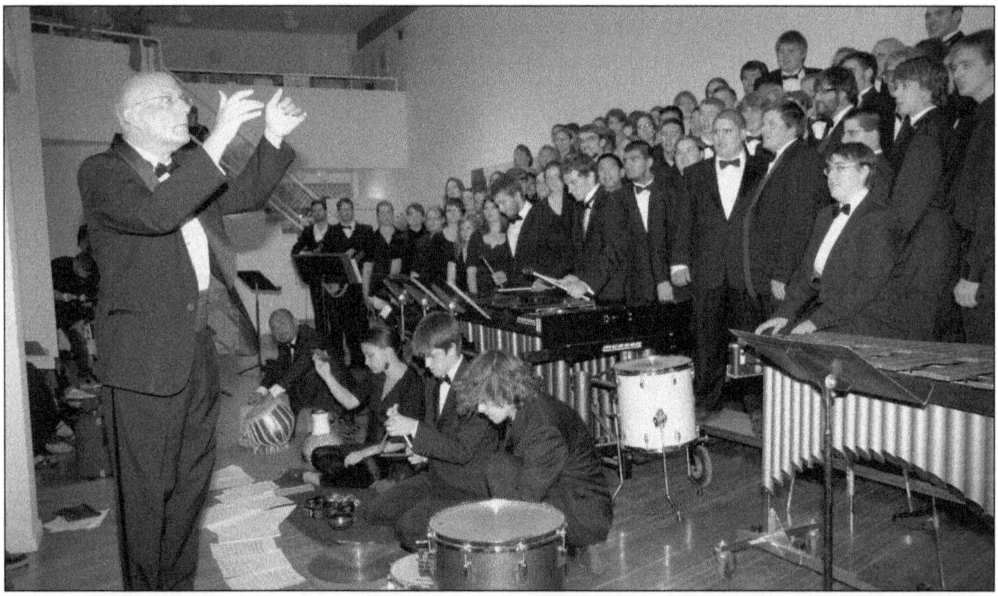

University Distinguished Professor Daniel Bukvich, known for his innovative pedagogy and enthusiasm, recruits music students from across the university; the jazz choirs are known for high-energy performances. Here, Bukvich directs the jazz choir in 2011 as part of Turning the Wheel, a yearlong humanities program funded through a National Endowment for the Humanities challenge grant under the direction of Prof. Rodney Frey. (SPEC, Turning of the Wheel Digital Collection.)

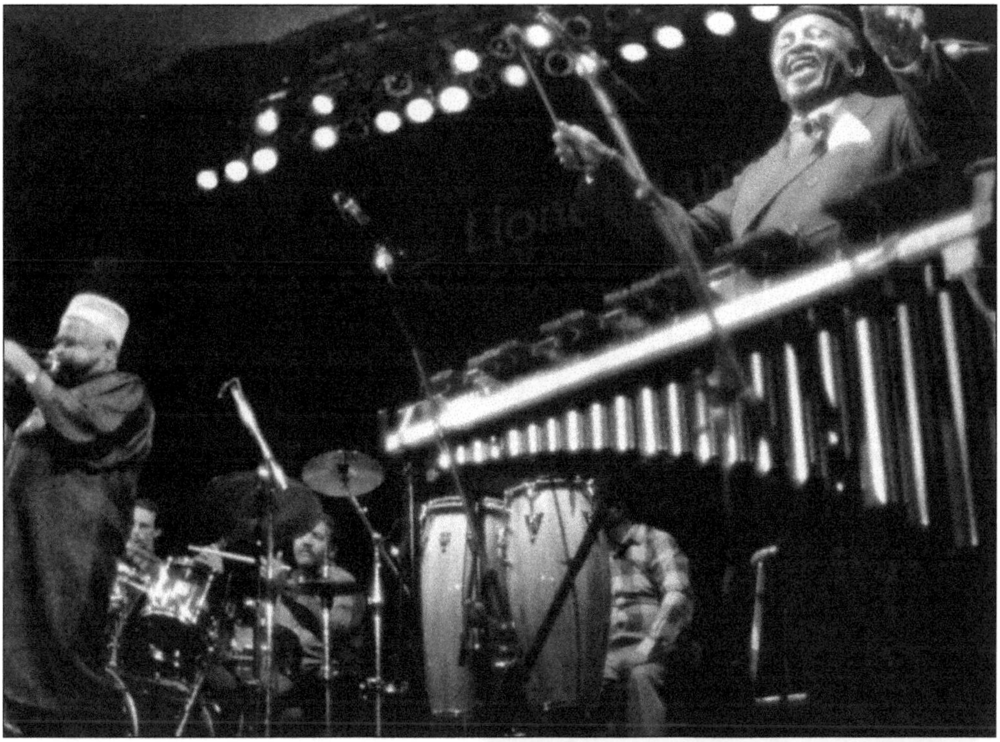

The first UI Jazz Festival took place in 1967; the program included a dozen student groups and one guest artist. Music professor Lynn "Doc" Skinner's dedication grew the festival, renamed the Lionel Hampton Jazz Festival in 1985. The festival has hosted thousands of students and featured guest artists including Ella Fitzgerald, Sarah Vaughn, Diane Reeves, and Dee Daniels. Pictured above are Dizzy Gillespie (left) and Lionel Hampton (right) at the 1999 festival; at right is John Clayton playing a tribute to perennial crowd favorite Ray Brown. Clayton was a Ray Brown protégé and still plays his bass. The Grammy-winning Clayton became artistic director of the Lionel Hampton Jazz Festival in 2007, the same year the festival was awarded the National Medal of the Arts. The International Jazz Collections are part of UI Special Collections and Archives. (Above, SPEC, UA 2003-015; right, UI Photo Services.)

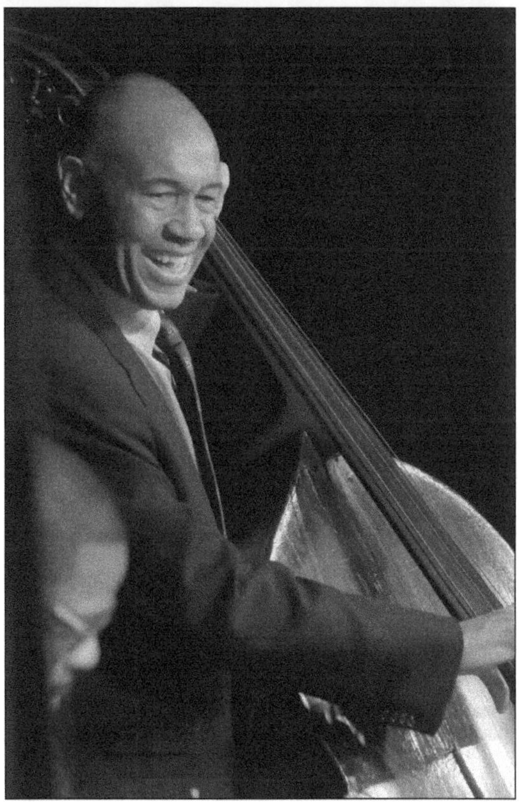

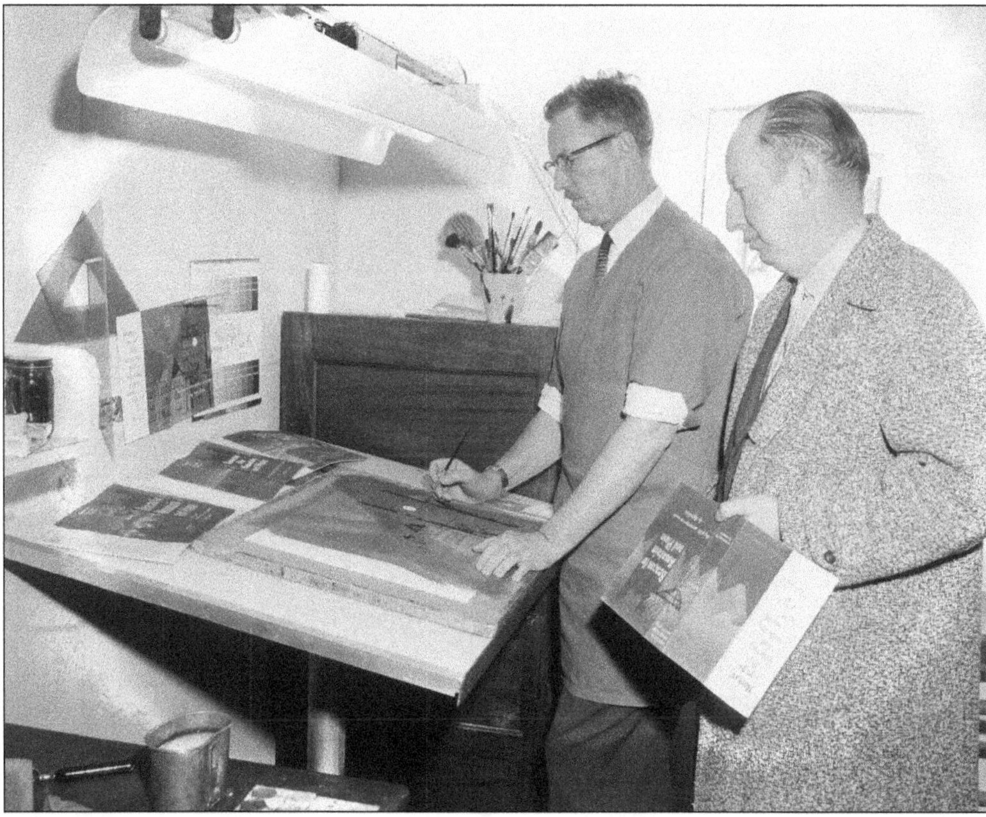

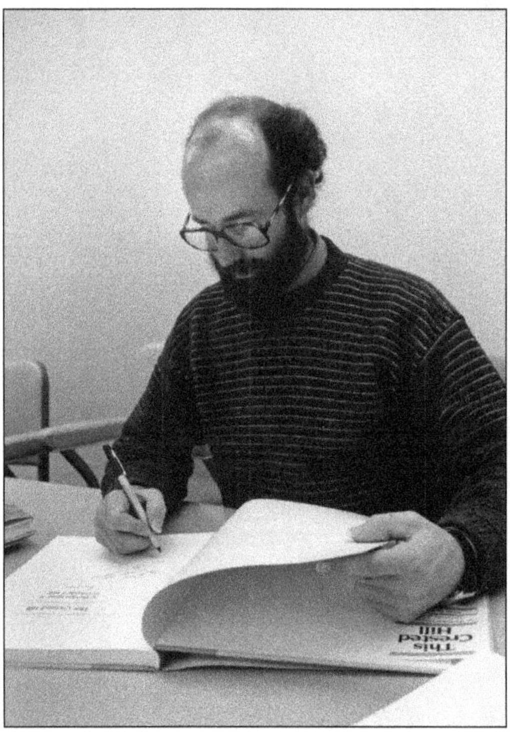

Rafe Gibbs's *Beacon for Mountain and Plain: Story of the University of Idaho* covers UI's first 70 years. Gibbs (1934) served as director of information, university editor, and professor. Alf Dunn (1936) joined the UI faculty in 1941 and designed the cover and provided illustrations for the book. His depictions of the University of Idaho are beloved. Here, they put the finishing touches on the dust jacket. (SPEC, PG 101-1996.)

As part of its centennial, the University of Idaho commissioned Keith Petersen's *This Crested Hill: An Illustrated History of the University of Idaho*. Petersen, the author of monographs and articles on Idaho history, served as the Idaho state historian and as Idaho State Historical Society associate director. In recognition of his contributions, the university conferred an honorary doctorate upon Petersen in 2014. Here, Petersen autographs his book. (SPEC, UA 1989-27.)

Bibliography

Gibbs, Rafe. *Beacon for Mountain and Plain: Story of the University of Idaho*. Moscow, ID: The Regents of the University of Idaho, 1962.

Lockery, Glen. *Songs of Idaho*. Moscow, ID: University of Idaho Press, 1988.

Petersen, Keith C. *This Crested Hill: An Illustrated History of the University of Idaho*. Moscow, ID: University of Idaho Press, 1987.

Reese, Garth, and Katherine G. Aiken. "The Homestead and Morrill Acts: Idaho's Federal Policy Foundations." *Idaho Landscapes* (March 2013): 32–45.

Reese, Nels, and Diana Armstrong. "The Olmsted Plan for the Campus." *Here We Have Idaho* (Spring 2014): 12–21.

University of Idaho Student Alumni Relations Board. *University of Idaho Traditions*. Moscow, ID: University of Idaho Student Alumni Relations Board, 2014.